THE
PUBLICATIONS
OF THE
SURTEES SOCIETY
VOL. CXCIV

Filmset by
Northumberland Press Limited
Gateshead, Tyne and Wear
Printed in Great Britain by
Fletcher and Son Ltd, Norwich

THE

PUBLICATIONS

OF THE

SURTEES SOCIETY

ESTABLISHED IN THE YEAR

M.DCCC.XXXIV

VOL. CXCIV

FOR THE YEAR M.CM.LXXXI

At a COUNCIL MEETING of the SURTEES SOCIETY, held in Durham Castle on 16 June 1981, the PRESIDENT, Professor H. S. Offler, in the chair, it was ORDERED—

'That the edition of Northern Petitions prepared by Dr Constance M. Fraser should be published by the Society as the volume for 1981.'

A. J. Piper, *Secretary*
The Prior's Kitchen,
The College,
Durham

NORTHERN PETITIONS

illustrative of life
in Berwick, Cumbria
and Durham in the
fourteenth century

EDITED BY
C. M. FRASER

PRINTED FOR THE SOCIETY BY
NORTHUMBERLAND PRESS LIMITED
GATESHEAD
1981

CONTENTS

INTRODUCTION

The reign of Edward I of England was notable for the establishment of machinery for dealing with complaints against faults
in royal administration. Many of these petitions were handled by
committees of 'triers' in parliament. Others were submitted to
the King's chancellor for a decision. Out of the stream of
grievances were consolidated the right of the representatives of
shire and borough to be heard in parliament, and the power of the
Chancellor to decide equitable remedies. Edward's reign also
saw the start of endemic warfare between England and Scotland,
which ceased only with the accession of James VI to the English
throne in 1603.

The line of the Anglo-Scottish border had advanced and re-
ceded according to military opportunity since the tenth century.
David I had apparently won recognition of his authority over
Cumbria and (through his wife and son) over Northumbria as
far as the Tees, and regarded the diocese of Durham as within his
sphere of influence. (He vigorously pressed the claim of William
Cumin to be bishop after the death of Geoffrey Rufus in 1138.)
There was a quick reversal of fortune when the death of Earl
Henry of Northumberland on 12 June 1152 was followed by the
death of his father, David I, a year later. While the crown of
Scotland passed to David's eldest grandson, Malcolm IV, Northumberland was inherited by his second grandson, William 'the
Lion'. By 1158 Henry II of England had re-annexed Northumberland and Cumberland, while recognising that Prince William had
special authority in North and South Tynedale. This was confirmed by the Treaty of York in 1237, when the lands were
defined as consisting of North Tynedale in Northumberland and
parts of Inglewood with Penrith, Castle Sowerby and Carlatton
in Cumberland. A general claim to overlordship over Scotland
was advanced by Henry II in the Treaty of Falaise of 1175; re-

tracted for money by Richard I; and re-asserted by Edward I at
the time of the arbitration over the inheritance of the Scottish
Crown in 1291.

In March 1296 Edward I invaded Scotland, storming and
capturing Berwick upon Tweed, routing a Scottish army at
Dunbar, and finally compelling the surrender of King John [de
Balliol] in July 1296. For the remainder of Edward's reign the cost
of war in Scotland was a drain on English revenue. Edward II
was forced to continue hostilities despite his preoccupation with
rebellious magnates led by Thomas, earl of Lancaster, and abortive
attempts by Pope John XXII to negotiate a truce. The Peace
of Northampton of 1328, with the Scottish repayment of 'repar-
ations', was of short duration, since in 1332 the 'Disinherited'
Scottish nobles attempted to proclaim Edward de Balliol king of
Scotland, and called upon Edward III for aid.

Fighting tended to be confined to southern Scotland at first,
including the recovery in 1333 of Berwick by the English, but
from 1340 the Scots regained the initiative and resumed the raiding
into England which had ruined the north of England between
1312 and 1322. Newcastle was blockaded and Durham stormed.
In 1346 David II led an army eastwards along the Tyne Valley,
but was checked in an advance south by his defeat of Neville's
Cross outside Durham. The Scottish king's capture led to a truce,
which was spasmodically observed until his conditional release in
1357.

For the remainder of his life David II was under an obligation
to continue repayments for his ransom. He maintained cautious
relations with Edward III but his nobles steadily re-asserted
control over Roxburghshire, Berwickshire and the other border
counties where the English claimed overlordship. After his death
in February 1371 there were outbreaks of hostilities in 1372 and
1377/8. Berwick upon Tweed briefly changed hands on three
occasions, 1355/6, 1378, and 1383. John of Gaunt was sent to
Scotland in 1380/1 to negotiate peace, and succeeded in rousing
the hostility of the new Percy earls of Northumberland. There
were further raids in 1383, 1384, 1385 and 1387; and a major
Scottish invasion in 1388, at the height of the domestic crisis of
the Lords Appellant, culminated in the battle of Otterburn, where
the earl of Douglas was killed but 'the Percy led captive away'.
Again, in 1402, another Scottish army of invasion came south

under the earl of Douglas, to be met at Humbledon Hill near
Wooler and defeated by an Anglo-Scottish force under the
(refugee) earl of March and Sir Henry 'Hotspur' Percy. The capture of leading Scottish magnates here and the royal refusal to
sanction their ransom was the ostensible cause of the Percy rebellion the following year, which ended with Hotspur's death at
Shrewsbury in July 1403.

Behind the panoply of international politics the people of
northern England had to adapt to a way of life where raiding was
normal, food supplies precarious, law enforcement uncertain,
taxes difficult to raise. That the English Exchequer recognized the
problem is confirmed by the new assessment for spiritual taxation
ordered in 1318, which reduced the tax liabilities of churchmen in
the dioceses of York, Durham and Carlisle. The majority of the
lay subsidies of the fourteenth century were not exacted from
Northumberland, Cumberland and Westmorland because of local
poverty. Other problems included the relations of the Palatinate
of Durham with the Crown, and the need at Berwick upon
Tweed, the only part of Scotland to remain permanently annexed
to England, to safeguard the property rights of both Scottish and
English house-owners.

The collection of Ancient Petitions which follows is the remainder of a collection whose first instalment was published by
this society as *Northumberland Petitions* (Volume 176) in 1966. The
documents relate to the counties adjoining Northumberland and
provide illustrations of the practical difficulties of life in the north
of England during the fourteenth century.

The method of presentation has been to provide a short
introduction of background history to each section. Each petition
is preceded by a calendar of its contents. It is followed by the
approximate date, and editorial comment on its relation to other
known material. Place-names occurring in the petitions are expressed where possible in their modern form in the calendar.
Scribal insertions in the text are indicated by brackets ⟨ ⟩, in
order that 'second thoughts' can be identified. Original use of
capital letters has been followed, but the punctuation is modern.
Occasionally a letter or word is introduced in italics where its
absence makes the sense obscure. Editorial glosses on the text are
also in italics. Conjectural readings are in square brackets. Long
lacunae are indicated by points. Where a petition is already printed

verbatim a calendar only has been included, and then only where required to round off a section.

It remains for me to thank all those who have helped me in any way in the preparation of this edition. Unpublished Crown-copyright material in the Public Record Office, London, has been reproduced by permission of the Controller of H. M. Stationery Office. Professor T. E. Hope of the Department of French, University of Leeds, and Professor H. S. Offler, lately of the Department of History, University of Durham, very kindly read through my typescript for linguistic points. Mr. Kenneth Emsley, lately of the Department of Law, Leeds Polytechnic, has discussed with me certain legal aspects of the petitions in relation to Durham. The General Editor, Mr. Alan Piper, has made a number of useful suggestions, by which I hope I have profited. The final content of this volume remains my own responsibility.

ABBREVIATIONS

AA   *Archaeologia Aeliana*

AP   Ancient Petition (PRO, Special Collection 8)

Bain   *Calendar of Documents relating to Scotland*, i–iv, ed. J. Bain (1881–88)

Barrow   G. W. S. Barrow, *Robert the Bruce and the Community of the Realm of Scotland* (1965)

Bek   C. M. Fraser, *A History of Antony Bek* (1957)

Boldon Buke   *Boldon Buke*, ed. W. Greenwell (Surtees Society 25; 1852)

Cal Inq Misc   *Calendar of Inquisitions Miscellaneous*

Cal Inq pm   *Calendar of Inquisitions post mortem*

Cal Pap Reg   *Calendar of Papal Registers*

CChR   *Calendar of Charter Rolls*

CCR   *Calendar of Close Rolls*

CFR   *Calendar of Fine Rolls*

CPR   *Calendar of Patent Rolls*

Cowan/Easson   I. B. Cowan and D. E. Easson, *Medieval Religious Houses: Scotland*, 2nd ed. (1976)

Durham   Muniments of the Dean and Chapter of Durham Cathedral

Fasti   *Fasti Dunelmenses*, ed. D. S. Boutflower, (Surtees Society 139; 1926)

FDP   *Feodarium Prioratus Dunelmensis*, ed. W. Greenwell, (Surtees Society 58; 1872)

HBC   *Handbook of British Chronology*, 2nd ed. (Royal Historical Society; 1961)

Knowles and Hadcock   D. Knowles and N. Hadcock, *Medieval Religious Houses: England and Wales*, 2nd ed. (1971)

Lapsley   G. T. Lapsley, *The County Palatine of Durham* (1900)

Lloyd   T. H. Lloyd, *The English Wool Trade in the Middle Ages* (1977)

North'd Pet   *Northumberland Petitions*, ed. C. M. Fraser, (Surtees Society 176; 1966)

NCH   *Northumberland County History*, i–xv (1893–1940)

PRO   Public Record Office, London

QR Mem Roll   Queen's Remembrancer Memoranda Roll (PRO, E159)

Reg Pal Dun   *Registrum Palatinum Dunelmense*, i–iv, ed. T. Duffus Hardy (1873–78)

Ridpath   G. Ridpath, *Border History* (1776)

Rot Parl   *Rotuli Parliamentorum*, i–vi (1783)

Rot Scot   *Rotuli Scotiae*, i–ii (1814–19)

Scott   J. Scott, *Berwick upon Tweed* (1888)

Scrip Tres   *Historiae Dunelmensis Scriptores Tres*, ed. J. Raine, (Surtees Society 9; 1839)

Surtees   R. Surtees, *The History And Antiquities of the County Palatine of Durham*, i–iv (1816–40)

VCH   *Victoria County History*.

Willard   J. F. Willard, *Parliamentary Taxes on Personal Property, 1290 to 1334* (Medieval Academy of America; 1934)

SECTION I

BERWICK UPON TWEED

Berwick upon Tweed was a captured town. In consequence the settlement of grievances arising from changing allegiances and contradictory titles to property figured largely in the petitions presented to the King and his Council. Also of concern was the encouragement of trade, especially after the town's natural hinterland of the Tweed valley had been partially lost by the redrawing of the national border (nos 1–8, 10, 12, 42, 44–50).

Until 1296 Berwick had been one of the most successful Scottish ports, a 'second Alexandria'. It exported the produce of Tweeddale, including wool and grain, the customs-dues in 1286 amounting to £2,190. 'There was scarcely an abbey in Scotland that had not property in Berwick.' There was a colony of Flemings in their Red Hall, and trade links with Norway. The town already had a reputation for its salmon (Scott, pp. 13–14, 23, 44–6). To the extent that their presence presumes a sizeable population, it should be noted that Berwick had attracted friaries of the following orders: Franciscan (1231), Trinitarian (pre-1240/8), Dominican (pre-1240), Carmelite (1270), Austen (pre-1299), and of the Sack (1267). In addition there was a Cistercian nunnery (Cowan/Easson, pp. 108, 116–17, 125, 136, 140–1, 142, 145).

The extent of the slaughter in Berwick at the storming of March 1296 was remarked on by many chroniclers, estimates of casualties varying between 7,500 and 15,000. The outer defences of palisade and ditch were totally inadequate. Edward I quickly sought to remedy this by providing a ditch 80 feet broad and 40 feet deep. He also established in the town the nucleus of a Scottish government, including an exchequer, treasurer, chancellor and justiciar, although nominally responsible for Berwick only. On 12 January 1297 he appointed a committee of nine merchants from English towns to join with the guardian of Scotland and the treasurer to regulate the state of Berwick and assess rents of houses and open spaces in the town for the encouragement of merchants, artificers and other suitable traders. In fact the town returned briefly under Scottish control in the winter of 1297/8, although the castle remained in English hands (Scott, pp. 25–6, 28–31).

Berwick was the appointed place of muster for the English invasions of Scotland in 1299 and 1303. Later Edward II used it from 1309 to 1314. By 1315 the town walls were completed and sufficient, despite unrest within the garrison (nos 30–32) and chronic shortage of pay (no. 33), to repel a fierce assault by the Scots in January 1317. The burgesses thereafter undertook in June 1317 to maintain the defence of the town on receipt of an annual subsidy of £4,000. The principal merchants gave hostages to ensure that the town would not be betrayed lightly to the Scots. Notwithstanding, in the spring of 1318 the Scots captured the town by assault and reduced the castle six days later. They remained in control until 1333, despite an abortive siege conducted by Edward II in 1319, when it was necessary for Thomas, earl of Lancaster, to swear on the Gospels that he was not in communication with the Scots (CPR 1313–17, p. 671; Scott, pp. 33–9, 43).

The Scots confiscated the lands of all Berwick inhabitants who had showed loyalty to the English cause by fleeing south with their goods. The English king was equally incensed with them, considering the loss of Berwick a proof of their treachery. The Berwick merchants were therefore caught between the two enemies, distrusted, and a prey to both (nos 36–38).

Whereas in 1296 and 1318 the town had surrendered unconditionally, in 1333 an agreement was reached on 15 July after a blockade of over two months. In accordance with the conventions of the time it was agreed that unless the Scots could formally relieve Berwick by 20 July, either by a battle or by reinforcements, the town and castle would surrender. The lives and possessions of the inhabitants and garrison would be spared, and such as wished to leave the town might have forty days in which to sell their goods. In addition, exporters of wool and hides would continue to pay the lower Scottish customs rates. The immediate result was a hasty attempt by the Scots to muster a relieving force, leading to the disastrous battle of Halidon Hill on 19 July (cf. nos 49–50, 59). The town then surrendered in accordance with the previous agreement. This enabled the inhabitants to claim security in their tenements (Ridpath, pp. 304–309; Scott, p. 62) (nos 42–44, 51, 54, 55).

Despite these rapid changes of 'nationality' Berwick had succeeded in retention of its trade and was still in 1330 the premier customs port in Scotland, with Aberdeen and Edinburgh at a respectful distance behind (cf. no. 40). The wool customs were £570, £484 and £400 respectively (Scott, p. 48). It had been the policy of Edward I to make Berwick conformable with English trading practice by appointing a committee of English merchants as governing body. He also gave special privileges to encourage incomers to the town, a policy which was sufficiently successful to arouse the alarm of existing Berwick merchants (nos 13–14, 21–22). Following the recapture of 1333 a Newcastle merchant was introduced as mayor to enable English trading customs to reassert themselves (nos 57–58).

As long as Berwickshire and Roxburghshire continued to accept English domination Berwick could maintain its position as a wool port (nos 20, 22–23, 26, 29). With the gradual erosion of English authority during the later fourteenth century, the volume of wool steadily fell until the burgesses were forced to plead for special customs rates to enable them to compete with Edinburgh and Newcastle (nos 27–28). Another burden was the cost of repairs to the town wall; to meet this expense a special tax was levied at the rate of 3s 4d for each sack of wool, 3s 4d for every 300 wool fells, and 6s 8d for every last of hides. Foreign merchants paid at double the rate (Scott, p. 63). There were total embargoes on trade in 1336, 1352 and later (no 26). The men of Berwick were able to persuade Richard II to grant them the right to export wool elsewhere than to Calais, and Henry IV and Henry VI permitted them to buy even in Scotland (Lloyd, p. 228) (nos 28, 29).

The Berwick petitions have been loosely subdivided into five themes, a) topography (nos 1–12), b) franchises (nos 13–19), c) trade (nos 20–29), d) defence of Berwick (nos 30–39), e) compensation (nos 40–44), and f) war damage (nos 45–59).

Topography

Ancient Petitions 1590, 3849, 4548, 4612, 4953, 5001, 5328, 5737, 6782, 7939, 8739, 9313.

I

Michael le Spicer of Berwick petitions the King and Council that John de Botelston by force and arms and against the King's peace deseised him of his free tenement in Berwick and of a site which he held by lease of Michael, which he has since sold to Walter de Gosewyk without agreement with Michael.

Also Michael petitions that he [?John] sold to Walter de Goscwyk at a time he forgets three shops for 10 marks, which he had of the King's gift against losses of £52 sustained after the capture of Berwick six years ago.

Furthermore Michael petitions that whereas he leased to Adam de Dunbar for six years tenements in the town for 20 marks, after which term Michael required their return and could get no answer, then Adam died and a William de Byntele entered them and holds them against Michael, who is unable to obtain re-entry.

Furthermore he petitions against a Richard le Barber with whom he lodged his strong-box, and Richard in collusion with John de Botelston who was obliged to Michael in £20 broke the strong-box in his keeping and took Michael's seal and made a quit-claim for John for the said debt so that Michael, a well-known man, was wholly ruined by the said John and Walter and has no means of livelihood (AP 4548).

A nostre seignur le Roy et a soen consail Mustre Michel le Spicer de Berewyk' sur Twede qe Johan de Botelston a force et arme et a contre la poes nostre seignur le Roy, li ad deseisi de soen fraunk' ⟨tenement⟩ en Berewyk sur Twede, et de vne place qil tient a terme des aunz, del les le vantdit Michel pus le terme passe ad vendu a Wautier de Gosewyk' en fee sanz ascun gre faire al vantdist Michel: dunt il prie pur deu remedie de ceste chose.

Ausi mustre le vantdist Michel qe come il auoit vendu a Wautier de Gosewyk' troys Shoppes pur .x. Mars en la ville avantdit en tiel houre dunt il ne fut en bone memorie, Le queux Shoppes Le vandist Michel auoyt de doun nostre seignur le Roy pur ses damages de .lij. li' qil auoit en temps apres qe le Roy auoyt conquis Berewyk' de ore a sis aunz; dunt il prie pur deu remedie.

De autrepart mustre Le vantdist Michel qe come il auoit baille a

Adam de Dunbar tenementz qil auoyt en la vile avantdite pur
.xx. Mars a terme de sis aunz, apres cel terme vint le vantdist
Michel e demaunda deliueraunce de les tenementz, e de rien ne
pout estre respundu: den apres murust le vandist Adam e entra
vn William de Byntele et detient hors le vantdist Michel qe nul
entre en les auanditz tenementz ne put auer e ceo oue grant tort;
dunt il prie pur deu remedie.

De autrepart mustre e se pleint le vantdist Michel de vn Richard
le Barber a qi il auoit baille son forcet a grader e vint le vantdist
Richard e par collusion feet entre li e Johan de Botelston, le quel
Johan fut tenu al vantdist Michel en .xx. li', si debrisa le forcet
qil auoit en garde e prist le seal aluantdist Michel e fit al
vantdist Johan vne quiteclamance de la vantdite dette, issi qe le
vantdit Michel, qi pur homme esteit conuz, par les auanditz
Johan a Wauter est tut destrut si qe rien nad ont viure par quei il
prie pur deu de ceste chose remedie.

                                                    Berewyk'

Endorsed: Scocia
    Ad omnes articulos infrascriptos habeat breue ⟨de Cancellaria
Anglie directum⟩ Cancellario Scocie quod faciat ei iusticiam per
communem legem parcium illarum.

c. 1302. The reference to the capture of Berwick must relate to
1296 as Walter de Gosewyk was dead by 1324 (*CCR 1323–27*,
p. 317).

                                2

    Hervey de Doway, burgess of Berwick, petitions the King's
council that whereas the agreement made at Berwick by the King
has been confirmed in all points whereby each burgess may have
his inheritance and possessions as had his forefathers in the time of
King Alexander, a John Leche sought a tenement in Narugate
which he [Harvey] had bought from the right heir who still
lives in Berwick (AP 5328).

    A bone Consail nostre seignur le Roy Mustre Heruy de Doway,
burgeoys de Berwic' sur Twede, pur ceo qu lez couenant' de
Berwic' fayt de par nostre seignur le Roy sunt affirme en tuttez

poyntis qu chescon burgez auerra sez heritage et sez possessiouns qu luy et sez ancestres auont el temps le Roy Alysander. Et vne Johan Leche ad purchese vne tenementz du dit Herui en Narugate le quele il ad catera de verey heyr qe volte onkore en la dyt vile de Berwic'. Pur quey le dyt Heruy pri pur dieu et pur la alme nostre seignur le Roy Edward qe dareyn seurreit qe dieu luy asoiel qe il peut auoire couenable Remedy et droyt si pleys vers sy.

Endorsed: Dicunt quod Eda snaw et ancessores sui fuerunt seisiti de tenemento infrascripto tempore Alexandri Regis etc. et idem Eda illud dimisit predicto Herui et heredibus ipsis qui inde seisitus fuit quo usque amotus fuit per Robertum de Brus per processum littere, et postmodum idem Robertus illud retradidit prefato Heruico et sic seisitus inde fuit quousque amotus fuit per vicecomitem Regis pro eo quod Robertus de Bruys illud dedit prefato Nicholo (*sic*) etc. et quod idem Heruicus fuit in villa tempore reddicionis etc et quod non remisit etc.

Habeat breue vicecomiti Berwic' ad liberandum ei dicta tenementa si occasione premissa et non alia in manu Regis existant, tenenda prout ea prius tenuit, saluo iure Regis et alterius cuiuscumque.

post 1333, when the Scots surrendered Berwick to Edward III on terms printed in *Rot Scot* i, 253–54.

3

Their liegeman of England, John de Chilton, petitions the King and Council that whereas he bought a burgage in Berwick when the town was in the hand of the King's father from a Nicholas Moyses, which Nicholas and his forefathers were seised of the same in the time of King Alexander, and also John by virtue of his purchase of the burgage was seised until the taking and betrayal of the town to Robert de Bruys; and now, since the town has been surrendered to the King, John brought an assize of novel disseisin against Stephen le Foubour, tenant of the burgage, and others where it was found that John was disseised as he complained and he recovered his seisin; and because it was found at the same assize that some named in the writ were unconnected with the disseisin John was amerced £10 by custom of the land for his false claim, which custom is that any man will be amerced £10 before the justices and no less. He requests pardon for this amercement because he lost all his goods at the taking of the town, totalling 2,000 marks, and ever since has lived wretchedly in Northumberland (AP 4953).

A nostre seignur le Roi et a son conseil prie Johan de Chilton soun homme lige de Engleterre qe come il achata vn burgage en la ville de Berewyk' tant come la ville feust en la mein le Roi qi mort est piere le Roi qore est de vn Nichol Moyses, le quel Nichol et ses auncestres furent seisiz du dit burgage du temps le Roi Alisandre, et auxint le dit Johan par vertu de son purchace auantdit du dit burgage feust seisi tant qe la dite ville feust prise et trahie par Robert de Bruys: et ore puis qe la dite ville feust renduz a nostre seignur le Roi le dit Johan porta vne assise de Nouele disseisine deuers Esteuen le Fourbour tenant de dit burgage et autres, par vertu de quele assise feust troue qe le dit Johan feust disseisi come il se pleint, par quoi il recoueri sa seisine: et purceo qe troue feust par mesme lassise qe ascuns nomez en mesme le bref ne furont mie a la disseisine le dit Johan feust amercie a .x. li' par la custume de la terre pur sa faux pleinte, la quele custume est qe chescum homme serra amercie deuant les Justices a .x. li' et ne mie a meins: qe lui plese de sa grace pardoner a lui le dit amerciement depuis qil perdist quant la ville feust prise touz ses biens et chateux, qe amounteront a deux Milles mars, et touz iours puis il ad esquy a meschief en la Countee de Northumbr'.

Endorsed: le Roi lui ad pardone de sa grace

1333–34. On 4 March 1334 the sheriff of Berwick was ordered to lift the distress from Chilton which had been imposed in respect of an amercement of £10 imposed by the King's justices in eyre at Berwick for a false claim against Robert Mauldesson and William son of Simon of Paxton in an assize brought by writ against Stephen Fourbour, James de Cologne, and the said Robert and William for a carucate in Nether Lamberton, the sum having been pardoned. On the same date another inquest found that John de Chilton had also suffered the loss of an oven in the vennel between Uddyngate and Ravensdene in Berwick at the time of the capture of Berwick in 1318. As Chilton's loyalty was unquestioned the sheriff was to restore him in possession (*Rot Scot* i, 264, 269). Chilton was mayor of Berwick in 1337 (Bain iii, 229).

4

Robert Wake of Bamburgh petitions the King and Council that whereas he took of the King a messuage in ... in Berwick for a year at a rent of 6 marks a year, which is in his hand through the [forfeiture] of a Peter Kymbri[gge]ham, and Robert wishes to stay in the town and dwell in the messuage—, he requests a grant of the same for a term of 10 years (AP 3849).

A nostre seignur le Roi et a son conseil prie Robert Wake de Baumburgh' qe come il ad pris de nostre seignur le Roi vn mees en ..... la ville de Berewyk' sur Twede pur vn an, rendant a lui pur mesme le an .vj. mars, le quel mees est en sa main par ..... vn Piers kymbri[gge]ham, et le dit Robert est en volente a demorer en la dite ville et enhabiter le dit mees sil auoit ..... outre en mesme le mees, qe lui pleise granter au dit Robert et a ses heirs mesme le mees rendant le ferme ..... au meyns a terme de .x. auns.

Endorsed: Eit le dit mees a terme de sis auns pur la ferme qil rend' aore, issint qil troefse surete au viscont de Berewyk' de enhabiter le dit mees [par] lui ou par ascune autre suffisant Dengleterre et qil sustendra le dit mees en auxibien estat come est aore et qil paiera sa ferme prestement au Roi.

1334. On 4 March 1334 the King granted to Robert Wake of Bamburgh a messuage in Soutergate lately of Peter de Kymbriggeham, enemy and rebel, for six years from Martinmas next, paying to the King's chamberlain of Berwick 6 marks, half at Whitsun and half at Martinmas: to be returned in as good state as found, and to be dwelt in by himself or by other sufficient Englishmen. He was to find surety for the payment of the farm (*Rot Scot* i, 264).

5

Adam de Corbrig' petitions the King that whereas Ralph Philyp his uncle, whose heir he is, was seised as of right and heritage of divers tenements in Berwick until ejected by war, to wit, eight tenements in Soutergate, another tenement lying in Uddynggate, three tenements lying in Briggate, a tenement lying in Waldef' gate, and a croft lying in Kergate, 3 crofts lying outside the walls of Berwick with a rent of 16s from the tenement lately of Adam de Banysclef and John Banysclef in Sayntmarigate and a rent of a mark from the tenement of Christopher de Coloyne in Crossgate, which tenements Sir Robert de Bruys, lately King of Scotland, gave after the death of the said Ralph to Sir Robert de Louwedre, because the said Adam was English and living in allegiance to the King of England, by reason of whose forfeiture they are now in the King's hand (AP 5001).

[A] nostre seignure le Rey dengleterre mustre Adam de Corbrig' qe come Rauf Philyp soen vnkel qi eir il [est feu seis]i cume de soen dreyt e soen heritage de diuers tenemence en la vile de Berwik' taunke il [est deseisi p]ar force de gere, cest a sauoir, de .viij. tenementz en Soutergate, une gisant entre le [d]e Coldingham vers le North' e la Rwe de Walkergat vers le Swe, vne autre gisant entre [la tere] iadyse Wiliam de Kergate vers le North' e la tere Roger Wyly vers le Swe, .vj. tenementz gisante [entr]e la tere iadys Wiliam de Kergate vers la North e la tere Robert de Irwyne vers le swe; vne [aut]re tenement gisant en Vddynggate entre la tere les Nonailes de Southeberwyk' vers le North' e la [r]we de Hydegate vers le swe; .iiij. tenementz gisance en Briggate .ij. entre la ter Johan de Lundres vers [l]e Est e la tere Steuyne Fourbur vers le West, le terce tenement gisant entre la tere de la Mesoundeu vers [l]e Est e la tere iadis Patrik' Schot vers le West; vne tenement gisant en Waldef' gate iust le tere iadys Waryne de Pebles vers le swe e vne croft' gisant en Kergate entre la tere Frere Wiliam Maydyne mestre del brighouse vers le Est e le Vikerwende vers le West; .iiij. croftes gisance dehors les moures de Berwyk' vne entre le Bardyke vers le North e le croft' Labbe de Meuros vers le swe, vne autre gisant entre le dist croft de Meurose vers le North e le croft del Brighous vers le Swe, le terce croft gisant entre le chemyne qe va del Bongat vers le Snoke vers le North' e le croft del Meusondew vers le Swe: Et de .xvj. souz de rent issance du tenement' iadys Adam de Banysclef e Johan Banysclef' en Sayntmarigate, E de vne Marche de rent issaunt du tenement

Cristolf' de Coloyne en Crosgat; les qeus tenementz apres la mort
le dist Rauf', pur ceo qe le vaunt dist Adam feu engles a la foy
le Rey Dengleterre demorant, Sire Robert de Bruys iadys Rey
de Escoce les dona a sir Robert de Louwedre, par qi forfeture
les tenementz sunt ore en la mayne nostre seignure le Rey: dount
il pri remedi e grace pur dieu.

Endorsed: Dicunt quod predictus Radulfus Philip fuit seisitus de
tenementis infrascriptis tempore Alexandri Regis etc et Johannis
Regis etc quousque villa de Berewico capta fuit per Regem auum
Regis etc, et quod idem auus omnia tenementa predicta dedit
diuersis tenentibus qui illa tenuerunt quousque dicta villa capta fuit
per Robertum de Bruys, qui omnia dedit Roberto de Lowedre
seniori [et Roberto] filio suo per [cuius] forisfactum nunc capta
sunt in manum Regis, et quod predictus Radulfus obiit tempore
dicti aui apud Berewik', et quod predictus Adam qui est
consanguinius et heres eius propinquior semper fuit ad fidem
Regis et non [inimicus].

Habeat breue vicecomiti Berewici ad liberandum ei omnia
tenementa infrascripta si in manu Regis occasione premissa et
non alia existant, tenenda prout predictus Radulfus ea tenuit,
salvo iure Regis et alterius cuiuscumque.

1333–34. Following an inquest returned before the King in
parliament it was found that Ralph Philip was seised in demesne
of two messuages, 11 tofts, 4 crofts and 29s 4d of rents in Berwick
in the time of Alexander and John, kings of Scotland, until the
capture of the town by Edward I, who gave them to divers
tenants who held them until its recapture by Robert de Brus,
who gave them to Robert de Lowedre senior, who gave them to
Robert de Loweder his son, on whose forfeiture they came to the
King. Ralph died in the time of Edward I at Berwick, and Adam
de Corbrigg is kinsman and heir. He was always loyal and neither
he nor Ralph had alienated their rights in the messuages etc. In
consequence on 4 March 1334 the sheriff of Berwick was ordered
to restore the lands to Adam de Corbrig provided that they were
held by him solely on these grounds (*Rot Scot* i, 264). It was noted
in June 1337 that a rent of 15s, granted by Ralph Philip for the
upkeep of Berwick bridge, was settled on a tenement in Briggate

then held by Adam de Corbrig and 'waste' (*ibid.*, 493). The petition
is calendared in Bain iii, 218–219.

6

Their liegeman, born in England, Simon de Bedenhale, burgess
of Berwick, petitions the King and Council that whereas a William
Spore his uncle, whose heir he is, was seised of a tenement in
Soutergate in Berwick as of fee and right until ousted by the war of
Sir Robert de Brus, and also a Simon Spore his father, whose heir
he is, was seised of a tenement in Seyntmarigate in Berwick as of
fee and right until ousted by the said war, and Simon de Bedenhale
after the surrender of Berwick sued an Adam Brekroue and
William Mayden, then tenants of the said tenements, and during
his suit they adhered to the Scots and thereupon the chamberlain of
Berwick seized the tenements into the King's hand as forfeiture.
He requests an enquiry and justice (AP 1590).

A nostre seignur le Roi et a son conseil prie le soen liege homme
nee dengleterre Symound' de Bedenhale, Burgeys de Berewyk sur
Twede, qe come vn William Spore vncle le dit Symound' qi
heir il est fust seisi dun tenement en Soutergate en la dite ville de
Berewyk' come de fee et de dreit tauntqil fust euste par la guerre
mue par sire Robert de Bruys: Et auxint vn Symond Spore pier
le dit Symond' de Bedenhale qi heir il est fust seisi dun tenement
en Seyntmarigate en la dite ville de Berewik' come de fee et de
dreit tauntqil fust euste par la dite guerre. Et le dit Symond' de
Bedenhale pres le rendre de la dite ville de Berewik' enpleda vn
Adam Brekroue et William Mayden adonqes tenauntz des ditz
tenemenz, et pendaunt son plee le ditz Adam et William sount
ahers a les enemis descoce, et sur ceo le Chamberleyn de Berwik'
ad seisi en la mayne nostre seignur le Roi les ditz tenementz come
sa forfeture: pleise a nostre seignur le Roi de grante bref au
Chaumberleyn de Berewik' denquer la verite et qil lui face dreit
et resoune.

Endorsed: Eit bref forme sur sa peticion au dit Chaumberlein
denquere sur les pointez de sa dite peticion et de returner lenquest
en chauncellerie, la quele returne et vewe le Chaunceller face

assauer au Roi ce qe serra troue par la dite enquest et le Roi lui face outre sa grace.

1333–34. Following an inquest as above it was found that William Spur was seised in demesne of a messuage in Seyntemarigate in Berwick in the time of King Alexander and that he was later amoved by war. After divers tenants it came by forfeiture of Robert de Loweder junior into the King's hands. Simon son of Patrick de Bedenhale was next of kin and heir, and was ever loyal. On 4 March 1334 the sheriff of Berwick was ordered to restore Simon de Bedenhale to possession provided he had not remitted his right to any other (*Rot Scot* i, 265–266).

7

John de Routhbiri, chaplain, petitions the King's council that whereas John de Routhberi, formerly burgess of Berwick, his uncle, died seised as of fee in the time of King Alexander of lands and tenements in the street of Our Lady in Berwick lying between the tenement of William de Poulwrth to the north and the tenement of the abbot of Kelso to the south, which holding is in the King's hand by reason of the forfeiture of Peter de Kymbregham: because John de Routhberi, chaplain, is nearest heir to his uncle he requests a remedy (AP 6782).

Al consayl nostre seignur Le Roy Mustre Johan de Routhbiri, Chapelayn, que Johan de Routhberi iadis burgois de Berwyc' son oncle, Murruste vestu et seysi ⟨com de fee⟩ en Le tens le Roy Alexander de [terres] e tenement' en La Rew nostre dame en Berwyc', gissaunt entre Le tenement William de Poulwrth' enuers le North' et le tenement Labbe de kelsow enuers le seu, Le quel tenement est en La Mayne le Roy par le forfecture Peris de kymbregham. Et pour ceo qe Le diste Johan de Routhberi chapelayn est plein prochayn aire Le diste son oncle, si pri il grace et remedie pour dieu.

Endorsed: Dicunt quod Johannes de Routhbire quondam Burgensis de Berewico fuit seisitus de tenemento infrascripto tempore Regis Alexandri etc et quod obiit inde seisitus, et post mortem suam intrauit Johannes filius suus et heres et illud tenuit quousque villa de Berewico capta fuit per Regem auum et tunc amotus fuit et semper hactenus, et quod dictus Johannes Capellanus qui nunc sequitur est consanguineus et heres Johannis filii Johannis propinquior et quod fuit in villa etc et [non] remisit etc.

Habeat breue vicecomiti Berewyc' quod liberet prefato Johanni tenementa predicta si occasione premissa et non alia in manu Regis existant, tenenda prout predictus Johannes auunculus suus ea tenuit saluo iure Regis et alterius cuiuscumque.

1333–4. Following an inquest as above it was found that John de Routhebury, lately burgess of Berwick, and his ancestors were seised of a messuage *in vico Beate Marie* in Berwick in the time of King Alexander and died so seised, and John de Routhebury as son and heir entered into possession and held the same until he was amoved by Edward I at the time of the capture of the town. John de Routhebury, chaplain, was kinsman and heir of the said John son of John, and the messuage was in the King's hand by the forfeiture of Peter de Kymbriggeham, then in occupation. John de Routhebury the chaplain was in the town at the time of its recapture. He and his ancestors had always had the right (*ius*). In accordance with the conditions of surrender the messuage should be restored; and on 4 March 1334 the sheriff of Berwick was so ordered, provided that the forfeiture was the only cause of the land being in the King's hand (*Rot Scot* i, 267).

8

Hugh de Hecham of Newcastle upon Tyne petitions the King and Council that whereas the King granted him by letters patent sealed under the seal of Berwick a messuage with appurtenances on the Ness in Berwick, which was of Peter de Kymbrigeham, and a messuage with appurtenances near Brideþurgh' gang in the same town, which was of Ralph de Staunford, lately the King's enemies, by whose forfeiture they came into the King's hands and so are, to have until Martinmas in his eighth year, rendering to the King 40s: Hugh requests a grant of the same to him and his heirs for ever at an annual rent to the King and his heirs of 40s a year in equal portions, and Hugh will live there and build them up (AP 5737).

A nostre seignur le Roi et a son conseil prie le son Hugh de Hecham de Noef Chastel sur Tyne qe come nostre seignur le

Roi ad grante par ses lettres patentes enseales de sous seal qil vse a
Berewyk' sur Twede au dit Hugh' vn mees od les appurtenaunces
sur la Nesse en la dite ville de Berewyk' qe feu a Piers de Kymbrigeham et vn mees od les appurtenaunces pres de Brideþurgh'
gang en la dite ville de Berewyk qe feu a Rauf de Staunford'
nadgairs [enemys] nostre dit seignur le Roi, et les queux par la
forfaiture mesme deux Piers et Rauf deuindrent a les mayns
mesme nostre seignur le Roi et issint sont en sa mayn a auoir
tanqe a la seint Martin lan du regne le dit Roi oitisme, reddant
au dit nostre seignur le Roi .xl. s.: qe lui pleise granter au dit
Hugh et a ses heirs a touz iours les ditz mees od les appurtenaunces queux sont sasetz, reddant chescun an au dit nostre
seignur le Roi et a ses heirs .xl. s. par eweles porcions, et le dit
Hugh' veot enhabiter et edifier illoqes.

Endorsed: 'Habeat tenementum predictum ad terminum sex annorum: Ita quod securitatem inueniat ⟨vicecomiti Berewic'⟩ ad
dictum tenementum per se vel per alios de Anglia sufficientes
melioritandum et ad reddendum firmam' *cancelled*
   Eit les ditz tenementz a terme de sis auns pur la ferme qil rend'
a ore: Issint qil troefse surete au viscunt de Berewik' de enhabiter
les ditz tenementz a lui ou par ascun autres sufficients Dengleterre,
et qil susten[t les dites] tenementz en auxi bien manere qe ils sont
a ore .... sa ferme present au Roi.

c. 1334. On 17 June 1334 Hugh de Hecham was granted a messuage
on *le Nesse* in Berwick lately of Peter de Kymbrigeham and a
messuage by *Bradthurghgang* in the same lately of Ralph de Staunford, who as enemies and rebels had forfeited their lands, to hold
for fifteen years from Martinmas following, rendering to the
chamberlain of Berwick 60s, half at Whitsun and half at Martinmas, to be kept as received and to be occupied by him or other
sufficient Englishmen (*Rot Scot* i, 273).

9

Their merchant Richard Colle of Norham petitions the King
and Council that he has well and truly served the King and his
father in his Scottish war at Berwick and stayed on the Scottish

marches, wherefore he requests a little messuage in Berwick on the corner of the Ness at a reasonable price, so that he can hence-forth have a certain income [to contribute to the] strength and defence of the town (AP 7939).

A nostre seignur le Roi et a son conseil pri son marchaund' Richard Colle de Norham, qui bien et leilment ad serui .... bien nostre seignur le Roi Edward' son pier cum en temps nostre seignur le Roi qi ore est, et fust demoraunt .... long temps en ayde de lui en sun guere Descoce au Berewyk' et au demure en la Marche des Escoces en ten .... de son vie: pur quoi le vandit Richard' pri qe vous pleise lui grantre vn ⟨petit⟩ mes en la vile de Berewyk' ...le qel mes est sur la corner del Nes pur vn raynabel pris, issint qil puisse de ci enauant auoir illoqes certein recetz .... afforcement et defens de la dite ville de Berewyk'

Endorsement illegible even under ultra-violet light

c. 1334. On 4 July 1334 Richard Colle of Norham was granted a messuage in *Le Fleshewerrawe* in Berwick, lately held by William Bette and forfeited as an enemy, for ten years from the Martinmas following, rendering to the chamberlain at Berwick 53s 4d, half at Whitsun and half at Martinmas, to be kept as received and occupied by him or other sufficient Englishmen (*Rot Scot* i, 275).

10

Ralph de Coldingham petitions the King that whereas Thomas de Coldingham his uncle, whose heir he is, bought a burgage in Berwick from Simon Frysel of which he was seised as of fee and right, free from all rent save 6d a year to the King, until he was ousted by Robert de Bruys: then Simon entered the same burgage and gave it to a Patrick Flemyng, who leased it to Giles de Myndrom in fee at a rent to him and his heirs of £4 a year, by forfeiture of which Patrick the £4 were seized into the King's hand. Since the town came into the King's hand Ralph has re-covered the burgage against Giles by writ of right before the mayor and bailiffs, and now the sheriff is distraining him for the £4. He lodged a petition in the last parliament held at York, requesting the King to have an enquiry so that he can hold the burgage quit like his ancestor held it, which enquiry, taken by the King's command and returned into Chancery, found that his ancestor held it free of the said £4. He requests an order that he can hold the burgage quit of the £4 like Thomas his uncle, and that a writ be sent to the sheriff to that effect (AP 8739).

A nostre seignur le Roi prie Rauf de Coldingham qe cum Thomas de Coldingham vnkle le dit Rauf qe heir il est purchasa un burgage en Berewyk' de Symon Frysel, de quel il feut seisi com fee e droit, descharge de tote manoir de rente saue .vj. deners au Roi par an taunke il feut de ceo ⟨burgage⟩ ouste par Robert de Bruys: en qi temps le dit' Simonde entre mesme le burgage e le dona a vn Patrik' Flemyng', le quel Patrik' lessa mesme le burgage a Giles de Myndrom en Fee rendrant a luy e ces heirs quatre liures par an, par la Forfaeiture (sic) de quele Patrik' les ditz quatre liures sount ia seizerz en la Meyn nostre seingnur le Roy. E le ⟨dit⟩ Rauf puys qe la vile vynt en la Meyn nostre seingnour le Roy aed recoueri le dit burgage uers le dit Gyles par bref de droit deuant le Maier e les balifs de la seisine le dit Thomas, e ia le vescount ilok' lyu destreynt pur les quatre liures, sur queu il Mist vne peticioune en le parlement dareyn tenuz a Eurewyk' en priant ale Roy qe il feist enquer la verite, ensi qe il pueit teneir le dit burgage descharge com son auncestre le tynt, sur quia par comaundement nostre seingour le Roy enquest est pris e retourne en Chauncelerie par quele est troui qe son auncestre le teynt descharge de ditz quatre liures: qe lyu plrra comaundre qe il pueit teneir le dit burgage descharge de les quatre liures com le ⟨dit⟩ Thomas son vnkle que heir ⟨il⟩ est le teynt, e sur ceo maunde son bref' a son vescount ilokes.

Endorsed: Soit lenquest [returne] en chancellerie *probably erased*
    Soient lenquestes returne en chancellerie vewes et examinez et si troue soit come les peticons (sic) supposse, adonqe soit droit fait en chancellerie.

1334. Following an inquest it was found that Thomas de Coldyngham, uncle of Ralph de Coldyngham who was his heir, acquired for himself and his heirs a tenement in Berwick from Simon de Frysel, who with his ancestors had held the same in the time of King Alexander and later until this acquisition free of all service save an annual payment of 6d in aid of the fee-farm of Berwick. Thomas held the same by this service until he was ousted by Robert de Bruys in war, when the heirs of Simon entered and alienated the tenement to Patrick Flemyng, who later leased it to Giles de Myndrom at a rent of 6 marks. Ralph by the King's writ of right sued against Giles before the mayor and bailiffs of Berwick after its capture according to the law and custom of those parts to recover seisin. Ralph was ever loyal and neither he nor his uncle had remitted any rights. The sheriff of Berwick was ordered on 6 July 1334 to supersede any collection of the rent from Ralph and allow him to enjoy the tenement without payment of the 6 marks, just as Thomas his uncle and his feoffees had before the war (*Rot Scot* i, 275). Parliament met at York on 21 February 1334 (*HBC*, p. 519). Thomas de Coldingham was a substantial wool-merchant who bought from the convent of Durham, from whom he also leased the fishery at Paxton (Durham, Bursars Accts 1302–14 passim).

II

Their burgesses of Berwick petition the King and Council that whereas they and their forefathers were in possession of the Belfrey of Berwick in the time of King Alexander and long before— the commons of the town had it in fee-farm on behalf of the good folk to them, their heirs and successors, burgesses of the town for ever from a Simon Maunsel, to whom the bare site was in fee, rendering 6d a year to the King and 20s a year to Simon, and furnishing the place at their own expense, Robert de Tuggal, sheriff, has seized the Belfrey into the King's hand and collected its revenues.

Also the burgesses petition that whereas cannage from the harbour used to be levied and kept in the time of King Alexander and before in the following form: the good-men of the commons each year elected two responsible men of good estate sworn to receive the cannage and, when repairs were needed, seek out workmen and set down the costs by advice and view of the wisest of the town, and render account once a year of receipts and issues, so that no money came to the King's ministers nor to the town's profit, but was allocated to *Holdeman*, which is a perilous entry for ships entering and requires much expense each year, Robert de Tuggal took all the issues of this toll so that the harbour is on the point of being lost.

Also the same burgesses petition that whereas at all times since the fall of Berwick Bridge they have been quit of ferry-charges as was found lately by inquest held between the King and the bishop of Durham, by order of Robert de Tugal the ferrymen will allow no burgess to cross without paying passage.

Also the said burgesses petition that whereas they were in the time of King Alexander and at all times quit of all kinds of gauging of wine and cloth, Robert de Tughal made them pay gauge and tronage.

Also the said burgesses petition that a grievously great custom was levied in England on the King's burgesses of Berwick, to wit that when they arrive with their merchandise in the towns and havens throughout England they are charged 3d from every pound of money and every pound of merchandise to their great impoverishment, being in low estate by reason of the war.

Also the said burgesses petition that whereas they were wont in the time of King Alexander and at all times to be quit of tonnage in the royal burghs of Scotland and those of the said burghs were free from tonnage in Berwick, now that the tonnage is levied on them at Berwick, they are levying it on those of Berwick when in their parts. They request a grant of quittance throughout England when they trade, and as much for English goods at Berwick, as used to be in the time of King Alexander (AP 4612).

[A nostre seign]ur le Roi et a son Conseil mostrent ces burgees de sa ville de Berwyk, qe por la ou eus et lour [auncestres] furent en possession de le Berfrai de Berwyk en le temps le Roi Alisander et grant ⟨temps⟩ deuant cum ... qe la comunaute de la dit ville aueyt pris a fe ferme pur les bones gentz qe adonqes furent a eus, a lour heirs et a lour successours burgeis de la dit ville pur totes iours de vn Symond' Maunsel a qe la place voide estoit en fee, rendaunt a nostre seignur le Roi .vj. deners par ane et au dit Symond' et a ses heirs .xx. soutz par anee et fesent a lour propres custage herbergier la dit place com il est ore: Ia est venu Robert de Tuggal viscunt et ad sessi le dit Berfreit en la meyn nostre seignur le Roi et leue les issues: de qoi il priount remedy pur dieu.

sewn to above

Ensement musterent les vantditz Burgees qe le Canage de la hauen de la vantdit ville solait en le temps le dit Roi Alisander et deuant son temps ester leue et garde en la furme qe ensute: Les bones gentz de la comunalte esleisoient chescun aune deuz prode hommes de bon estat iurrez de receiuer la Canage et en temps qe amendement dust ester mys de purchascer ouerrons et de metter Les Custages en la mendement de Holdeman par le Consail et la Weu des plus sage de la ville et de render aconte vne feez par an de lour recepte et despense, issi qe nul dener ne veent au minister le Roi ne au profit de la ville forke tanke soulement fust reserue a Holdeman qe est vn perilious entre pur le nefs qe venunt Et chescun an demande grant Custage; Ia Roberd' de Tugal vaunt dit recepte totes les issues, par qoi la dit Hauen est en poynt destre perdu: de qoi il priount remedy pur dieu.

Ensement mustreint meismes les Burgeys qe par la ou ⟨en⟩ tous temps pus qe le Punte de Berwyk' chaij il ount este fraunche et quyt de paier passages al ferry cum il fust troue nadgaires par lenqueste ⟨qe⟩ passa parenter nostre seignur le Roi et le Eueshe de Durrem, Ia par commandement Robert de Togal les passagers ne suffrent nul Burgeis passer saunz paier passage: de qoi il priount remedy pur dieu.

Ensement mustrent les dites Burgeis qe par la ou il ount este en le temps Roi Alisaunder et en totes temps quites de tote manere de gaugages des vines et de draps, Ia Robert de Tughal les fet paier gaugage et ensement tronage ... il furent totes jours quites; de qoi il priount remedy pur dieu.

Ensement mustrent les dites Burges qe vn grant Custume greueus est leue en Engleterre sur les Burgeis nostre seignur le Roi de sa dit ville de Berwyk, cest asauoir qe come il arriuount eu lour marchandises en les villes et as hauenes sur la mere par tote Engleterre il leuent de chescun liuer de deners et de chescun liuere de marchandises treis deners, qe est vn grant enpouerisment a les gentz nostre seignur le Roi de sa dit ville qe sunt en simple estat par lencheson de la gere: de qoi il priount remedy pur dieu.

Ensement mustrent les dits Burgeis qe com il soloient en temps Roi Alisander et de tote temps en touz les Burgs le Roi en escoce ester quites et frans de tounages, et eaux de les dites Burgh' furent franches de tounages en la dite ville de Berwyk', Ia pur ceo qe lein leue tounage de euz en Berwyk', ils leuent de touz eaux de Berwik' cum ils sount en lour partyse: de qoi il priount remedy pur dieu. Et pur ceo, Trescher seignur, nous vous prioms pur lamur dieu si com nous … Burges qil vous plest de vostre grant grace grantter qe nous purroms ester quites en totes partie Denglettere ou noz marchaundises, et les marchaundes Dengleterre quites dever nous, si com il solaint ester en le temps Roi Alisander.

Endorsed: Peticiones de Scocia liberate apud Nouum Castrum super Tynam.

1337. On 24 June 1337 Antony de Lucy, keeper of Berwick and justice of Lothian, and Thomas de Burgh, chamberlain there, or their deputies, were ordered to hear the suit of the mayor, bailiffs and commons of Berwick and summon before them Robert de Beverlaco as its present keeper to hear reasons for restoration of *le Berfreyt*, following a petition from the mayor, burgesses and commons of Berwick before King and Council in Parliament. This alleged that they had acquired a vacant space in the town and built thereon a house called *le Berfreyt* to hold prisoners of the town in custody and used it as a prison from before the time of Alexander, lately King of Scotland, and later until the capture of the town by Edward I, who had granted the house to William de Keythorp. Later Edward I was more fully informed of the right of the mayor, burgesses and commons and was asked to restore it to them, and after the keeper made enquiry on oath into the truth from men of Berwickshire and it was confirmed that the mayor, burgesses and commons had it in fee before the time of King Alexander from Simon Maunsel at a rent of 20s and were in peaceful seisin until Edward I had given the house to William de Keythorp, he restored the house, which they held in peace until Robert de Tughale, lately chamberlain, took it into the King's hand after the surrender. For this reason it was in the King's custody and now in the custody of Robert de Beverlaco, the house being held for 6d annual rent and worth 100s (*Rot Scot* i, 493–94). Tughale, who was appointed sheriff of Berwickshire on 27 July 1333, was replaced before 2 August 1338, by which date he was keeper of the King's victuals at Berwick. He was appointed chancellor of Scotland on 5 February 1342 (*ibid*, 256, 531, 541, 637).

12

His liegeman Henry de Chesham, merchant of London, petitions the King that whereas Thomas de Swanlend and he took in fee-farm by the King's charter from the chancellor at Berwick an empty site on the High Street within the gateway called Watergate, which lately was of Simon de Saltoun and is now forfeit, which is 52 feet long and renders annually at the rate of 12d a foot, which is too dear for an incomer to make his profit, he requests the King to grant them and their heirs by charter the said empty site for 6d a year, just as another burgage would render in the town, and then Henry could build on it and incur expenditure and live on it to the strengthening of the town (AP 9313).

A nostre seignur le Roi prie son lige home Henri de Chesham Marchant de Loundres Come Thomas de swanlend et ledit Henri eunt pris en fee ferme par Chartre nostre dit seignur de Chanceller en Berewik' sur Twede vne voide place en la Haute Rue dedenz la porte appelle Watergate qe fu nadgueres a Symon de Saltoun et ore forfaite, qe contient en longure .lij. pies rendant pur chescun pie par an .xij. d. qest trop chier a home de nouel venu a faire son profit, pleise a nostre dit seignur le Roi graunter as ditz Thomas et Henri et leur heirs par Chartre la dite voide place pur .vj. d. par an sicome vne autre burgage rende en la dite ville, et adonke le dit Henri purra edifier et mettre custages et inhabiter en afforcement de la dite ville.

Endorsed: Eyt pur .L. s.

temp Edward III. Royal letters of protection were issued for Simon de Saltoun of Berwick on 26 July 1333 (*Rot Scot* i, 255). Thomas de Swanlend was collector of customs at London in 1339 (*CPR 1338–40*, p. 313).

Franchises

Ancient Petitions 1614, 1615, 2153, 2185, 5211, 8247, 13028.

13

The burgesses of Berwick petition King and Council that whereas they are new men come into the town and had and have great need of the King's aid and have several times asked him, for his own benefit and the profit of his town of Berwick as well as of the burgesses inhabitant, to grant them certain kinds of franchises which are contained in the bill attached: these franchises were promised them by the King at Roxburgh to have and confirm at his next parliament, and by reason of the franchise many merchants and other sufficient persons have come and stayed there since then. They request King and Council to have the matter at heart, for they have stayed a long time on this suit (AP 1614).

A nostre signour le Roi et a soen Cunsoyl prient les Burgeys de Berewyk' sur Twede, que cum eux soyent noueles gentz veniz en la dite ville, et graunt mester auereyent et vnt del ayde du Roy, E eus plusures feze eyent priee a nostre signeur le Roy ausiben pur soen prou et amendement pur sa ville de Berewyk' cume pur les Bourgoys enhabitantz que il lur voillet grauntier certeynes articles des franchises, lesqueux sont contenues en la Bille que est attachee a ceste: Lesqueux fraunchises nostre segneur le Rey leur promist a Rokesborgh' de auer et confermer a soen procheyn parlement, et par la reson de la fraunchise multz des marchantz et altres gens suffisantz sunt illeuques venuz et demorrees puys ceu temps. Et ceste chose prient il pur dieu, que le Roy et soen Cunseil voleyent aueir au quoer, kar il vnt lungement demorree entur ceste suyte fere.

Endorsed: Coram Rege quia de Scocia
Further endorsement illegible

c. 1306. See no. 14 below.

14

Draft of proposed charter enclosed in above: confirming that Berwick be a free burgh with free burgesses, an elected mayor, bailiffs and other officers. Disputes arising from elections would be

settled on the oath of 24 senior townsmen. These officers would
swear to be faithful to the King and the town and the duties of
their office. The burgesses and their heirs should have their lands
freely. They should have return of writs where it concerned
burgesses' business. No sheriff, bailiff nor officer should enter the
burgh unless in case of default by the mayor, reeves, bailiffs or
town officers. Pleas should be held only in the burgh before the
mayor, etc in suits arising from land, trespass, debt etc, who might
entertain all pleas moved in the burgh without a writ. The
burgesses and their heirs should elect a burgh coroner, who would
take his oath before the mayor and burgesses. They should not
answer elsewhere appeals or any other charges, but only before
the mayor etc. None in the burgh arrested or charged with a
crime should be imprisoned nor tried other than in the burgh
by the burgesses. No outside merchant might buy wool, hides or
fells within Berwickshire save from a burgess of the town. The
burgesses might freely grind all their grain and malt wherever
they would. No outside ship laden with salt might discharge its
cargo for sale by the boll or smaller measure unless it was sold
to a burgess of the town. No outside merchant might sell or cut
any cloths in the town by the ell but only by the whole cloth:
and if he did not wish so to sell he could remove his wares freely
on payment of the usual customs, and so with all other outside
merchants and their wares. No abbot nor prior nor men of religion might have any fulling-house within the county or town of
Berwick. If any of the castle garrison wronged any burgess, he
should seek remedy at the gate of Berwick castle and the accused
after trial would be amerced according to his offence: and if any
burgess incurred a forfeit to one of the castle garrison the latter
would seek justice at the town's tolbooth. None of the castle
garrison might take prises from articles on sale in Berwick against
the will of the burgesses. No burgess might be distrained outside
the burgh for a debt where he was not the chief debtor or a
pledge. There should be a prison in the burgh for the punishment
of malefactors, and the mayor etc should exercise jurisdiction over
infangenetheves and *utfangentheves*, saving the King's right to their
chattels. The burgesses should be exempt throughout the kingdom from payment of toll, pontage, passage, pessage, murage,
[pavage, canage], lastage, cariage, pickage, quayage, rivage,
wreck, waif, ward and ward-penny and all other customs leviable

from their wares. All inhabitants of the burgh, both men of religion and others, should freely enjoy their lands etc in the burgh, and share with the burgesses in any aids imposed on the burgh according to their means. Any who disregarded this concession would have their lands etc seized by the mayor etc until they made satisfaction. The burgesses should have a weekly market on Monday and Friday, and a fair annually from Easter until Michaelmas. They should be quit of prise taken for the King from wine bought for their own use. If any burgess died, having a legitimate son under age, the child with all the lands etc should be entrusted to the next kin onto whom no benefit of inheritance would devolve, to keep until he reached age, and the guardian should render account of his receipts to the mayor etc. Any hindering these privileges should incur forfeiture to the King (AP 1615).

Edwardus dei gracia etc Archiepiscopis Episcopis salutem etc. Sciatis quod ad emendacionem et melioracionem ville nostre de Berewyco super Twedam et vtilitatem ac comodum Burgensium nostrorum eiusdem ville volumus et concedimus pro nobis et heredibus nostris quod predicta villa liber Burgus sit et homines eiusdem ville liberi sint Burgenses et habeant omnes libertates et liberas consuetudines ad liberum Burgum spectantes. Preterea volumus et concedimus quod Maior prepositi balliui et ceteri ministri in eadem villa per transacciones eiusdem ville eligantur. Et ita quod si aliqua controuersia inter comunitatem predicte ville in eleccione Maioris prepositorum balliuorum ac ministrorum predictorum fieri contigerit, tunc fiat eleccio per sacramentum viginti et quatuor de melioribus et discretioribus hominibus dicte ville, per quos villa tucius regi et negocia eiusdem ville comodius tractari poterunt et terminari. Et quod predicti ministri prestant sacramentum corporale super sacra dei Ewangelia quod ipsi erunt fideles nobis et heredibus nostris ac comunitati dicte ville et omnes libertates eisdem Burgensibus et Burgo predicto a nobis concessas pro viribus suis conseruabunt illesas, et fideliter ac diligenter facient omnia ea que ad eorum officia pertinent in Burgo predicto. Concessimus etiam pro nobis et heredibus nostris quod predicti Burgenses et eorum heredes ac successores sui terras *et* tenementa sua que habent infra predictum Burgum et habituri sunt inposterum tam de eorum hereditate quam de perquisito in eorum vltima voluntate libere et absque impedimento nostri vel heredum seu ministrorum nostrorum quorumcumque dare libere possint quibuscumque voluerint. Et quod habeant retornum omnium breuium nostrorum Burgum illum et Burgenses eiusdem qualitercumque tangencium. Et quod nullus vicecomes balliuus seu minister noster Burgum illum ingrediatur ad officium aliquod ibidem de aliquo ad Burgum illum pertinente faciendum nisi in defectum Maioris prepositorum balliuorum ac ministrorum eiusdem ville. Et quod non inplacitent seu inplacitentur alibi quam infra eundem Burgum coram Maiore prepositis balliuis supradictis de aliquibus terris possessionibus tenuris intrincesis (*sic*) transgressionibus debitis conuencionibus seu contractibus infra eundem Burgum factis. Et si quis versus eos placitare voluerit, ipsi non respondeant neque placitant extra Burgum illum. Et quod possunt se cognoscere de omnibus placitis causis et querelis sine breui nostro infra eundem Burgum motis vel mouendis. Et quod ipsi Burgenses et eorum heredes per breuia nostra de Cancellaria inmediate eis dirigenda Coronatorem eligant de se ipsis qui prestet sacramentum Maiori et Burgensibus dicte ville quod fideliter faciet et conseruabit ea que ad officium Coronatoris pertinent in Burgo predicto. Insuper volumus et concedimus quod dicti Burgenses et eorum heredes non respondeant aliquibus forinsecis super aliquibus apellacionibus rettis iniuriis transgressionibus criminibus calumpniis aut forisfactis eis inpositis vel inponendis nisi solummodo per Burgenses nostros dicte ville et hoc coram Maiore prepositis balliuis et ministris supradictis. Concessimus etiam quod nullus de Burgo predicto pro secta sua captus vel rectatus de aliquo crimine vel forisfacto pro quo debeat inprisonari non inprisonetur nec adiudicetur alibi quam in Burgo predicto per predictos Burgenses. Volumus et concedimus quod nullus extraneus mercator emat aliquas lanas corea seu pelles lanutas infra Comitatum Berewyci nisi a Burgensibus eiusdem ville tantum. Et quod predicti Burgenses libere possint molere omnia blada sua et brasium suum vbicumque voluerint, sine impedimento et calumpnia nostri et heredum nostrorum. Et quod nulla nauis extranea carcata sale discarcabit in aliquam domum ad vendendum per bollas vel paruas mensuras seu per celdr' nisi vendatur Burgensibus eiusdem ville. Et quod nullus extraneus Mercator vendat nec cindat aliquos pannos suos in dicta villa per vlnas set per pannos integros. Et si sibi non placuerit pannos suos in dicta villa modo supradicto vendere, licitum erit sibi adire partes cum pannis suis vbicumque voluerit sine impedimento aliquo, soluta prius consuetudine sua: et ita fiat de omnibus aliis Mercatoribus et mercandisis suis. Et quod nullus Abbas seu Prior nec aliqui alii viri religiosi habeant aliquam domum fullonum ad fullendum pannos infra Comitatum seu villam Berewyci. Et si aliquis castellanus alicui Burgensi in aliquo vel aliquibus forisfecerit aut deliquerit, ipse Burgensis adibit portam Castri Berewici ad prosequendum et petendum iusticiam, quam ibi optinebit et reus amercietur secundum quantitatem delicti. Et si aliquis Burgensis alicui castellano forisfecerit, ipse castellanus veniet ad Tolbotham eiusdem ville ad ius suum petendum et optinendum et eodem mode predictus reus amercietur. Et quod nullus castellanus habeat captionem seu prisam rerum venalium in villa Berewyci vel apud Berewycum ven[ientum vltra] voluntatem Burgensium eiusdem ville. Et quod nullus Burgensis per aliquem distringatur extra eundem Burgum ad reddendum alicui aliquod debitum vnde non sit Capitalis debitor vel plegius. Volumus [et con]cedimus quod quedam prisona fiat et habeatur in eodem Burgo ad malefactores ibidem deprehensos castigandos (sic), ita quod predicti Maior prepositi et balliui de Infangentheues et vtfangentheues quando eis pl[acuerit iusticiam] facere possunt, saluis tamen nobis eorum cattallis. Volumus etiam et concedimus pro nobis et heredibus nostris quod predicti Burgenses et eorum heredes per totum regnum et potestatem nostram de theolonio pontagio passagio pessagio mura[gio, pauagio, canagio], lastagio, cariagio, pickagio, cayagio, riuagio et omni wrecto et wayf, tam per terram quam per mare, warda et wardepeny et omnibus aliis consuetudinibus secularibus et demandis de rebus mercandisis suis ... in perpetuum sint quieti. Et quod omnes illi de Burgo predicto tam viri religiosi quam alii terras tenementa redditus et possessiones infra predictum Burgum habentes libertatibus et liberis consuetudinibus predictis gaudere vole[ntes] ... et auxilium in omnibus cum eisdem Burgensibus quociens Burgum illum talliari seu auxiliari contigerit secundum eorum facultates: et si contingat aliquos vel aliquem premissorum contra hanc concessionem .... tenementa redditus terre et possessiones sue capiantur et detineantur in manu Maioris prepositorum et ministrorum predictorum quousque de eorum delicto et defectu eis plenarie fuerit satisfactum. Concedimus etiam .... prefatis Burgensibus mercatum suum et quod libere habeant et possideant illud per duos dies singulis septimanis, videlicet per diem Lune et in die Veneris: et quod habeant feriam suam singulis annis in villa predicta cum omnibus ad eam p[ertinenciis] ... a festo Pasche vsque ad festum sancti Michaelis Archangeli plene completum duraturam. Et quod de propriis vinis suis de quibus negociantur quieti sint de recta prisa nostra, videlicet de vno doleo ante malum et alio post ma[lum] ... [Et] si aliquis Burgensis de legitimo thoro habeat aliquem liberum infra etatem existentem et de ipso Burgense contingat humanitus, ipse liber positus erit cum omnibus terris redditibus possessionibus ac cattallis suis sub custod ... viri proximioris parentele sue ad quem hereditas dicti liberi descendere non poterit, qui inueniet securitatem ad conseruandum dictum liberum terras redditus et possessiones suas bone et fideliter ... [vsque] ad etatem peruenerit legitimam secundum disposicionem et ordinacionem Maioris prepositorum balliuorum ac ministrorum predictorum, qui custos eisdem fidelem reddet compotum de omnibus et singulis exitibus receptis ... Et prohibemus ne quis eis super hoc faciat impedimentum molestiam dampnum aut grauamen super plenam nostram forisfacturam. Has vero consuetudines et libertates eisdem Burgensibus nostris ville Berewyci super Twedam et eorum heredibus concessimus et hac presenti carta nostra confirmauimus, tenendas at habendas de nobis et heredibus nostris sibi et heredibus suis bene [et pacifice] libere quiete plenarie integre et honorifice in omnibus locis et rebus sicut factum est inperpetuum. In cuius rei etc.

c. 1306. Four petitions were presented by the burgesses of Berwick in the parliament of 1306, the first for the fines imposed on burgesses in the Mayor's Court, the second for the profits of the courts merchant, tolls and petty customs, the third for liberty to use the Statute Merchant as in London and elsewhere in England, and the fourth for a grant of customs, farms and profits of mills and fisheries at Berwick for 12 years, saving the Great Custom on wool, in order to build a stone wall around the town, towards which they would contribute £501 (*Memoranda de Parliamento 1305* [1893], pp. 178–9). On 4 August 1302 Edward I had granted a charter providing for a guild merchant and markets, and a fair from Easter to Michaelmas (*CChR* iii, 27–29). The amended charter enclosed with the petition had no reference to a guild but stipulated that strangers should not buy wool in Berwickshire, and added wreck and waif to the levies from which Berwick merchants should be exempt. On 30 March 1307 Edward I granted the mayor and burgesses the town with its mills, lands, tolls, amercements etc for an annual fee-farm of 500 marks (*ibid.* iii, 89–90). Cf. no. 22 below.

15

Louis, Bishop of Durham, petitions the King and Council that whereas the water of Tweed is boundary in many places between England and Scotland the King of Scotland had passage by boat to transport men and other things from Berwick to Tweedmouth, where they reached the bishop's soil in England: and the bishop ought to have similar passage rights, which used to be worth more than £20 a year to him and his predecessors *sede plena*, and now the King of Scotland maintains the passage by force and disturbs the bishop, who cannot enjoy it, to his loss and to the disinheritance of his church and of the Crown. And whereas the King of Scotland has the river bank ... who ought not to anchor in the Tweed for more than an hour, those from Scotland anchor ... whereby the bishop loses the profit of his fishery, to which he is entitled *sede plena* and the King loses *sede vacante*, for whereas the franchise of Norham is held of the bishop as by right of his church of Durham a site called ... in the water of Tweed, part of the said manor of ?Ord, has always been held of the said town, and this has been drawn to the King of Scotland, to the damage of the bishop and the disinheritance of his church and of the Crown. He has sued Sir Robert de Brus in his time and the keepers of Scotland since about the wrongs ... to make amends and redress and he can have no justice, wherefore he requests the King to ordain a remedy for the right of his Crown (AP 5211).

A nostre seignur le Roi e a son conseil moustre Lowys Euesqe de Duresme qe la ou Lewe de Twede est Marche en plusours lieux entre Engleterre e Escoce issi qe le File del Ewe iloqes parte les deux roialmes, le Roi descoce ad eu passage par Bate de passer gentz hors de la ville de Berewyk' e autres choses ..... Twede-muth' e illoqes arriuent sur le soile le dit Euesqe en Engleterre ....

doit le dit Euesqu auoir au tieu passage e arriu ..... Berewyk' le
queu passage valeit au dit Euesqe e a ces predecessours pluys de
vynt liures par an le see pleyn e au ta ..... e valant au Roi
deschoce meinteint son passage par pouer e par force e desturbe
le dit Euesqe qil ne peot .... en damage de lui e desheritaunce de
sa Eglise e de la Corone. E sire ceo la ou le Roi Descoce ad la
riuail ..... ok' les queux ne deyuent ancreer de cea le File del
Ewe de Twede forsqe vne hour la venoi[ent] ... i Deschoce e
ancreont de cea le File del Ewe ..... par quei le dit Euesqe perde
le profit de sa pecherie qe .... [de]uoient auoir de droit le see
plein e le Roi .... [Fra]nchise de Norham est tenu de le dit
Euesqe come le dreit de sa Eglise de Duresme vne place de terre
qest appelle ..... en Lewe de Twede e est parcele de dit Manoir
de Derd' e ad este de tote temps ... tenuz dela dite ville .....
atreit la dit place au Roi Deschoce au damage le dit Euesqe e
desheritance de sa Eglise e de la Corone ..... vsqe eit suy a sire
Robert ⟨de⟩ Brus en son temps a ales gardeinz Deschoce qe
puis en cea ont este qe les tortz e les ..... faissent amende e redresces si ne poait il vnqes vnqor reson auoir: par quoi il prie a
nostre seignur le Roi ... voleit de cestes choses ordeiner remedie
e pur le droit de sa Corone.

Endorsed: Coram Rege et magno consilio
   Quant le Roi verra temps, il ordeinera de remedie en ceste
partie, mes aore ne poet il mie.

?1331. On 3 February 1331 Edward III informed King David II
of Scotland and Thomas, earl of Moray, keeper of Scotland during
the king's minority, that Bishop Louis de Beaumont had made
to him a formal complaint of breach of the Treaty of Northampton (1328). In particular, although it had been agreed that church
lands occupied during the war should be restored without
prejudice West Upsetlington, situated west of Norham but on the
north bank of the River Tweed, was still held by the Scots, despite
frequent letters from the English king requesting its deliverance
to the bishop of Durham as an estate of the church of St.
Cuthbert. Patrick de Dunbar, earl of March, was hindering the
bishop by armed force from taking possession and receiving the
issues (*CCR 1330–33*, p. 283). In a petition on the subject (AP
7233) it was noted that 'the township of West Upsetlington near

Norham is part of England and annexed to the Crown from time immemorial. The writs of the bishop of Durham run there *sede plena* and the writs of the king of England *sede vacante*, as in the bishopric of Durham. No bishop of Durham ever owned suit or fealty or any other service for the said township. . . . Furthermore, whereas the lords of Tweedmouth have their boats to ferry men and other things and anchor (*arivere*) opposite Berwick, and the lords of Berwick anchor opposite Tweedmouth with their boats, the Scots come and claim the whole water as parcel of the kingdom of Scotland. They anchor their boats on English land and will not suffer English boats to anchor on Scottish land, thereby appropriating a right appurtenant to the English Crown. The wardens of the truce will not afford any remedy'. Cf. Bain iii, 187–88.

16

Richard, Bishop of Durham, petitions the King and Council that whereas the bridge between Berwick and Tweedmouth was broken in the time of King Edward the King's grandfather it was agreed between the then King of Scotland and the Bishop of Durham that the King would send by boat men and other things from Berwick to Tweedmouth and in the same way [the Bishop] would send men from Tweedmouth to Berwick, and the profits would be shared equally between the King and the Bishop. So it was until the sixth year of the present King in the time of Louis, the lately dead bishop of Durham, when David de Bruys levied war against the King and the residents of Tweedmouth, and burnt and destroyed. And when Berwick came into the hands of the King, then the temporalities of the bishopric of Durham were in his hands through the death of the said Louis, at which time the ministers of the King at Berwick took the entire profits of the crossing . . . by their boats on the Bishop's soil at Tweedmouth to the disinheritance of his church of Durham (AP 13028).

A nostre seignour le Roi e a soun counseil [moustre] Richard eueske de Durem' [qe com]e le pount entre Berewik' sur Tuede e Twedemuth' fuit enf[rait] a temps le Roi Edward ael nostre seignour le Roi qe ore est, accord se prist entre le Roi descoce qe adonqes fuit e leuesqe [de Durem'] . . . le dit Roi passereit par

batz les gentz e autres choses hors de Berewik' iusqe a Tuedemuth' e qe [leueske de Dure]me yn meisme la manere passereit
les gentz de Tuedemuth' tant qe a Berewyk' e qe le profit del
dit passage durr .. ewelment de parti entre les ditz Roi e leueske,
e issi fuit vse tant qe lan sisme de nostre seignour le Roy qe ore
est [en] temps sire Lowis qe dreyn moreust eueske de Durem', qe
Dauy de Bruys leua de guerre contre le Roi ... achaca, e les
tenantz e les reseauntz de Tuedemuth' e ardist e destruyt. E apres
quant la dite vile de Berewik' deuy[nt en] la mayne nostre
seignour le Roi adonqes furent les temporaltes del euesche de
Durem' en sa mayn par la mort le dit L[owi]s, du quel temps les
ministres le dit nostre seignour le Roi de Berewyk' pristront le
profit du passage entierement ..... par lour batz sur le soil de dit
eueske en Tuedemuth', en desheritaunce de sa eglise de Durem'
...... dont il prie remedie.

Endorsed: soit mande au viscount e autres les ministres de Berewyk'
que sils puissent trouer par bone enqueste a sibien gentz
Dengleterre come Descoce que Leuesque feust seisi de la passage
decea auant le temps Robert de Br[uys] e adonque ils soeffrent
les Ministres le Euesque par decea auer le dit passage come ses
predecessours lauoient e qils surseessent de faire tieles oppressions
sur le poeple.

1334. On 12 March 1337 an exemplification was made of a writ
of 15 June 1334 directed to the King's chamberlain of Berwick
and his sheriff there, to allow the bishop of Durham passage with
his boat from Tweedmouth to Berwick and to receive the profits,
and to restore any taken for the King's use since the previous 7
September when the temporalities were restored. It was found by
an inquisition that in the times of Alexander and John, former
Kings of Scotland, the bridge of Berwick over the Tweed had
been entire and that there was no ferry over the river. Later
when the bridge was broken any man could cross in his own or
another man's boat at will. Later Antony Bek, then Bishop of
Durham, had a boat made for the crossing and received its profits
during his life. Then Edward I had a boat for the passage from
Berwick to Tweedmouth, which Edward II granted to John Hayward together with the bishop's boat during the vacancy of 1311.
When the temporalities were restored to Bishop Kellawe so was

the ferry, and he was so seised as was Bishop Beaumont until stopped by Robert de Bruys (*CPR 1334–38*, pp. 395–6). Cf. no. 18 below.

17

Roger de Lue and Joan his wife petition the King and Council that whereas King Edward I formerly gave to John Hayward, who was his chief butler for twenty years and more as can be testified by the magnates there present and father of the said Joan, whose heir she is, by charter for his good service the crossing of the Tweed to Berwick, to have and to hold to him, his heirs and assigns, until a bridge between Berwick and Tweedmouth be sufficiently repaired so that men on foot or horse or in carts or with loads might pass there safely: and John had no other reward for his long service, and by virtue of the said charter and its confirmation by King Edward, as they are ready to show, was peacefully seised of this crossing, to take its profits, until they were ejected by Sir Robert de Brus, when by force and treason he took the town of Berwick and Scottish land on . . . And Roger to aid the present King of England and Sir Edward Bailliol, King of Scotland, to recover their lands found an armed horseman at his own expense, as can be testified by the magnates present, to follow and challenge his right from the beginning to the end. May it please the King to deliver to Roger and Joan the crossing as Joan's inheritance, to hold according to the form of the charters of his ancestors, as they have [a duty to find] an armed man ready in the manner aforesaid.

Furthermore they petition that whereas John Heyward had from the King's grandfather certain burgages in Berwick in Hudgate where they lodged, and then leased to . . of Boston, burgess of the same town, at an annual rent of 7 marks to John and his heirs, of which he had peaceful seisin until Sir Robert de Brus by force and treason took the town: they may have a grant of their seisin of the said tenements or the rent as the inheritance of the said Joan, as they found an armed man at their own expense from the beginning to the end, [when] the King entered Scotland with armed men (AP 8247).

A nostre seignur le Roi et a son consail prient Rogier de Lue et Johanne sa femme come le Noble .. Roi sire Edward [ael nostre seignur le Roi] nadgairs auoit done a Johan Hayward qe estoit son chief boteler pur sa bouche par vynt aunz et plus contin[uellement, si come] purra estre testmoigne par les grantz qi adunqe feurent, piere la dite Johanne qi heir ele est, par sa chartre ..... de la ville de Berewyk' pur son bon seruice le passage de Twede a Berewyk' pur auoir et tenir au dit Johan et [ses heirs et assignes] tauntqe vn pount entre Berewyk et Twedemouth feust suffisalment reparaille issint qe gentz a pee et a chiual et charrue .... summages peussent illoeqes saluement passer. Et le dit Johan nul autre regerdoun auoit de lui a demorer pur ses .... son lung seruice forqe le dit passage, et par vertue de la chartre auantdite et par confermement le .. Roi Edward ..... sont prestes amostrer a vostre volunte, estoit pesiblement seisi de cel passage et de prendre de ce les profistz tauntqe [ils sont] ostee par sir' Robert de Brus quant il par force et par tresoun prist la ville de Berewyk' et la terre Descoce sur le ..... Et sur ce le dit Roger en eyde nostre seignur le Roi Dengleterre qore est et de monsieur Edward Baillol Roi Descoce pur les [dits] .... reconquere les eyt troue vn homme arme a Chiual a ses custages, si come purra estre testmoinge par les grantz qi illoeqes [feurent] ... son droit suyre et chalanger, del comencement tauntqe a la fyn, qil pleise a nostre seignur le Roi de sa grace rendre as ditz Roger [et Johanne] le dit passage come leritage la dite Johanne a tenir solon la forme de les chartres de ses Auncestres de si come eux ounte ... prest vn homme arme en la Manere auantdit.

Estre ce prient a vostre seignurie les ditz Roger et Johanne si le vous plest pur ce qe le dit Johan Heyward auoit de son ... de vostre Ael ascuns burgages en la dite ville de Berewyk' en Hudgate, les queux il meismes herbergea et puis les lessa a .. de seint Botolf, burgeys de meisme la ville, rendant au dit John et a ses heirs sept Mars par an, dont il est en pesiblement seisine [tauntqe le] dit sire Robert de Brus par force et par treison prist la ville auantdite, qe vous veullez de vostre grace granter as ditz Roger et Johanne qe eux peussent auoir leurs seisine des tenementz auantditz ou de la Rente auantdite come del heritage la dite Johanne de [sicome ils] ont troue vn homme arme a leurs custages del comencement tauntqe a la fyn ... nostre seignur le Roi entra par genz darmes .... le terre Descoce auantdite.

Endorsed: Soit ceste peticion mande en Chancellerie et la vewes lour chartres et munimentz qils ont del dit passage et des tenementz contenuz en la peticion, et quant le Chanceller serra enfourme il avise le Roi et le Roi ent comand' sa volunte.

1333–37. The crossing was claimed before April 1337 by Richard Bernard as nephew of Hayward and his next heir. He claimed that Heyward had been seised of the ferry until June 1307, when Bishop Bek forcibly ejected him from the Tweedmouth end. He had successfully sued before Edward II at Berwick in 1311, when a jury of English and Scots affirmed that the ferry was in the King's gift and denied that the Bishop of Durham had any rights (Bain iii, 258–259). After the capture of the town by the Scots the deeds were lost, but with its recapture Bernard was reinstated as cousin and heir of Hayward. The Bishop of Durham, however, had resumed occupation and he claimed the King's aid. An enquiry ensued before Antony de Lucy, the warden, in the presence of the mayor and bailiffs of Berwick, which found that Hayward had been in occupation for 15 years until the capture of the town by the Scots. On the strength of this and a local verdict that Bernard was next heir Edward III granted him the ferry until a new horse and foot bridge was built, in reward for his good service to himself and to John, the late earl of Cornwall (*CPR 1334–38*, p. 422). Bernard was still seeking restitution in April 1345 (*ibid. 1343–1345*, p. 462). Cf. no. 25 below.

18

The bishop of Durham petitions the King and Council that whereas the water of Tweed separates the kingdoms of England and Scotland, of which the bishop is lord as by right of his church of St Cuthbert of Durham as far as the mid-stream adjacent to his lands, and he and his predecessors were at all times seised of all profits deriving from the river as far as the mid-stream until Master John de Bolton, lately chamberlain of Berwick, seized the profits of the ferry there without cause: as appears by the certificate of Robert de Tuggale, chamberlain, returned into Chancery by writ *super modo et causa* stating that Master John seized the ferry because he believed and understood that it ought to belong to the town of Berwick. Ever since then he requested the King and Council to grant him restitution of the issues, having regard to the fact that Richard de Bury, his immediate predecessor as bishop, on his petition to the King in his eighth year (1334) had restitution of the same ferry because Robert de Bruys had ejected him by force, it having been found by inquest by men of Scotland and England that his petition was true. He then died seised and the present bishop was so seised until his unreasonable ejectment by Master John (AP 2153).

A nostre seignur le Roi e son conseil moustre leuesqe de Duresme qe come lewe de Twede departe les Roialmes dengleterre e Descoce de quelle le dit Euesqe est seignur tanqe a file dycelle par tout ou ses terres sont ioignantz e son soil come de droit de sa esglise de seint Cutbert de Duresme, e lui e ses pre-decessours de tout temps seisiz de touz les profitz prouenantz de le soil de le ewe tanqe au file dycelle tanqe Mestre Johan de Bolton' nadgairs Chamberleyn de Berwyk' seisist les profitz de le passage illoqes sanz cause, come piert par la certificacion de Robert de Tuggale, Chamberleyn, par brief super modo et causa qe certifia en la Chancellerie qe le dit Mestre Johan seisist le dit passage quia credidit et intellexit qe le dit passage deueroit appurtener a la ville de Berwyk; pur quai del houre qe le dit passage feust seisi sanz cause il prie a nostre seignur le Roi e son conseil de lui granter restitucion oue les issues, eiant regard qe Richard de Burry darrein predecessour le dit Euesqe, sur sa peticion quelle sui a nostre dit seignur le Roi en lan oitisme de son regne, auoit restitucion de mesme le passage pur tant qe Robert de Bruys lui ousta par force, e ensi troue feust par enqueste sibien par gents Descoce come Dengleterre qe sa peticion feust veritable, e puis morust seisi e leuesqe qore est seisi tanqe le dit Mestre Johan lui ousta nounresonablement.

Endorsed: soit cest bille mande en Chancellerie e appelle le Chamberlein e autres qe sont appeller, soit fait droit.

c. 1367. A commission dated 12 February 1367 was issued to Henry de Percy, Ralph de Nevill, John de Stryvelyn, John de Moubray, Thomas de Ingelby and William de Fyncheden to enquire in Berwick and in the county of Northumberland touch-ing an information on behalf of Thomas, bishop of Durham, to

the effect that whereas the Tweed was the boundary between
England and Scotland and the bishop was lord of the bed of the
river as far as midstream wherever it adjoined his demesne, and he
and his predecessors were ever seised of the same where the water
adjoined the land of their lordship of Norham and Tweedmouth,
and took all profits arising, such as fisheries, fixings of weirs and
mills, and passage tolls of ships and boats, as of the right of their
church of St. Cuthbert of Durham, Master John de Bolton, late
chamberlain of Berwick, had taken into the king's hand all profit
of the passage of ships and boats in the bishop's lordship without
reasonable cause (*CPR 1364–67*, p. 427).

19

The bishop of Durham petitions the King and Council that
whereas the water of Tweed separates the kingdoms of England
and Scotland the bishop is lord of it and of the adjoining lands
as far as midstream, and he and his predecessors have been seised of
all profits arising therefrom, Master John de Boulton, lately
chamberlain of Berwick, seized the profits of the Tweedmouth
crossing which abuts on the bishop's land on the English side, on
the understanding that the profits of the crossing belonged entirely
to the town of Berwick: which is to the detriment of the King
and the English crown, and deprives the bishop of his right:
whereupon the bishop sued a petition in parliament for remedy,
which was endorsed and sent to the chancery for right to be done,
and then the bishop sued in chancery from one day to another
and could get no final answer, which he requests of the King and
Council according to law and reason (AP 2185).

A nostre seignur le Roi e son counseil moustre leuesqe de
Duresme qe par la ou lewe de Twede depart les Roialmes
Dengleterre e Descoce, de quele ewe le dit Euesqe est seignur tanqe
au fyl de ycele par tot oue ces terres sont ioignantz a ycele, e lui
e ses predecessours seisitz de tote les profitz prouenantz de la dite
ewe tanqe au fyl sanz destourbance tanqe maistre Johan de
Boulton' nadgers Chaumberleyn de Berewyk' seisit les profitz du
passage de Twedemouth, quiel passage est fait sur la terre le dit
Euesqe de part dengleterre, entendant qe les profitz de passage del
ewe de Twede apurtinentz entierement a la ville de Berewyk',

quel chose est en desheritance de mesire le Roi e de sa Corone
Dengleterre, e oustant le dit Euesqe de son droit; sur qoi le dit Euesqe
suyst peticion en parlement dauoir remedie en cel partie, quel
peticion fuist endosse e mande en la Chauncellerie de faire droit
illoeqes, e puis le dit Euesqe ad suy en la dite Chauncellarie de
iour en autre e ne poet nul fyn auoir, dount il prie a nostre
seignur le Roi e son conseil comander qe finale discussion ent
soit faite solonc lei e resoun.

Endorsed: Soit qe ceste bille vewe en la Chancellerie, cy soit fait
droit.

c. 1374. A commission dated 28 November 1374 was issued to
Thomas de Ingelby, Roger de Kirketon, Donald Heselrigg,
Bertram Monboucher, Robert de Umframvill and Roger de Fulthorp to take an inquisition in the county of Northumberland
touching a petition for restoration exhibited by Thomas, bishop
of Durham, before the King and Council in parliament, showing
as before his rights in the Tweed and the fact that he had taken
all profits and emoluments arising from boats taking men or things
to Scotland and from all other things crossing until Master John
de Bolton, chamberlain of Berwick, seized into the King's hands
the passage of the said water on both sides as pertaining to the
town, by which pretext the bishop was removed from the passage
within his lordship at Tweedmouth on the English side (*CPR
1374–77*, p. 64).

Trade

Ancient Petitions 1205, 1616, 1627, 2386, 2470, 4114, 4425, 4426,
4749, 4760, 11930.

20

His burgesses of Berwick upon Tweed petition the King and
Council that whereas the King granted them for the growth of
the town and for his own profit the crofts and empty sites lying
within the town's pale, Master Nicholas de Kardoyl, the King's
buyer, and others asked to hold these same crofts and sites of the

King in fee, to the detriment of the King and his heirs, and to the prejudice and great loss of them and the diminution of the town, when merchants coming daily there wanted the empty spaces to lodge because of the great franchises given by the King to the town. If the King granted to any the empty places it would block the town from the sea. Furthermore, if he granted away the sites, the town of the beneficiaries would be larger than the King's own town. They request some remedy (AP 1616).

A nostre seignour le Roy e a son counseil moustrent ses Burgeis de la vile de Berewyk' sur Twede qe par la ou nostre seignour le Roy auoit ordine e graunte pur la cresaunz de la dit vile e pur son profit les croftes e les voides places qe gisent dentz le paliz de la vile: Ore vent Mestre Nichol de Kardoyl akatur nostre seignour le Roy e plusurs autres e demandent meismes celes croftes e places a tenir de nostre seignour le Roy en fee, a deshericesun nostre seignour le Roy e de ces heirs e a preiudis e greef damage de eux e a menusement de la dit vile: Cume Marchauntz veignent a la dit vile de iour en iour e si demandent les voides places pur herberger pur les graunt fraunchises qe nostre seignour le Roy ad graunte a la dite vile: E si nostre seignour le Roy graunt a akuny les voides places il serra forclos entre la vile e la Meer, issint qe ceux de sa vile ne auerunt nul issu de vers la Meer: E sil graunt les places hors de sa meyn, la vile de ceux qi prendrunt les places si serra plus graunt qe la vile le Roy meismes; dunt il prient pur son graunt pru e le profit ses heires qil ordeyn acun remedy qe seit pur eux e la dite vile.

No endorsement

1302. On 30 July 1302 an inquest was taken to ascertain by what services Nicholas of Carlisle, the King's sergeant at Berwick, held a burgage and 4 'places', and whether 40 acres lying between the town and its fosse, extending from the old place formerly of the Friars Preachers of Berwick outside the streets of Burghgate, Sutergate, and Sissorgate towards ..., held by many men at the King's will, might be granted to Nicholas to hold of the King without damage. The jurors testified that Nicholas held the burgage of Ralph Phelipe in Briggate, a vacant place on the Ness lately of the Bishop of Moray, another there of William le

Scriptor, and another of Henry of Stirling. In the time of Alexander the land was held freely by the burgesses as appurtenant to their burgages. When the burgh was founded the burgesses had leave to build if they wished, and there were streets on the ground arranged for this. They were now held of the King for 2s an acre. The ground could not, without the greatest injury to the King and the confusion and destruction of the town, be held solely by Nicholas or any other: for he might build as good or a better town there than the present, and the burgesses had no other place within or without the town for common pasture, and it was divided in small parts among the burgesses. If they ceased to be appurtenant, there would be room for 160 burgages (Bain ii, 332–333). On 30 March 1307 a grant of the 'vacant places' was made to the burgesses (CChR iii, 89–90) Cf. nos 13 and 14 above.

21

Roger de Gosewyk' and John de Chilton, burgesses of Berwick, petition the King and Council that whereas they bought in Northumberland 32 sacks of wool and took them to Berwick and loaded them on a ship of Beverley and paid their great new customs due to the King, as is witnessed by Sir Robert Heron, parson of Ford and keeper of the said customs, and took them to Aardenburgh in Flanders, there Sir John de Courtreye, burgess of Bruges, and two Germans, one called Herman Sidentop of Lubeck and the other Tidman Felescape of *Goten*, came and arrested the 32 sacks because the King had sent his sailors of Sandwich with a ship called *la Plente* and a barge, of which William Langeters was master, to keep the Scottish sea so that no ship might enter to sustain his enemies; this ship *la Plente* with the barge took off Aberdeen a Flemish ship laden with wool and brought it to Berwick and sold the wool. Sir John de Courtreye and the Germans said that the petitioners had bought the wool from the said sailors, and for this reason they detained the 32 sacks, worth 18 marks each, by assent of the échevins and commons of Aardenburgh in Flanders, to their loss of £300, for which they request a remedy (AP 2470).

A nostre seignur le Roy e a son consayl Mustrent Roger de

Gosewyk' et Johan de Chilton', Burgeys de sa vile de Berewyk'
sur Twede, qe par la ou il auoient achatez en Northumberlount
Trente deus saks de Leignes, e mesmes ceaux Leignes amenerent
tanqe a Berewyk', e la les chargerent en vne Nief de Beuerleye
et loiaument payerent lours grantz noueles Custumes dues a nostre
seignour le Roy auxsint come il temoigne par sire Robert Heron
parsone de Forde e gardeyn de mesmes le Custumes, e mesmes
ceux leignes amenerent tanqe Darneburgh' en Flaundres, la vindrent sire Johan de Courtreye Burgeys de Brugges et deus
Alemaunz, leun a noun Herman Sidentop de lubyk' e lautre
Tidman felescape de Goten, e mesmes ceux Trente deus Sakes
aresterent par encheson qe nostre seignur le Roy auoyt maunde
ses Mariners de Santwych' ou vne Nief' qe feust appellez la
Plente e vne Barge de mesmes la vile Dunt Willmen Langeters
estoyt mestre par Comaundement nostre seignur le Roy pur
garder la Meir de Escot' qe nul Nief' ne luj entrat pur sustoiner
ses Enemyes: la vint mesmes cele Nief' le plente oue la Barge
et pristrent deuant Aburdein vne Nief' de Flaundres chargez de
Leignes e mesmes cele Nef' amenerent tanqe ala vile de Berewyk'
e les leignes venderunt la ou bien lour fust: Par quey qe sire Johan
de Curtreie e les Alemaunz disoient qe nous auioms mesmes ceux
leignes achatez de les ditz Mariner. E par cele encheson mesmes
ceux leignes detenent il les Trente deus saks, pris de chekun Sak'
dys et vt Mark' par assent des Esquiuines e la Comune de Arden-
burgh' an Flaundres, a nos greues damages de .ccc. li' pur la quele
chose nous vous prioms si vous pleise de ceste chose grace et remedye.

Endorsed: Habeat breụe Comiti Flandrensi in forma communi.

c. 1305. A summary of this petition is printed in *Mem de Parl*,
p. 193. Roger de Gosewyk was keeper of the King's exchequer
at Berwick, 1311–12 (Bain iii, 433). William, brother and heir of
Robert Heroun, lately rector of Ford, was summoned to appear
at the Michaelmas session of the exchequer in 1317 to account for
the time Roger was controller and deputy of the chamberlain of
Scotland and keeper of the King's customs in Berwick (PRO, QR
Mem Roll 90 m 131d).

22

The same burgesses [of Berwick] petition the King and Council
that Tweedmouth market be abated as it used to be in the time
of King Alexander, which market was erected without warrant
to the great hurt of the King and of his town of Berwick.

The same burgesses also petition the King and Council that
whereas they were granted by charter a fair from Easter until
Michaelmas, that they will change the date and grant the fair from
Holy Cross in May [3 May] until the feast of St. John the Baptist
[24 June] following, for it will be of greater profit to the King
and the town (AP 1627).

Ensement priount memes les burgez au Roy e ason conseyl
qe le Marche de Twedmouth' seyt abatu cum soleyt estre en tens
le Roy Alexaundre, le quel Marche il vnt leue saunz garant en
grant damage du Roy e de sa dite vile de Berwyk

Assigenentur (sic) Johanni de Sandale Camerario Scocie et
Thome de Sheffeud' ad inquirrendum vtrum forum solebat esse
ibi ab antiquo an non et per quot tempus vsi sunt ibidem foro,
et inquisitis istis et omnibus aliis circumstancibus certificent
Regem et consilium suum.

Ensement priount memes lez burgez au Roy e ason conseyl
desicum il lour ad grante feyre par sa chartre de la Pasche iekes al
seynt Michel qe il lour voille sily plest ceste poynte changer e
grantir feyre du iour de la seynte Croyce en May iekes a la feste
de seynt Johan le Baptist' procheyn suaunt, kar ceo serreyt
greinour profit au Roi e amendement a sa dite vile de Berwyk'.

Videatur Carta per quam habent feriam et si ita sit, fiat eis
secundum peticionem suam et restituant aliam cartam

The Latin 'endorsements' are added below each petition.

1307. The alteration of the dates for Berwick fair was approved
in the Carlisle parliament of 1307 (*CChR*, iii, 29). The longer
period had been requested as recently as 1305; cf. no. 14 above.

23

William Gettour of Berwick petitions the King and Council
that certain Flemings of the power of the count of Flanders on

Saturday, the eve of Palm Sunday, 8 Edward II (15 March 1315), took his ship called *le Messager* of Berwick off Dunwich near the shore, while passing from Berwick to Flanders, and took from the ship goods of himself and his fellows, namely, 100 sacks of wool worth 11 marks a sack, to a total of 1100 marks, 400 hides of ox and cow worth £50, 10 sacks of wool-fells worth £50, and the ship worth £80, and 100 salmon worth 10 marks, and steered to Flanders, and killed 13 men found in the ship. He craves an arrest of Flemings until restitution be made for his goods so purloined (AP 2386).

A nostre seignur le Roi et a son conseil moustre William Gettour de Berewyk' qe certeyns gent de Flaundres del poer de la seignurye le Counte de Flaundres le Samady en la veille des Palmes En lan du regne nostre seignur le Roi Edward filz le Roi Edward vtisme pristrent vne Nef del dit William qe hom apela le Messager de Berewyk deuaunt donwych' pres de la Coste ⟨de⟩ la Mer, passaunt de Berwyk' vers Flaundres et les biens le dit William et ses compaignouns en mesme la Nef trouez, cest asauoir Cent sacks de Layne pris le sack de vnze Marcks La summe Mil et Cent Marcs, quatre Centz du quirs des boefs et des vaches pris du Sinkaynte Liueres, .x. saks des pealus du Layne pris du synkaynte Liueres, et la Nef qe valust .iiij.ˣˣ liueres, et Cent Saumonz qe valerent diz Marcs, pristrent et amenerent tauntqe a Flaundres, et .xiij. genz en la Nef trouez tuerent: par quei le dit William prie a nostre seignur le Roi et a son consail qe la-Rest se face deuers les ditz Flemyngs taunqe restitucion lui soit fait de ses biens et ses chateus suthdites en tele manere amenez et enportez.

Endorsed: Quia negocium istud tangit Flandrenses tradatur domino Willelmo de Ayremyne qui se de negociis Flandrensibus intro-mittit.

1315. Styled 'admiral' in 1311/12, William Gettour was com-missioned to seek and seize all ships sailing with victuals to Scot-land without the King's licence and bring them to Berwick. On this service he received pay at the rate of 2s a day. The master of his 'barge' *la Messagere* and its 'constable' both received 6d a day, and the boatswain and 26 others 3d a day (Bain iii, 401). On 28 November 1312 he was bailed to answer at the exchequer an accusation of robbery brought against him by various Flemings (PRO, QR Mem Roll for 6 Edward II, m 92 [Bain iii, 58]). On 10 April 1315 a request was sent to the count of Hainault, Holland and Zeeland and lord of Friesland to hear the petition of William Getur, burgess of Berwick, and to do justice in his complaint that having loaded at Berwick his ship *le Messager de Berewyk* with hides, wool etc of certain merchants of the town to be taken to Flanders to trade, certain of the King's enemies of Scotland laid in wait for his ship, attacked it, and slew all but one of the crew and took the ship and cargo to Middelburg in Zeeland, where they still detained it. He was asked to write back by the bearer what had been done (*CPR 1313–18*, p. 227).

24

William de Ayremynne, clerk, petitions the King and Council that whereas the King was lately obliged to Walter de Gosewyk, burgess of Berwick, in £300 received as an advance, and in 125 marks which Walter borrowed to pay on the King's behalf to Sir Roger de Moubray, which sums the King wished to be paid Walter from the customs of Hartlepool, as is shown more clearly by letters patent sealed with the King's privy seal, of which a transcript is sewn to this petition: then before Walter received anything from the custom William with the assent of Sir John de Sandale, then chancellor, and Sir Walter de Norwich, then treasurer, delivered to Walter a wardship which he had bought from the King, and took the letters of privy seal from him: and because he was assigned the marriage of John, son and heir of John de Londeham', worth 100 marks, the treasurer and barons of the exchequer are unwilling to make allowance or payment on these letters because no mention was made of the recipients of the money from Walter. He requests a remedy (AP 4425).

Attached: Privy seal letter of Edward II, recognising debts of £300 and 125 marks payable to Walter de Gosewyk from the first issues of the Hartlepool customs, dated 14 July 1311 (AP 4426).

A nostre seignur le Roi et a soun Counseil prie William de Ayremynne, clerk, qe come le dit nostre seignur le Roi nadgeres estoit tenutz a Wautier de Gosewyk Burgeys de Berewyk en trois

Centz liures qil resceust de lui daprest et en Centz et vynt et cynk' marcs, les queux le dit Wautier emprist apaier pur nostre seignur le Roi a monsieur Rogier de Moubray, des queux sommes nostre seignur le Roi voleit et granta qe le dit Wautier eust este paiez de la custume de Hertelpol, sicome plus pleinement piert par les lettres ouertes sealees du priue seal nostre seignur le Roi dount le transecrit est cusu a ceste peticion: et puis auant qe le dit Wautier resceust rien de la dite custume le dit William par assent de sire Johan de Sandale adoncs Chauncelier et de monsieur Wautier de Norwicz adoncs Tresorer liuera au dit Wautier de Gosewyk' vne garde, qil auoit achate de nostre seignur le Roi, et prist les dites lettres du priue seal deuers lui: et sur cel lui eit este assigne auant ces houres le marige Johan filz et heir Johan de Londeham' en value de Centz mars, Le Tresorier et Barons de Lescheker ne volent faire allouance ne paiement de celes lettres pur ceo qe mencion nest pas faite qi resceut ceux deniers du dit Wautier, par quoi le dit William prie a nostre seignur le Roi qil lui pleise comander ent sa bone grace.

Endorsed: Soit maunde as Tresorrer et Barons de Lescheqer qe serchez roulles et remembrraunces de Lescheqer et autres remembrraunces tochauntz la dite matyre et appelles a eux qe sount appeller facent son gre en due manere de tant come li est arere ou par paiement ou par assignement.

Attached: Edward par la grace de dieu Roi Dengleterre, seignur Dirlaunde et Ducs Daquitaine, a touz ceaux qui cestes lettres verrount saluz. Sachez nous estre tenuz a nostre cher Marchaund' Wautier de Gosewyk' Burgeys de Berewyk' sur Twede en treis Centz liures qui nous receumes de lui de prest, et Cent et vint et cynk' mars les queux il emprist a paer pur nous a monsieur Roger de Moubray, des queux soumes nous voloms et grauntoms qe le dit Wauter soit paez des primeres issues de la graunt custume de Hertelpol, entesmoignaunce de queu choses nous auoms fait faire cestes noz lettres patentes. Doun souz nostre priue seal a Berewyk sur Twede le .xiiij.^{me} iour de Juyl, lan de nostre regne quint.

Endorsed: Irrotulatur   Coram rege

post June 1318. William de Ayreminne started as a clerk of the

King's exchequer, and was master of the Rolls by August 1316. Among his preferments he was rector of Whitburn in 1312 (cf. no. 140 below) and Bishopwearmouth in 1316. He was a canon of Lincoln (1314), Dublin (1315), London and Salisbury (1316), warden of St. Leonard's Hospital, York (1318), keeper of the Privy Seal (1324), acting keeper of the Great Seal (1326) and Treasurer of England (1331). He was consecrated bishop of Norwich by papal nomination in September 1325, and died in March 1336 (*HBC*, p. 84; *Fasti*, p. 7). Walter of Goswick had been appointed deputy butler in the port of Berwick on 14 September 1309, and on 16 January 1311 a safe-conduct was issued for his men trading in divers parts of the realm. On 13 July 1311 Goswick was granted the issues of the great custom on wool, hides and fells at Hartlepool for four years as from the following Michaelmas, in part payment of the King's debt (*CPR 1307–13*, pp. 190, 327, 377). John Sandall was Chancellor of England from 26 September 1314 to 11 June 1318, and Walter Norwich was Treasurer between 26 September 1314 and 27 May 1317 (*HBC*, pp. 84, 101).

25

John Hayward petitions the King and Council that whereas Walter de Goswyk, lately mayor of Berwick, and other burgesses of the same town for themselves and others of the commons of the town recognised in the late king's chancery in his 35th year [1306/7] that they were obliged to John in 80 marks a year for the passage, pesage and tronage of Berwick and certain lands and tenements in the town leased to them, by which recognisance the burgesses owe him £300 from issues received before the loss of the town, wherefore he sued a royal writ to the chancellor of Scotland to send to the chancery in England the said recognisance, and he did so. John Hayward has sued a writ from the English chancery to have his debt met from the goods and chattels of the burgesses and commons of Berwick where found in England, but he is hindered in chancery until now from having this writ (AP 4114).

A nostre seignur le Roy et soen consail prie Johan Hayward qe come Wauter de Goswyk' nadgeres Meir de Berewyk' et autres

Burgeises de mesme la ville pur eaux et les autres comuners de
mesme la ville se eusent reconuz en la Chauncellrie soen pere qe
dieux assoille Descoce, Lan de soen regne trentequinte, destre tenu
audit Johan en quatrevyntz mars par an pur le passage pesage et
tronage de Berewyk' et ascuns terres et tenementz en mesme la
ville a eaux lessez, de la quele reconisance lez ditz Burgeises lui
sont tenuz en .CCC. li' des issues de ce rescues auant la ville
perdue, parquoi ledit Johan sui bref' nostre seignur le Roy qe ore
est a soen Chaunceller' Descoce qil feyt venir en sa Chauncellrie
Dengleterre la reconisance auantdite et il issint ad fet, parquoi ledit
Johan Hayward ad sui dauer bref' hors de sa Chauncellrie
Dengleterre pur sa dite dette leuer dez biens et chateaux dez
Burgeyses et comuners de la ville de Berewyk' auantdite trouez
en Engleterre, mes ledit Johan ieskes enca est destorbe en sa dite
Chauncellrie de ce bref' auer, dont il prie remedie.

Endorsed: Il bosoigne qil demoerge ci la qe autre chose soit ordene.

Coram magno consilio

?c 1320 Following the capture of Berwick by the Scots in 1318
the refugee merchants found themselves liable for a variety of
debts, ranging from the undertaking to defend the town down-
wards (*CPR 1313–17*, p. 671). For Hayward's tenure of the ferry
at Berwick see nos 16 and 17 above.

26

The mayor and good men of Berwick petition the King and
Council that whereas all wool growing in Scotland in the lordship
of the King, which was wont to be shipped from Berwick, by
reason of the embargo is now taken and traded with the Scottish enemy to the great loss and handicap of the town and
sustenance of the enemy: may it please the King and Council to
order writs to the chancellor, chamberlain and sheriff of Berwick
to enquire by good men to obtain an estimate of wool growing
within the lordship in a year, and may the amount found be
assigned for export in aid of the town and more (AP 11930).

A nostre seignur le Roi et son conseil moustrent le Maire et

les benes gentz de sa ville de Berwyk' Pur ceo qe touz les leynes
cresceantz en escoce dedeinz la seignurye nostre seignur le Roi qe
soloient estre eskypez a Berwyk par cause de noun passage sont
ore meintenant amener et tratez de iour en autre as enemys descoce
a grant perte et arrerissement de sa dite ville et en meintenance
des ses ditz enemys: Pleise au Roi et a son dit conseil maundier
ses briefs a Chaunceler, Chamberleyn et viscontes de Berewyk
denquere par bones gentz qaunt des leynes crescent en mesme la
seignurye par estimacion en vn an et qe la somme trouez pusse
passer en outres et amendement de sa dite ville et mout plus.

slits for closure

Endorsed: Soit respondu comment homme quide qe lestaple et le
passage des leines serra ouert en Engleterre a la Goule daugst', et
adonqes serra le passage enter a Berewik' et en le meen temps
soit enquis des choses compromises en ceste bille.

1352–53. The embargo was imposed in September 1352, prepara-
tory to the introduction of home staples on 1 August 1353 (Lloyd,
pp. 205–6).

27

The poor burgesses of Berwick petition the King that whereas
they have sustained many losses and damage in the town both by
the enemy from Scotland and from Normandy and the sea, and
that above all in Flanders they lost 170 sarplers of wool worth
£2,000 to their great detriment, may it please his lordship to
consider the great losses and hurts that they have sustained in the
town and grant of his special grace 2,000 sacks of wool grown in
Northumberland to ship from Berwick at a customs rate of 13s 4d,
whereas they pay at present 26s 8d, for the comfort and relief
of the burgesses (AP 4749).

A nostre tresredoute seignur et tresexcellent seignur le Roy
supplient voz poures lieges Burgeys de vostre ville de Berewyk'
sur Twede qe come ils ont sustenuz plusours perdes et damages
en vostre dite ville sibien par enemys descoce come de Normandie
et le Mere et ala sumour en Flandres ils perderont .viij^{xx} et
.x. sarplers de layn a value de deux Milles liures a tresgrant

aneyntissement de lour estat, dont plese a vostre tresgraciouse seignuris considerer les grantz perdes et meschefs qils ont sustenuz en vostre dite ville et granter as aux de vostre grace especiale deux Mils saks de layn de la cressance de Northumbr' deskypper a vostre dite ville de Berewyk, apaier pur chescun sak' a custume .xiij. s. .iiij. d. la ou ils paiont au presente .xxvj. s. .viij. d., en confort et relefe de vos ditz Burgeys pur dieuy et en oeure de charite.

Endorsed: le Roi de sa grace especiale ad grante as suppliantz en releuacion de lour estat qils puissent achater Milles sakes de layn en le Counte de Northumbr' de lancressance du dit Counte et les carier a la ville de Berewyk' sur Twede et el port illoeqes charger et dilloeqes a quelle partie qe lour plerra del amitie le Roi amesner, paiant pur chescun sake .xiij. s. .iiij. d. et nient plus: Niencontresteant qils furent charge par lettres patentes du Roy a eux autre foith grantez de paier pur chescun sake de mesne la cressance .xxvj. s. .viij. d.: Issint tante .... es qils ne chargent el dit port namesnent des ditz parties ascuns layns de la cressance de nulle autre lieu dengleterre ne greindre nombre de la cressance du dit Countee, sur peyne de forfaiture de touz les layns auant-ditz.

c. 1392. On 30 May 1392 Gerard Heroun, collector of customs and subsidies in the port of Berwick, was ordered to suffer the merchants and burgesses there dwelling to load and take to foreign ports wool, hides and fells on paying 26s 8d a sack and as much on every pack of 240 fells, and 4 marks on each last of hides originating between Tweed and Coquet: paying 13s 4d a sack and pack, and 26s 8d a last where originating in Tevydale and parts of Scotland in the King's obedience: and 6s 8d a sack and pack and 13s 4d a last where originating in parts in obedience to the King of Scotland. This concession was in consideration of their losses by wasting and weakness and the fewness of men there dwelling, in order that merchants and others might be drawn to dwell therein. The King granted to any man of those parts in his allegiance that he might sell them wool, fells and hides, carry them to the town, and there expose them for sale, provided that an indenture be made between buyers and sellers certifying the true place of growth and the quantity thereof on the oath of the

merchants and burgesses, to be shown and given to the chamberlain and customers there, in order that a full and true answer
could be made for the customs and subsidies due from the town in
accordance with this ordinance (*CCR 1389–92*, p. 465).

28

The poor burgesses of Berwick petition the King that following
the burning and destruction of the town he provided relief, since
when they had rebuilt their houses in the town at their own cost,
but they had received only £33 of the 1000 marks promised from
the hands of the customs' collectors, to their great impoverishment. They request full and speedy payment of the residue as
otherwise they can no longer stay there.

Item, the burgesses petition that they pay different customs for
wool, hides and wool-fells coming to the port, namely for each
sack of wool, hides and wool-fells growing between Coquet and
Tweed in the county of Northumberland, 26s 8d, and from each
sack of wool, hides and wool-fells grown in Tevydale 13s 4d, and
for each sack of wool, hides and wool-fells grown in Scotland,
6d 8d. They request the removal of this variety to aid the burgesses and make them stay and live in the future, by granting
to them licence henceforth to buy wool, hides and wool-fells
growing in the three parts aforesaid and take them to the port
of the town and ship them, paying for custom 13s 4d a sack only,
as otherwise it will be necessary for them to evacuate the town
and live elsewhere where they can manage better. May the King
consider that King Richard, his immediate predecessor, granted
them, when they had no losses, leave to ship 1000 sacks of wool,
hides and wool-fells of the growth of Northumberland, paying
at the rate of 13s 4d a sack.

Item, the burgesses petition that whereas the town walls are
broken and wasted and in many places fallen to the ground so that
there is no defence against the enemy without his instructions
and help, may it please his lordship to order the amendment and
repair of the walls in a short time, for the safety of the town and
comfort and relief of the burgesses and defence against his enemies
(AP 4760).

A nostre tresexellent et tressouereigne seignur le Roy Supplient

voz poures Burgeis de vostre ville de Berewyk' . . . apres lar[son]
et destruccion de vostre dit ville en comfort et releue de vos ditz
Burgeys et en . . . les maisons deinz mesme la ville de vostre
grace especial' et . . . de voz custums deins le port du dit ville
par les mayns de vos custumers illoeqes . . . depuis quel temps . . .
les ditz Burgeis conferantz de vostre tresgracious doun sont edifiez
de nouel lour maisons deinz la dite ville a lour propres costages
et mys ent'rompe ne puissent . . . nulle paiement de ditz Mill'
marcz forsqe tauntsoulement .xxxiij. li' a grande empouerisment
et anyentisment de lour poures estate: Plese a vostre tresgracious
descrecioun ordeyner qe plein et hastiue paiement soit fait as ditz
Suppliauntz de la residue de les Mille marcz auauntdites en eide
Comfort et releue de cez ditz Burgeys ou outrement ils ne puissent
pluis longement demurrer illoeqes.

Item supplient voz ditz Burgeys qe come ils paient a vous
diuerses custumes pur leyns quirs et pealx lanutz venaunez au
port du dicte ville, cest assauoir pur chescun Sak' des leynes quirs
et pealx lanutz cressaunt parentre les ewes de Coket et Twede
en le Countee de Northumbr' .xxvj. s. .viij. d., de chescun Sak
des leyns quirs et pealx lanutz del cressance de Tevydale .xiij. s.
.iiij. d., et pur chescun Sak des leyns quirs et pealx lanutz del
cressance descoce .vj. s. .viij. d. en grande diuersite et ambiguite
des paiements de vostre dicte custume parentre voz custumes
illoeqes et voz Burgeys auauntditz: Plese a vostre tresgrante roialte
pur ouste lambiguite des paiementes de voz ditz custumes illoeqes,
en comfort et releuement de voz ditz Burgeys de eux faire demurrer et enhabiter vostre dit ville en temps auenir, de vostre
grace especiale granter a voz ditz Burgeys licence qils et chescun
de eux de cy enauaunt purront et purra achater leyns, quirs et
pealx lanutz del cressance de les troys parties suisditz et eux
amesner tanqe al port du dicte ville et la eux eskipper, paiantz a
vous pur la custume de chescun Sak' .xiij. s. .iiij. d. tantsoulement, ou autrement eux couyent de necessitee envoider et remuer
del dicte ville et enhabiter en autre villes ou mielx lour purra
ordeigner, considerant tresredoubts seignur, si vous plest, qe le
Roy Richard vostre darrein predecessour, qe dieux assoille, granta
a eux quant ils nauoient nulles perdes ne mischiefs licence de-
skipper Mille Sake de leyns, quirs et pealx lanutz del cressance del
Countes de Northumbr', paiantz a luy pur chescun Sak dicels
.xiij. s. .iiij. d. sanz pluis en eide et comfort de eux.

Item supplient vos ditz Burgeys qe come les mures du dicte
ville sont debrisez et degastez et en plousours lieux cheitz a terre,
issont qe nulle defence y poet estre encontre vos enemys illoeqes
sinon de vostre tresgracious ordinaunces et secour en celle partie:
Plese a vostre tressouerain seignurie, de vostre tressage discrecioun,
issint ordeigner qe les ditz mures purrent estre amendez et repar-
ailez deinz brief temps, en saluacioun de vostre dit ville, comfort
et releue de voz ditz Burgeys, et en defence encontre voz enemys
auauntditz.

Endorsed: Especiales peticiones
Touchant le second article de ceste peticione, le Roy veullant
conforter les Burgeuses, Marchants et enhabitantz de la ville de
Berewyk' et autres ensi y vorront venir pur enhabiter, de sa grace
especiale voet qils aient leffect de cest article, adurre pur trois
ans proscheins aduenirs: Pur . . . toute foitz qe des leynes cressantes
decea leawe de Coket ils ne facent eskipper en le . . . . . . sur peine de
forffaiture dicelles durant le terme suisdit.   *Galled throughout*

1410. On 8 May 1410 a grant was made for the removal of
certain differences and ambiguities which had arisen concerning
the payment of custom, in consideration of the burning and destruction of the town of Berwick and losses suffered. This allowed
burgesses and merchants resident in the town to buy wools, hides
and wool-fells grown between Coquet and Tweed, in Teviotdale
and Scotland, and to take them to the port of Berwick and ship
them to foreign parts, after payment to the King of 13s 4d for
each sack of wool or last of hides and every 240 wool-fells
(*CPR 1408–13*, p. 194).

29

The burgesses of Berwick petition the lord regent of France,
the duke of Bedford, that whereas Henry V his brother by the
advice of Council, having regard to the weakness and ruin of the
town and scarcity of men inhabitant, of his special grace granted
by letters patent to the burgesses and merchants there in aid, that
they could for a limited time buy wool, hides and wool-fells
from whomsoever they pleased, from between Coquet and
Tweed as well as Teviotdale and Scotland, and ship them to

foreign parts, paying for each sack of wool and each last of hides and every 240 wool-fells, 13s 4d, as the letters patent more fully contain. And since the present King by the advice of Council by his letters patent for the six years following granted the burgesses that they could buy wool and wool-fells from the said areas and ship them to Middelburg or Bruges, and nowhere else, paying the said custom: now the burgesses cannot buy wool, hides or wool-fells in Scotland because the King of Scotland has proclaimed throughout his kingdom that none of his lieges may sell wool, wool-fells or hides of Scottish origin to the English under certain penalty, to their great hurt unless they have aid. They request consideration of the matter, and for the help of the burgesses and the improvement of the town and the growth of customs there to grant them by the advice of Council for the next twenty years leave to buy wool, wool-fells and hides from between Blyth and Tweed, which water of Blyth is about 9 miles beyond the Coquet: in view of the fact that they cannot buy wool in Scotland because of the said proclamation, nor may they ship it thence wherever they will on paying the said custom: and that there is no other merchandise in the neighbourhood in which the burgesses can invest to the profit of the King and of themselves (AP 1205).

No endorsement

1426. The petition is entered verbatim on the parliamentary roll (*Rot Parl* iv, 309–10). The necessary licence was issued on 15 July 1426, quoting how Henry V on account of the great destruction of the goods of the burgesses of Berwick by Scottish inroads, weakness and lack of inhabitants had granted them leave for a certain term to buy and ship wool, wool-fells and hides from any, whether they originated from between Coquet and Tweed, Tevy-dale or Scotland, on payment of customs of 13s 4d. As their state was no better and on the advice of Council the King gave them leave for the next eight years to buy etc as before (*Rot Scot* ii, 256).

Defence of Berwick

Ancient Petitions E275, E276, E374, E378, E383, E393, E412, E970, 9231, 10342

30

Randolph de Benton petitions the King and Council that whereas sir Maurice de Berkeleye, keeper of Berwick, and sir Stephen le Blount were commissioned to enquire whether he had issued the King's victuals in his custody to the garrison of Berwick by false measure and whether he had changed good victuals for bad and taken money to do so: and whereas the commission was intended to ensure that an enquiry was taken by good men and true, the original instigators in their false association came and banded together and all the garrison with them and said that they would maintain what they had started or die in the attempt, and so they procured an enquiry by the most false men of the garrison and town. The enquiry was held contrary to the terms of the commission and Benton was threatened so that he dared say nothing on his own behalf, as he would have been killed. He requests the King and Council that this enquiry may not be prejudicial to him and that it be stayed until the King's coming in those parts, or that some keeper be willing to hold the enquiry by form of law and with loyal men, when he will prove that the enquiry was taken by false men against the form of their commission (AP E970).

A nostre seignur le Roi et a son conseil moustre Randolf de Benton' qe come monsieur Morice de Berkeleye gardein de la ville de Berewyk' et sire Esteuen le Blund auoient commission denquere si ieo eusse liuere les vitailles le Roi qe ieo auoi en garde as gentz de la garneson de Berewyk' par fauses Mesures et si ieo eusse change les bons vitailles por mauueis et pris lower por faire leschange, et par la ou la commission voleit qil eussent pris lenquest par bons et loiaux viendrent par leur fause alliance et procurrerent les primers Abettours et se cuilleront ensemble et tute la garneison ouesqe eux, et disoient qil voleint meintenir ceo qil auoient commence por morir en la peine et issint procurerent lenquest des plus fauses gentz de la garneison et de la ville et de celes gentz pristeront il lenquest encontre la forme de leur commission, et ieo estoi manace qe ieo ne oseie riens parler por mon esta demeyn, qe si eusse parle iea eusse este tue: par qei ieo pri a nostre seignur le Roi et a son conseil qe cele fause enquest issint passe fausement encontre moi ne me courge en preiudice, mes qele demoerge en pees tant qe

a la venue le Roi en celes parties ou de asqon gardein qe voille et ose
et force de poer de prendre lenquest en forme de lei et par loiaux
gentz, qar deuant le Roi et son conseil ieo ateyndrai lenquest estre
prise par fauses gentz et encontre la forme de leur commission qil
auoient.

No endorsement

1315. An enquiry was returned into the Exchequer by John
Carbonel under the seals of Simon Warde, keeper of Berwick,
master John de Weston, chamberlain of Scotland, John de
Wysham, marshal of Berwick, and Ranulph de Holme, mayor,
which stated that on the Friday before the Purification [31 January]
1315 in their presence the knights and others in garrison alleged
that the clerks deputed by the King to keep his victuals were falsely
issuing and selling these victuals to the detriment of the King
and the impoverishment of the men in garrison, and that
liveries of victuals were made by undermeasure, and that the
victuals received were exchanged for those of poorer quality, the
difference being taken from the merchants in money. The enquiry
found that Ranulph de Benton, keeper of the King's victuals in
Berwick, and Nicholas de Acton his clerk and Alan, Ranulph's
[?servant], sold the King's victuals and stock at Berwick and
disposed of them by sending them to Newcastle upon Tyne at will,
as was more fully described in the enquiry. Furthermore the
keepers of victuals sent back to Newcastle the good stores at
Berwick. They sold off victuals, and issued them using false
weights, and kept the advantage of about a fifth, for example
Henry Mortone issued 40 quarters of wheat where the keepers had
received 40 quarters, and yet 11 quarters were still left. The keepers
also bought inferior victuals for the garrison and sold the good
victuals they had received (cf. Bain iii, 80–81).

Benton then appeared in the court of Exchequer and explained
that he had sold victuals amounting to £152 18d on divers
occasions in the 6th and 7th years [1312–14] to have money in hand
for various necessary expenses, and he delivered a schedule and
offered to verify the truth by his account and however else the
court required. As for sending grain to Newcastle he admitted that
he had sent wheat there and elsewhere on the order of the steward
of the King's household and the keeper of the wardrobe on the

household account before the King went to Stirling in his 7th year, to make flour as there were not enough mills at Berwick, and John de Hereford, varlet of the King's pantry, was assigned to do this. He also sent malt to Newcastle for brewing, the ale to be returned to Berwick, and William le Ale Nymere was assigned to receive the malt at Newcastle. As for the King's store of stockfish sent to Newcastle, he acknowledged sending it in the 5th year on the orders of the steward of the King's household and had the acquittance of the clerk of the King's kitchen. As for the sale and disposal of victuals and stores, he said that he had issued them against bills of the wardrobe and bills of the chamberlain of Scotland, which commodities later were sold to divers persons in divers parts, and he handed over various particulars. He denied that he sold other victuals or stores or otherwise disposed of them, and offered to prove it. As for use of false measures, he said that he used the same measures as he received, and he denied any exchange of victuals in order to gain advantage. The hearing is entered under 'Recorda', Easter 1315 (PRO, QR Mem Roll 88, m 150).

31

The mayor, bailiffs and commons of Berwick greet the King and inform him that John le Iirois came to Berwick on the Monday before mid-Lent and sought leave of the Keeper to go to western parts to harass the enemy, and did so, and then returned to Berwick on 12 April with 38 men at arms and 54 hobelars, well equipped, and John and his men are staying in defence of the town up to the date of this letter and still remain. Written on 20 April (AP E276).

A tresnoble et treshonourable seignur le son liges Maire Baillifs et la communalte de sa ville de Berewyk' seur Twede honure reuerences et seruices duez a vostre seignourie: sire sil vous plest fesoms a ententer qe Johan le Iirois vint a Berewyk' auauntdist' le Lundy deuaunt dimy quarrem darrayne passe et demaunda conge du Gardein quil poait aler vers les partiez del West pur vos enemys greuer et si fait a son pouer et puis reuynt a Berewyk' le douzsme iour de Auerill' oue .xxx ⟨viij⟩ homes de armes et .liiij. hobellours bien aparaillez et si ad le dist' Johan oue ses gentz en la defense de la dist' ville demore tauntque au iour de la confeccione de ceste lettre et vncore demorent ses gentz. Sire dieu vous doint bone vie et long et victorie de vos enemys. Escristis le .xx. iour de Auerill'

No endorsement

1317. The Monday before mid-Lent fell in 1317 on 7 March. This and the following petition appear to refer to the same incident, but their dating cannot be completely reconciled as 12 April 1317 was the *Tuesday* after the octave of Easter. John the Irishman was a turbulent mercenary against whom a posse of knights, squires etc was sent from Clipston to Barnard Castle in November 1315 for the rescue of Lady Clifford, while the inhabitants of Bamburgh petitioned the same year against his depredations while in garrison there (Bain iii, 86, 88; cf. no. 180 below).

32

Information from the [keeper of Berwick] to the King that John le Hireis came to Berwick on Sunday in mid-Lent and left his men in Northumberland and sought leave to go to the parts of Carlisle to harass the enemy as the eastern borders were distant, and he was given leave and returned to his men and went, and they halted the enemy and much grieved them. Then John returned on the Monday after the octave of Easter and staged a muster before the chamberlain and [the keeper] of 28 men suitably mounted and armed with aketon, hauberk and bacinet (where sufficient men less well provided in garrison receive 12d a day), and 26 hobelars normally equipped. It seemed to John that his men were not receiving appropriate pay, but the petitioners had been ordered to treat all as hobelars except John himself, who was allowed 12d a day. May the King recompense John as one who has deserved reward, having grieved the enemy to the utmost of his power. God give you good news of your heir. Written on 22 April (AP E275).

Treshonure seignur, vostre vadlet Johan le Hireis veint a nous a Berewyk' il memes le Dimenche en mi quarreisme et lessa ses genz en Northumberland et nous pria counge daler deuers les parties de Carleyle pur greuer les enemys pur ceo qe noz marches furent lointeynes et nous li donasmes le counge et il se returna a ses gentz et alereit et firent vn bon eschek' sur les enemys et mout anoeaunt.

Et puis mon seignur reuint le dit Johan a nous le Lundi prochein apres le vtaues de la Pasqe et fit vne moustreson deuaunt le Chamberlein et nous de .xxviij. hommes couenablement mountez et armes Daketoun Hauberioun et bacinetz, dount assez de peuvres genz qils ne sount receiuent douze deners le iour en la Garnesoun, et de .xxvj. Hobelers couenables. Et semble au dit Johan, sire, qe come il fait volunte de ceo qe ses genz ne sount mie receuz solome lestat qil sount a ceo qil dit, mes nous ne li poums autre chose faire sire pur ceo qe vostre mandement parla tout de Hobeleurs, sauf qe le memes fut alowe a .xij. d. le iour. Dount sire sil vous plest voillez auer reward du dit Johan come de cesti qe bien le uaut a mon iugement et touz iours ⟨ad⟩ greeve as enemys a son poeir. Mon Seignur dieu uous doint bones nouelles de vous eir. Escrit le .xxij. iour Aueril.

No endorsement

1317. See no. 31 above. The accepted rate of pay for a hobelar on royal service in 1319/20 was 6d a day, the 'captain' generally receiving 12d a day (PRO, Exchequer Accts E101/15/27 m 2).

33

His varlet William de Weston petitions the King that whereas he served the King's father in Flanders and in all his wars in Scotland and now at his castle of Berwick, and his horses and armour are pledged at Newcastle for £10, being the costs of his horses since the beginning of the siege of Berwick castle, he requests that against his expenses since entering the castle he will order his treasurer to pay for the release of his horses and armour.

Item, he petitions the King that whereas he is owed for arrears of the wages of himself and his fellows and for restoration of horses lost in his service within the said time, as is shown by bills sealed in the wardrobe and the office of the chamberlain of Scotland, to a total of £600 and more, and he has lost both lands and rents in Scotland worth 100 marks a year and all his movable goods through the Scottish enemy, wherefore he has nothing to maintain him or his fellows unless by royal aid: he requests an order to the treasurer to make some assignment for payment of his debt and maintenance in order that he can serve him in due fashion as previously.

Item he petitions the King to order maintenance for him and his fellows to serve him as previously, and arrange how and where they should stay.

Item he petitions the King to grant him some office where he can serve him honourably, such as the bailiwick of Holderness for life (AP E378).

A nostre seignur le Roy prie le soen vallett William de Weston' qi ad serui a nostre seignour le Roy son treshonourable piere de bone memorie qe deux assoille et a ly en Flaundres et en totz ces guerres Descoce et ore en son chastell' de Berewic sur Twede, pur ceo qe ces cheuax et ces armours sount engages a Noef Chastel sur Tyne pur dix liueres pur les costages de ces chivax puis le comencement du seege de soun chastell' de Berewic auauntdit, por lor despences puis qil vindrount de Chastell', voile si le plest comaunder a son Tresorer qil ly face paiement pur aquiter ces chiuax et ces armours auauntiditz.

Item a nostre seignur le Roy prie leuauntdit William de Weston' pur ceo qil ly est tenuz pur arrerages de ses gages et de ces conpaignouns et por restor de lor chiuex perduz en son seruice dedenz le temps auauntdit, sicomme piert par billes qil ad seales de seales de sa garderobe et del office de sa Chaunbleynrie Descoce en six Centz liuerez et plus, et ces terres et rents qil auoit en Escoce qi ly solent valer par an Centz Marcz et touz ces biens moble ad perdu par ses enemis Descoce, Dount il ni ad riens pur sustener ly ne ses conpaignouns sinoun la seignurie de ly et son bon eide: qil voille si ly plest comaunder a son Tresorer qi a ly face assigner en ascune manere coment il porra estre paiez de sa dit dette et auoir ces sustenaunces pur ly seruir en due manere sicomme il ad fait cea en arrere.

Item a nostre seignur le Roy prie leuauntdit William de Weston' qe, si ly pleise qe il et ces conpaignouns ly seruent a sa volunte sicomme il ount fait cea en arrere, voille comaunder lour sustenaunce et ordeiner lour estate en quel manere et en quele estat ly pleise lour demore.

Item a nostre seignur le Roy prie leuauntdit William de Weston' qe, sil pleise a sa seignorie de ly graunter ascun Office dount il ly porra le plus honurablement seruir, ly voille si ly plest graunter la bailie de Holdurnesse a sa vie.

Endorsed: Coram Rege et consilio

1318 Berwick castle was besieged and captured by the Scots in the spring of 1318. Weston was a war-captain under Sir Ralph Monthermer at Berwick in 1311/12, handling a payroll of £295 18s (Bain iii, 397–98). His bay horse was appraised at 40 marks on the Berwick roll for 1311–12, and another, described as 'black liard' and worth £10, was lost at Linlithgow, when he ranked as a squire (*ibid.*, 411–412, 423). Weston, described as 'King's yeoman', subsequently petitioned in parliament that Edward I had been indebted to him in £600 and Edward II in 300 marks and 75s for wages when in their service in the Scottish wars and for horses lost then, as shown by bill of wardrobe of Edward I and certain bills of the late King's chamberlain of Scotland in his possession, for which he was not yet satisfied. Having besought the King to order payment or assignment he was given an order dated 8 February 1331 to the treasurer and barons of the exchequer and the chamberlains, for them to examine his bills and pay them if owing, or to cause an assignment to be made (*CCR 1330–33*, p. 198).

34

John Baudewyn, son of Sir Thomas Baudewyn, former burgess of Berwick, petitions the King and Council that whereas he was at horse and arms since the first conquest of the town, inflicting on the enemy what harassment he could within and without, without taking a penny, and he never agreed that the burgesses of the town should undertake its safe-keeping but always warned that they would lose the town through their great meanness and lack of expertise, and requests this be enquired into for the King's great profit, so that it may be known who were guilty of the loss of the town and pity be taken on those who were not: wherefore he requests maintenance for himself, his wife and children as one who has lost all in the town and then ransomed his wife and children from captivity, his eldest son being still a hostage (AP E374).

A nostre seignur le Roi et a son consail prie Johan Baudewyn fuiz Thomas Baudewyn chiualer, iadis Burgeys de Berewyk, Come il ad demore as chiuaux et as armes puis la primer conqueste de la dite ville, enfesaunt sur les enemys la greuaunce qe il poeit dedeins et

dehors saunz nul denier prendre, ne vnqes ne assentist qe les
Burgeys de la dite ville la garde enpreissent mes touz iours encriaunt
sur eux qe la ville se perderent pur lour graunt couertise et noun
sachauntie, et ceo prie il qe seit enquis pur graunt profit le Roi, issi
qe vous poiez certifie de ceux qe coupes ne auoient qe la ville se
perdi et pite auoir de ceux qe coupes ne auoient. Par quei le dit
Johan Baudewyn requert vostre grace de sustenaunce pur lui et sa
femme et ses enfauntz, come celui qe perdist en la dite ville qaunt
qil auoit, et puis sa femme et ses enfauntz hors de prison raunsouna
dount son eigne fuiz en hostage vncore demoert.

Endorsed: Coram Rege

Post—1318. The burgesses of Berwick agreed on 4 June 1317 to
undertake the defence of the town for 6000 marks a year, the
consequent arrangements including the surrender to Edward II of
hostages, either the eldest son or other near kin. The responsibility
dated from 1 July 1317 (*CPR 1313–17*, p. 671). On 17 November
1316 Geoffrey son of William de Roseles acknowledged a debt of
£20 owed to John son of Thomas Baudewyn of Berwick, to be
levied on his lands etc in Yorkshire (*CCR 1313–18*, p. 440).

35

Robert de Blakeburn petitions the King and Council that
whereas he had served the King and his late father at Berwick and
in the Scottish war for 22 years and more, and then was in the castle
there in the company of Roger de Horsle until its loss and was
taken prisoner of war and wounded near to death, and at the battle
of Stirling lost his brother, and for the past ten years lost the issues
of all his lands in the Scottish march worth 80 marks a year, so that
he had nothing to live on beyond £20 a year from a fishery in the
Tweed held of the town of Berwick, and he lived on this until the
loss of the town and now has nothing to uphold him. He requests
the King that for his long service and great loss he order
honourable maintenance until he can recover his lands (AP E383).

A nostre seignur le Roi et a son conseil moustre Robert de
Blakeburn' qe come ledit Robert eit serui nostre seignur le Roi et
son bon pere qi mort est dieus assoille en la ville de Berewyk et ensa

Guerre Descoce .xxij. aunz et plus et ore demorra en le chastel enla compaigny' Roger de Horsle tauntqe le chastiel fust perduz et ad estie pris de Guerre en son seruice et naufre tout ala mort et a la bataille Destriuelyn perdist son frere et tout ces .x. aunz ad il perduz les issues de ⟨toutes⟩ ses terres en la Marche descoce qe soleient valer par an .iiij^{xx}. mars, issint qil naueit riens dont viure forsqe .xx. liures qil prist par an dune pescherye qil aueit en lewe de Twede, taunt comme la ville de Berewyk' se tynt, et de cel ad il vesqui taunt ala perte dela dite ville et ore nad il riens dont il puist estre sustenuz: Par quei il prie por dieu a nostre seignur le Roi qe por son lung' service et la grant pierte qil ad eau et ad de ses dite terres qil lui voelent ordener honurable sustenance dont il purra estre sustenuz tauntqil porra auer ascun recouerir de ses terres par leide de dieu et de nostre seignur le Roi.

Endorsed: Coram Rege

post 1318 Calendared with one error in Bain iii, 118. On 25 July 1333 a protection was given to Ada, widow of Robert de Blakeburn of Paxton (*Rot Scot* i, 256).

36

His liege Walter de Gosewic petitions the King that he lost all his goods and chattels in the betrayal lately done at Berwick, and he, his wife and household were taken then ransomed by his friends. He requests that in consideration of his good service and his losses and damage as result of his good faith and loyalty to his liege lord he be admitted to his grace and granted that he may live in his realm without harm to body or goods, for otherwise he and his wife and children will perish (AP E412).

A nostre seignur le Roy pri son lige home Wauter de Gosewic qi en la treson nadgers faite en la ville de Berewic' perdist tous ses biens et ses chateux, et lui et sa femme et meigne pris, et puis par aide et le meschief qil poiant quer de ses amis reintz, qe lui pleise por dieu et por pite auer regarde al bon seruise qe le dit Wauter lui ad faite a son poiar, et a les perties qe il ad eu, et del meschief ou il est pur sa foi et por sa loiaute sauuer deuers son seignur lige qe il lui voille receiuere a sa grace et granter le, qe il puisse sanz empeschement de son corps ou de ses biens par cele encheson viuere denz son roiaume et son poiar et marchander, qar autrement lui et sa femme et ses enfanz perireint, de quoy il prie a son seignur lige qil ent eit pite.

Endorsed. Coram Rege   per Adam de Standon'

1318–19. A pardon dated 28 May 1319 was granted to Walter de Gosewyk for good service, remitting the King's anger and rancour of mind because Berwick had been captured by the Scots when he and others were expected to guard it. He was not to be molested in person and goods for the loss of the town unless he could be charged with sedition etc. A concurrent mandate was sent to the mayor and bailiffs of York to release his son Thomas, one of the hostages for the safe custody of the town, then in their prison (*CPR 1317–21*, p. 340).

37

The former burgesses of Berwick petition the King and council to grant them leave freely to stay and trade within the realm without arrest or attachment of them and their goods, such as they are, and to have their children released from prison, for their bodies will be ready at the King's pleasure (AP E393).

A nostre seignur le Roi et a soen conseil prient ses ligez gens qi iadis furent burgayses de Berewyck' qil voille pur lamur de dieu graunter a eux qe il puissent fraunchement demorer ⟨et marchaundier⟩ dayns son Realme, saunz areste ou atachement de eux ou de lour biens, teles comme il sount, et auer lour enfaunz hors de prison: Car lour corps serrount prestes a la volunte nostre seignur le Roi.

Endorsed: Coram Rege et magno Consilio

c.1318. Cf. no. 36 above.

38

The petition of his lieges Walter de Gosewyk, John de Chilton, John de Ponfreit, Randolph de Holme, Roger de Butilstane,

Henry de Dene, Simon de Skindelby, John Wake, William de
Scothou, William de Botilstane, Thomas de Duxfelde, Gilbert de
Duxfelde, Geoffrey de Frodesham, Thomas de Scothou, William Thoraud, Adam de Bolton, Robert de Loundres, Ralph
de Belford, Henry de Knapton, Richard de Overton, Robert
de Holande, Walter Storm, William de Donewyz, William de
Derby, William del Burne, Richard le Barbeer and Robert
Hauxey, lately burgesses of Berwick, to the King on behalf of their
fellow-burgess, Alan Scot, taken and imprisoned at Bordeaux on
suspicion of complicity in the betrayal of Berwick. They repudiate
the charge, affirm his constant loyalty and request his release.
Written at Newcastle on 10 June 13 Edward II (1320) (AP 9231).

A tresnoble, trespuissant et tresexcellent Prynce nostre seignour
sire Edward, par la grace de dieu tresnoble Roi Dengleterre,
Seignour Dirlaunde, et Ducs Daquitein ses homes liges si lui plest
Water de Gosewyk', Johan de Chilton', Johan de Ponfreit, Randolph de Holme, Roger de Butilstane, Henri de Dene, Simon
de Skindelby, Johan Wake, William de Scothou, William de
Botilstane, Thomas de Duxfelde, Gilbert de Duxfelde, Gefrei
de Frodesham, Thomas de Scothou, William Thoraud, Adam
de Bolton, Robert de Loundres, Rauph' de Belforde, Henri de
Knapton, Richard de Ouerton', Robert de Holande, Water
Storm, William de Donewyz, William de Derby, William del
Burne, Richard le Barbeer, et Robert Hauxey, ses Burgois iadys
demorauntz en la ville de Berewyk' sur Twede, corps et auoir et
quantqe il ont, oue tote manere de honours, reuerences, et seruyses
prestz et apareilliez a ses comandementz comme a lour seignour
lige: Treshonurable seignour, por ceo qe nous auoms entenduz
qe vn vostre lige homme et nostre cher veisyn et Comburgois
Aleyn Scot est pris et detenuz en prison en la ville de Burdeaux, por
suspecione qe ascunes maliciouses gentz lui ont susmys maliciouse-
ment qe il duist auoir este assentant dauoir trai la dite ville de
Berewyk'. A vostre real poer treshonurable seignour sil vous
plest, fasoms assauoir et loiaument vous tesmoignoms en bone fei
par cestes nos lettres, qe le dit Aleyn vnqes ne fu assentaunt ne
voillaunt ne sachaunt a la dite ville trair en nule manere: Mes
voilliez cher seignour sauoir sil vous plest qe le dit Aleyn touz iours
bien et loiaument se ad porte a vostre foy en touz pointz comme il
feire deuoit: Par quoi sire prioms a vostre seignourie et requeroms

sil vous plest por dieu qe vous voilliez de vostre grace, por la deliuerance du dit Aleyn couenable remedie ordiner. Treshonurable seignour, dieu vous doynt bone vie et lounge et victoire de touz vos enemys. En tesmoignance de qeu chose a cestes lettres patentes auoms mys nos seaulx: Escrites a vostre ville de Noef Chastell' sur Tyne le disme iour de Juyn, lan de vostre regne sire, trezisme.

tags for seals; no endorsement

10 June 1320. Cf. nos 36, 37 above.

39

John de Burdon, chamberlain of Berwick, petitions the King and Council to discharge him from the office of chamberlain and replace him with another as he can no longer bear the great expense to which he has been put to the detriment of his condition, as all past keepers can testify. The King should know that for all this time he retained 10 men-at-arms and 12 hobelars, for whom he took no payment save for four weeks (AP 10342).

A nostre seignur le Roy et a son conseil prie Johan de Burdon' Chamberlein de Berewyk' qe pleise a eaux descharger Luy de son office de Chamberlein et mettre vn autre en son leu qe il ne poet endorer le grant costages qe il ad mis auant ces hours sil ne soit a defesance de son estate, sicom touz les gardeyns qe ont este le pount tesmoigner. Et pleise a nostre seignur le Roy sauer qe il ad retenu tote le temps qil ad demore dysze homes darmes et dosze hoblurs pur les queux il ne prist vnke rend' sauf pur quart semayns.

Endorsed: Le Roi serra auise.

1340–43. John de Burdon, parson of Rothbury, was appointed in parliament in 1340 as chamberlain of Berwick at will at a fee of 100 marks a year in succession to Robert de Tughale, who had held the offices of chamberlain and victualler jointly at a fee of £100. Tughale was to continue as victualler at 50 marks (*Rot Parl* ii, 115). Subsequently on 28 April 1340 Burdon was appointed with John de Fenwick, Gilbert de Boroughden and Thomas de Heppescotes as collector of the ninth in Northumberland (*Rot Scot* i, 590).

On 6 May 1343 Burdon, now described as 'late chamberlain of Berwick', was to pay the wages of William del Wode, King's sergeant at arms, whom the King had granted for life the wool tronage at Berwick, with ulnage and gauging of wine, as held by the late Richard Thurlewall (*ibid.*, 638).

Compensation

Ancient Petitions 3712, 7064, 7073, 7076, 10319.

40

John Taillour, burgess of Berwick, petitions the King's Council that whereas he came to England to [Bishop's] Lynn on pilgrimage to Canterbury with letters of safe-conduct from the wardens for maintenance of truce on the March, namely from the earl of Prudhoe and from Sir Roger de Horsle, the bailiffs of the bishop of Norwich came and arrested him and his goods, and his letters of safe-conduct were taken from him, so that he could not depart. He requests a remedy lest Englishmen be arrested with their goods in Scotland through his detention (AP 3712).

A consail nostre seignur le Roy moustre Johan Taillour Burges de Berewik et prie grace qe come il vint en Engleterre ala ville de Lynne en pelyrynage vers Cantewarbures par lettres de Conduit de les gardeyns de la Marche a meyntenir la Trewe, cest assauoir la lettre le Counte de Preddu (*sic*) et la lettre monsz Roger de Horsle de salf' conduit de passer et retouner saluement sauntz de-stourbaunce, vindrent les baillifs Leuesqe de Norwz et soun corps ount arestu et ses biens et ses lettres de Conduyt lui ount tollu qil ne poet issir en nul liu: Par quei il prie pur dieu qe remedie lui soit ordine qe nules gentz Dengleterre ne soient arestuz ne lour biens en Escoce pur sa demoere.

Endorsed: Habeat breue Maiori et Balliuis de Lenn' continens effectum peticionis quod si Johannes tales habuerit litteras de con-ductu quales peticio supponit, quod permittant ipsum curialiter abire quo voluerit et restituant ei litteras suas.

1324. On 30 March 1324 the bailiffs of John, bishop of Norwich, at Bishop's Lynn, were ordered to permit John Taillour, burgess of Berwick, to go where he would, if he had letters of safe-conduct under the seals of Robert de Unframvill, earl of Angus, and Roger de Horsle, keepers of truce with the Scots in the parts of Northumberland. They were also to restore his letters and goods following his petition to Council (*CCR 1323–27*, p. 85). The Scottish (titular) earl of Angus was lord of Prudhoe and Redesdale in Northumberland. The use of the title of earl under-lines the importance attached to the rank, cf letter of Henry de Percy (PRO, S.C. 1, Ancient Correspondence XLI, 77).

41

John Marchaunt of Berwick petitions the King and Council for an order to the treasurer and barons and chamberlains of the Exchequer for payment or suitable assignment of £42 11s for wheat bought of him for the needs of the King's father by Roger de Horselee, former constable of Bamburgh castle for provision of the castle, as is shown by Wardrobe books of sir William de Melton, archbishop of York, the then keeper, whose account has been rendered at the Exchequer. The payment was ordered, but he could obtain neither payment nor assignment, to his grave hurt and he craves a remedy (AP 10319)

A nostre seignur le Roi et a son counseille prie Johan Marchaunt de Berwyk' qe leur pleise comander au Tresorer et as Barouns et as Chaunbreleyns del Escheker qe le dit Johan peust auer paiement ou couenable assignement de .xlij. li' .xj. s. pur fourment de dit Johan achate al oeps nostre seignur le Roi, piere nostre seignur le Roi qe ore est, par Rogier de Horselee, iadis Conestable du Chastiel de Baunburgh' pur le dit Chastiel vitailler, sicome piert par les liueres de la Garderobe du temps qe sire William de Melton' Erceuesqe Deuerwyk' fuist Gardeyn de la dite garderobe, dount lacompt est rendu en lescheker, et le dit paiement ad este maunde et nul paiment ne assignement peust il auer a ses greues damages, dount il prie remedi pur dieu.

Endorsed: Coram Rege   Soit mande as Tresorer, Barons et Chaumberleins de lescheker qe veue la compte le dit garderober, sil troessent qe le Roi feust respounduz du ditz blez et qe largent soir vncore du, qe adonqe lui facent ⟨auoir⟩ paiement ou couenable assignment.   Irrotulatur

1331. On 2 May 1331 the treasurer, barons and chamberlains of the Exchequer were informed of Marchaunt's petition that the late King owed him £42 11s for wheat, which sum was still outstanding. They were to search the rolls and memoranda and take appropriate action (CCR 1330–33, p. 236).

42

Adam Schankis, burgess of Berwick, petitions the King's council that he leased all the salmon fisheries in the Tweed belonging to the abbot and convent of Dryburgh for a term of 5 years beginning at Whitsun 1332, and one year was completed the previous Whitsun. As burgess and neighbour and within the conditions of the town he requests that he may have the completion of his term (AP 7076).

A noble Consaille nostre seignur le Roy Mustre Adam Schankis burgez de Berwic' sur Twed' qe il ad ferme totez les pecheris de salmon en la Ewe de Twede qe pertenent a labbe et le Couent de Dryburgh' de les dytes Abbe et couent pur les termes de .v. aunez [l]ur primer terme en comensand' al Pentecost' lan de grace .M.CCC.xxxij. dank' qe .v. annis soyent plenement complies, et si est passe de sez termez vne Aune a pentecost darreyn passe: Pur quoy il prie qe il est burges ⟨et veyson⟩ et en les condiciones du dit ville de Berwic' qe il put auore ces termes enterment Complies si vous plest.

Endorsed: Dicunt quod predicti Abbas et Conuentus per scriptum suum ostensum hic Curie dimiserunt prefato Ade piscarias predictas vsque ad finem quinque annorum reddend' per annum .ix. marcas ⟨et .xij. salmones⟩ et quod vnus annus inde elapsus fuit ad festum pentecost' proximum preteritum et quod seisitus fuit de termino illo quousque amotus fuit per vicecomitem et quod fuit in villa de Berwic' die reddicionis eiusdem et quod non remisit etc.

Habeat breue vicecomiti Berwic' quod liberet ei piscarias

predictas ⟨ea occasione⟩ habend' vsque ad finem termini predicti
Ita quod soluat Regi redditum predictum durante termino saluo
iure cuiuslibet.

July–November 1333. Adam Shankes, burgess of Berwick, was
granted royal letters of protection with Clement Todd on 25 July
1333. He held a tenement in Ravensdene liable to pay 4s rent for
the upkeep of Berwick bridge (*Rot Scot* i, 256, 493). The Berwick
exchequer rolls record for 1333/4 receipts totalling £23 12s 9d
from escheated salmon fisheries on the north bank of the Tweed.
These included Totingford, Law, and various others leased to
Thomas de Bamburgh and Robert de Tughale (Scott, pp. 250,
428).

43

Adam Scankys, burgess of Berwick, petitions the King's council
that he took to farm the Tweed salmon fisheries called *Totyngford* and *le Lawe* and *Callet*, which belonged to the hospital of
St. Mary Magdalen of Berwick, from the master of the hospital for a term of three years commencing at Martinmas 1332,
of which terms one year will be completed next Martinmas and he
had paid money in advance. He is a burgess and neighbour of
the town and covered by the King's conditions, and requests that
he may have the rest of his term (AP 7073).

A tresbone Consaile nostre seignur le Roy Mustre Adam
Scankys burges de Berwik sur Twede qe il ad pris aferme les
pecheris de salmon les quex sunt apelles Totyngford' et le Lawe et
Callet' en lewe de Twede les quex pertenent al hospitalle de seynt
marie Magdeleyn de Berwic' du Mester du dyt Hospitalle pur
les termes de .iij. aunes del fest de seynt Martin Lan de grace
.M.CCC.xxxij. Et si est passe de ces termes vne Aune al fest de
seynt Martin procheyn, et le dyt Adam son argent ad paye deuant
Mayn vne party: Pur *ceo* il prie il est burges et veysyn du dit ville et
dedens les condicions nostre seignur le Roy, qe il put auore ces
termes enterment complies si vous plest.

Endorsed: Dicunt quod Magister dicti Hospitalis dimisit dictas
piscarias predicto Ade ad terminum trium annorum per scriptum

suum quod ostendit hic Curie, reddend' per annum .xxiij. marcas, et quod vnus annus est elapsus et quod seistus fuit de termino illo quousque amotus fuit per vicecomitem et quod fuit in villa de Berwico super Twedam die reddicionis eiusdem et quod non remisit etc.

Habeat breue vicecomiti Berwic' quod liberet ei piscarias predictas ⟨si ea occasione⟩ habend' vsque ad finem termini predicti, ita quod soluat Regi redditum predictum durante termino saluo iure cuiuslibet.

July–November 1333. See no. 42 above.

44

Adam Schankes and Clement Todd, burgesses of Berwick, petition the King's council that Robert de Tughalle, sheriff of Berwick, seized as the King's escheats two of their salmon fisheries in the Tweed, called *Ald Waterstelle* and *Outer Waterstelle*. These were leased from the abbeys of Dunfermline and Dryburgh for a term of five years starting from Whitsun 1332, of which term two years are now gone. As they are within the King's conditions they request they may complete their term (AP 7064).

A bon consayle nostre sengnur le Roy Moustrunt' Adam Schankes et Clement Todde Burgoys de Berwyk' sur Twedde qe Robert de Tughalle Wyscount' de Berwik' Avandist pryst' deux lour pecheryes deu salmon en lewe de Twede Com eschet nostre seynur le Ray (*sic*) queus sunt appellez Ald Waterstelle et Outer Waterstelle, Le quelles Pecheryes eux pristerent au ferme del Abbe de dunfermelin et de Dryburgh' pur terme de Cynk' aunz des pentecost Lan de grace .M.CCC.xxxii.et sy sunt passes de lur terme deux aunz: Dount le dyt Adam et Clement vous pry pur dewe Com eux qe furent en le condiscioun nostre seynur le Roy qe dewe garde qe vous vollez ordyner Remedy sur ceo sy vous plest, qe eux pussynt auoir Lour terme Comply.

Endorsed: soit mande par bref de la Chauncellerie au seignur de Percy, gardein de Berewyk' et a sire William de Beuercote Chauncellor de Berewyk' et a Robert de Tughale viscont de Berewyk' denquere des choses contenues en cest peticion, et sil trouent lour suggestion verroie, et ils soient des condicions des gentz de la ville, qe les pescheries lur soient restituz a tenir com ils les tient a deuant sauue le droit le Roi et de chescun autre, Rendant au Roi la rente durante le terme auandit.

c. Whitsun 1334. See nos 42, 43 above.

War damage

Ancient Petitions 424, 428, 591, 1608, 1609, 1659, 4599, 5736, 7673, 10341, 10343, 10345, 10346, 11299, 11310.

45

Adam de Ryston complains to the King and Council of Sir Osborn de Spaldynton, keeper of Berwick, touching the great trespass done to him in Berwick and seeks some remedy for the fact that Osborn came to his houses in Berwick and ejected his men and delivered them to other men to his great hurt. He requests letters to Osborn to restore his houses as before and that he may hold them at rent by the customary service as other people of the town hold. May they instruct the treasurer of Berwick to provide him with a charter as others have, as he cannot go to obtain their letter. Osborn has received 28 shillings of his rent (AP 7673).

A Rey e A son consayl Adam de Ryston' senpleynt de syre Oseberun de Spaldynton' Gardayn de la vile de Berewyk' de grant trespas qe il luy ad fet en meyme la vile de Berewyk' e de ceo il vous pri mercy qe vous luy facez Remedi, si vous plest. Et vous Mustre syre qe meymes celuy Oseberun vyent a ses Mesons en la vile de Berewyk' e veleynement e hautise . . . . [deh]ors iete sa genz de ces Mesons e les ad Bayle as Auterene gentz a ses greuez damages. E pur ceo Chere syre il vous prie vostre lettre a meymes celuy Oseberun qe il luy deliuere ces Mesons cum il auant aueyt, e qe il les pusse tenir pur la Rent pur la seruice qe apent solum la taxacyon cum autre genz de la vile tenint. E si vous pleise comaoundez (sic) au Tresurer de Berwyk' qe il luy face auer Chartre cum les Auteres de la vile vunt, qe ieo ne pu my aler la e purpri de vostre lettre si vous plest. E seyniur celuy Oseberun ad Receu .xxviij. souz de ma ferme.

Endorsed: Habeat breue ad Thesaurarium de Berewyk quod inquirat et super hiis de quibus conqueritur faciat sibi fieri iusticiam.

?1296. Spaldington was appointed sheriff and keeper of Berwick during the King's pleasure on 16 May 1296 (*Rot Scot* i, 23). On 22 June 1295 Adam de Ryston, King's yeoman, was granted a burgage and 40 acres in Rhuddlan lately held by William le Marshal and Alice his wife, in the King's hands as an escheat and of the yearly value of 1 mark as shown by an enquiry by the justice of Chester (*CPR 1292–1301*, p. 137). A protection with clause *volumus* lasting until Michaelmas was issued on 16 November 1299 for Adam de Riston, going to Scotland on the King's service (*ibid.*, p. 457)

46

Alan son of Richard of Corbridge petitions the King for delivery of a messuage and three shops with appurtenances in Berwick which he had before the Scottish war began and which have been held by the King ever since, so that he cannot have reseisin; because he is English-born and at all times lived faithful to the King in England, doing service with horse and arms at the capture of the town and throughout Scotland, and has done nothing to justify exclusion from his land; that true Englishmen with lands in Scotland be not excluded from those lands (AP 424)

A nostre Seignur le Roy prie Alayn le fiz Richard de Corbrige quil si luy plest luy voille rendre vn Mes' e troys shopys oue les apurtenaunces en Berewyk' les quels il auoit deuant la gere Descoce comencee e les quels vnt estez en vostre mayn pus le dit conquest e vncore sunt, si quil ne poat vnqes sa seisine rehauer; desicome sire i est de Engleterre ⟨ne⟩ e en tutz temps en Engleterre demorant e a vostre fay, e seruise vous fist a cheuaus e armes al conquest de la dite vile e par tut le Reaum Descoce, ne rien sire nad forfayt par quei il doyt estre de sa terre foringe, plus qe vos bones gentz Dengleterre qui terres auoient en la terre Descoce ne sunt de lur dites terres foringez.

Endorsed: Adeat custodem et Camerarium etc., audiatur, et fiat sibi iusticia. Coram Rege pre–1307. See no. 47 below.

47

Alan son of Richard de Corbridge petitioned the King in his last parliament for restitution of a messuage and three shops with appurtenances in Berwick which he had before the war and which since then had been in royal hands *as above*. Following this the King granted him a writ to sir John de Segrave and sir John de Sandale to hold an enquiry and provide a quick remedy. These found by inquest attached, sealed with their seals, that Alan had always been of the King's faith and peace in England, but they could do nothing because divers men had been enfeoffed with the said messuage and shops by royal charters. He petitions the King to order restitution as he has done nothing against the King or anyone for which he should be excluded (AP 428).

A nostre seignur le Roy a son drayn parlement pria Alayn le fiz Richard de Corbrigge par sa peticion qe le dit nostre seignur le Roy vousist comander qil vst restitucion de vn Mees e treis Shopes oue les apurtenaunces en la vile de Berewyk' sur Twede les quels il auoit deuant la guere commencee, e les quels, puis qe la dite vile fust prise, ount este e vncore sont en la mayn nostre seignur le Roy, desicome le dit Alayn est Dengleterre ne e tut temps ad en Engleterre demurre a la foy le Roy e fist al Roy son seruise a la prise de la dite vile. Par la quele peticion le Roy li graunta vn breif a sire Johan de Segraue e sire Johan de Sandale, le quel est cosu a ceste peticion, qe eux faite sur ceo bone enqueste luy feissent faire hastyue remedie; les queux sires Johan e Johan tut trouerent il par enqueste, la quele est ausint cosu a cest peticion enseale de lur seals, qe le dit Alayn tut iours ad este a la foy e la pees le Roy demurrant en Engleterre, neqedent rien ne poeient faire par la resun qe diuerses gentz sunt feffez de dites Mees e Shopes par les chartres le Roy: par quei le dit Alayn prie a nostre seignur le Roy qil pur lamur de deu voille commaunder qe ses tenementz luy soient rendutz, desicome il nad rien fait encountre le Roy nencountre autre par quei il doit estre de eux foringe.

Endorsed: Sequatur coram tenente locum Regis in Scocia et Camerario et vocentur partes, et si inueniatur quod non fuit contra pacem Regis, non obstante carta, restituantur ei ⟨illa⟩ Messuagium et tres shope ⟨que petit⟩ indilate. Et ad hoc habeat breue.

The writ and inquest are missing

pre–1307.

48

The mayor and burgesses of Berwick petition the King and Council that whereas the King's grandfather with his Council after the first capture of the town had regard for the foundation and patronage of the Maison Dieu, which was granted in perpetuity to twelve of the better sort in the town of the governing class and its possessions protected by grievous sentences in the papal bull of confirmation, and quitclaimed by his charter under the great seal for him and his heirs for ever any claims to the detriment of its privileges and possessions: to avoid these grievous sentences they request a confirmation of the foundation and patronage (AP 10345).

A nostre seignur le Roi Dengleterre et son bon counsail moustrent ses liges gentz Meyr et Burgeys de la ville de Berewyk sur Twede qe com nostre seignur le Roi lael od son bon consail apres la primere conqueste de la dite ville auoient regard a la fondacione et douesone de la meson dieux en la dite ville, qe purement et perpetuelment si est graunte as .xij. des meillours de la dite ville par queux la ville si est gouerne et deit estre a touz iours et des greuouses sentences enbullez par bulle de nostre seignur le Pape sur la confirmacionem (*sic*) de les possessions a la dite meson appurtenantz, quitclama par sa Chartre enseale du grant seal pur lui et ses heyrs a touz iours de rien claimer la fondacion ne douesone de la dite meson en blemisement des priuileges et possessions qe a la dite meson appendent: qe de sa bone grace et en oeuere de charite en eschuauntz les auantditz greuouses sentences les voille par ses graciouses lettres la fondacion et douesone de la dite meson graunter et confermer.

Endorsed: Moustrent ceo qils ont pur eux.

c. 1333. An inquest of 1333/4 found that Philip de Rydale was founder of the hospital in the time of Alexander III, endowing it with 20s in rent derived from a messuage in Uddyngate subsequently forfeited to the King. There were two other rents, also forfeited. Rydale's gifts had been confirmed by Edward I on 24 November 1300. It appears to have been a hospital for the sick poor, rather than for lepers (Cowan/Easson, p. 171; cf. Scott, pp. 348–9). Rydale was mayor of Berwick in the 1280s and 1290s (G. W. S. Barrow, 'The Aftermath of War', *Transactions*, Royal Historical Soc., 5th ser. 28 [1978] p. 107).

49

The poor brothers and sisters of the Maison Dieu of Berwick petition the King and Council that whereas a Philip de Ridale founded the house and ordained a master chaplain and another four chaplains to sing in perpetuity and seven choir-men to sing the mass of Our Lady and five poor sick persons to have their board and clothing, and to maintain this chantry and almshouse he bought 100 librates of land and rents in England and Scotland and furthermore ordained that when the house was vacant by reason of the death of the master-chaplain the mayor and commons of Berwick should choose a sufficient replacement, failing which the King would intervene and appoint: for which cause the King's father gave the house to a master Thomas Paynton, clerk, who held it until the battle of Bannockburn, and then gave it to one of his own chaplains, sir Edmund de Londres, who held it until ejected by Robert de Brus. Robert de Brus asked it of the commons of Berwick for a William de Rokesburgh, who held and still holds it. During his time only one chaplain was provided, and no poor man received sustenance, he lying with his concubine and spending the goods of the house. They request the King to remedy this because William has always been a chief opponent of the King in aid and counsel and ere now in time of peace killed two men and wed two women in Berwick. For such reasons the poor people request the King to consider the unsuitability of William and the ruin of the house, and make orders for the maintenance of the chantry and the provision of the poor people, as they are all begging for their bread (AP 1659).

A nostre seignour le Roy et a soen consaille moustrent les pouers freres et soeres de la maison dieu de Berewyk' sur Twede qe la ou vn Phelip de Ridale feunda la dite meson et ordina illusques vn mestre chapelain et autres quatre chapelains de chaunter illusques perpetuelment, et sept clergeonetz de chaunter a la messe de nostre dame et quinque pouers langisantz dauoir lour sustenance en la dite meson en viuere et vesture, et pur cele chaunterie et cel almosne sustenir il purchacea .C. liuerez de terre et de rente en Engleterre et en escoce, et outre ceo il ordona que a quel houre que la meson se voidast par la morte dascun mestre chapelayn le Mair et la comunalte de Berewyk elirrent vn autre suffissant en soen lieu, et si ceo ne feusent le Roi mettreit la mayne et ordinereit solonc ceo que bon serroit. Et par defaute que le Roi pier nostre seignur le Roi que ore est troua il dona la meson a vn Mestre Thomas Paynton, Clerk, le quiel Thomas la tient tantque a la Bataille de Bannokburn' et peus la dona a vn de ses chapelayns demeisne sire Esmon de Londres, le quiel sire Esmon la tient tantqil fust oste par Robert de Bruys. Et le dit Robert de Bruys pria a la comunalte de Berewyk' pur vn William de Rokesburgh' que peus en cea lad tenu et vncore tient, issint que vnques en son temps chapelayn fust troue forsque vn, et a la foitz nul ne pouer homme sustenance nauoit, mes gist oue sa concubine et despend les biens de la meson. Et voille nostre dit seignour le Roi emendre si li pleise que le dit William tous iours en cea ad este capital encaux nostre seignour le Roi en ead et counsaille et deuant ceux houres en temps de pees tua deux hommes et espousa deux femmes en la ville de Berewyk'. Par quoi les ditz pouers prient que nostre dit seignour le Roi voille auoir regarde al noun ablete du dit William et a la destruccion de la meson et issint ordoner que la chauntrie peusse estre maintenu et les pouers auoir lour sustenance, kar ils vont touz mendinantz lour payn.

Endorsed: [Pur ceo qil] est tesmoigne qe la douison del Hospital appent de Meire e Baillif' de Berewik', soit mande a eux par bref qil facent tieux redres e amendement sur les choses contenues en ceste peticion qe le Roi ne mette mie la mein en defaut de eux.

1333–34. cf. no. 48 above. In 1335 the mayor and bailiffs of Newcastle were ordered to release Rokesburgh from prison in

Newcastle on his finding security not to depart from England nor communicate in any way with the Scots (Scott, p. 349).

50

The master, poor brothers and sisters of the Maison Dieu of Berwick petition the King and Council that whereas during the siege their church and houses were struck down by siege-engines so that they had no place of refuge, and the master at his own expense repaired the said church and houses and so spent more than he received, and pledged his chalices and vestments for the repairs, and the building is so weak that it cannot withstand the winter without rotting for ever: and the master with his slender resources cannot accomplish the work quickly without great help, wherefore he requests the King to provide alms for repair that the work be not lost, since if the King and Council will not help there is no other aid (AP 1608).

A nostre tresexcellent seignur le Roy e a som consoille Moustrent le Meistre, le pouers frers e soers de la meisonedieu de Berewik sur Tuede qe com en temps de lassege leur eglise e leur meisouns furent abatuz par engynes, si deueite qe il ny auoit nule quarter reinys esseaunt seyn, e le dite maistre ad mys ses costages pur les auauntdit eglise e maisouns repareiler, si quil ad pluys mys que resceu, e ad engage ses chalices e vescemuntz pur lauauntdit redrescement, que loureigne est si tendre en luy meismes quil ne pute endurer le Ivere sauntx estre porry pur touz iours, e le dit maistre est encuraunt de iour en autre a soen poure poeirt ne ne pute lauauntdite oure si en hasty porfournire sauntz grant aide, purquei tresgraciouse seignur il prie a vostre tres haute realte quil vous plest pur lamoure de dieuy e pur la saulucte de vostre alme de vostre grace e de vostre charite commander de vostre almoigne ceo que vous plest pur lauantdit oure repareiler, quil ne soit legerment perdu a remenaunt, que treshonurable seignur si vous e vostre bon conseile noliez eider, autre aide ny ad en terre que les voet eider.

No endorsement

1333–34. Calendared in Bain iii, 199. Cf. nos 48 and 49 above.

51

The executors of the will of Thomas le Hatter of Berwick petition the King and Council that whereas Thomas was in Berwick when the town was surrendered to the King and then until his death, and should have enjoyed the conditions granted by the King to those in the town on the day of its surrender, Thomas in his lifetime and since the surrender had certain of his goods taken by certain Newcastle wrongdoers from a ship at sea sailing to Berwick. These goods were carried to Newcastle and subsequently taken to York and delivered to the King's wardrobe: and Thomas sued by writ of great seal directed to the mayor and bailiffs of Newcastle for release of those goods in their hands but could have nothing, wherefore the executors request that the goods be restored to them according to the aforesaid conditions (AP 5736).

A nostre seignur le Roi et a son conseil prient les executours du testament Thomas le Hatter de Berewyk' qe come le dit Thomas fuist en la ville de Berewyk' au temps qe la ville feust rendu a nostre seignur le Roi et puis long temps tanqe il morust, por qoi le dit Thomas doit enioyer les condicions grantez par nostre seignur le Roi a ceux de la ville le iour qele feust rendue, et puis en la vie le dit Thomas puis le rendre de la dite ville certeins meffesours de Noef Chastel sur Tyne pristrent diuers biens et chateux le dit Thomas en vne nef sur la Meer, siglant deuers Berewyk' et les amenerent a la dite ville de Noef Chastel, les queux biens sont puis menez a Euerwyk' et liuerez a la Garderobe nostre seignur le Roi: et le dit Thomas ad suy par bref du grant seal as Meir et Baillifs de Noef Chastel tanqe les biens feurent en lour mayns dauer deliuerance et il ne poeit rien auer, par qoi les dits executours prient qe les ditz biens lour soient restorez selonc les condecions auantdites.

Endorsed: Pur ce qe tesmoyne est deuant le conseil qe le dit Thomas feust en la vile de Berewik' le iour qele feust rendue.

post 1333. On 5 October 1333 the mayor and bailiffs of Newcastle were ordered to deliver to Hatter his goods worth £45 6s 6d, captured on the high seas between Flanders and Berwick in the charge of his servant Adam and carried to Newcastle. Adam was also to be released from prison (*CCR 1333–37*, p. 137).

52

Robert de Tughale petitions the King that whereas all his houses in Rock and Scremerston in Northumberland have been burnt and destroyed by the Scots on their last coming into England, and standing grain, namely 80 acres of wheat, 160 acres of oats and 40 acres of barley, were destroyed by the King's army when he lay about Berwick, and 100 oxen and cows were taken by the Scots the night they came suddenly to Tweedmouth, that he may give him a tenement in the Berwick shambles in the King's hand by reason of the forfeiture of Emma Bettes, against the divers losses and damage received by him, or ordain some certain relief (AP 591).

A nostre seignur le Roi prie le son lige Robert de Tughale qe comme touz ses mesons qil auoit en les villes de Rok' e de Scremerston' en le Counte de Northumbr' ..... ars e destrutz par les enemys descoce a lour drein venue en Engleterre, e ses bledz de .... cest assauoir .iiij.^{xx} acres de fourment, .viij.^{xx} acres des aueins e .xl. acres dorge cresanc' en terre furent destrutz par les .... del hoast nostre seignur le Roi quant il gust entour la ville de Berewyk', et ses bestes cest assauoir .c. boefs e vaches pris e fraies par les dits enemis .... descoce la noet quant les dites enemys vindrent sodeinement a Twedemouth', qe li ples doner au dit Robert vn tenement qest en la meine le Roi par la forfaiture Emme Bettes en la boucherie de Berewyk' en allowaunce de plusours pertes e damages qe le dit Robert ad resceuz par les ditz enemys lescoces ou ordeiner ascuns [certein remedie] en releuance de son estat.

Endorsed: Habeat antiquam firmam ad terminum vit[e sue et] quod post .... Robert' et hered' *the endorsement is virtually illegible even under ultra-violet light.*

c. 1335. The siege of Berwick lasted from 12 April to 20 July 1333 (Ridpath, pp. 303, 309). On 22 May 1335 the treasurer and barons of the exchequer were ordered to allow respite until the following Michaelmas to Robert de Tughale, staying in the King's service at Berwick, for all debts owed at the exchequer and to cause without delay his release from any distraint made for that cause (*CCR 1333–37*, p. 487). Tughale served as sheriff of Berwick from

1333–37 (Bain iii, 199, 323, 368). In 1333 he and John de Denton were collectors in Newcastle of the King's wine custom. At the same time he was a collector of wool in Northumberland with Richard de Emeldon (*CCR 1333–37*, pp. 58, 61).

53

Robert de Tughall petitions the King to grant him the hamlet of Edrington and a fishery in the Tweed called *Edirmouth* for his lifetime against his expenses at Berwick, and may he appreciate that Robert has lived there since the town surrendered, and found at his own cost eight armed men and four hobelars, for whom he has taken nothing except that the eight were paid for eight weeks, and he vouches for this all the keepers who have been and the chancellor, chamberlain and mayor [of Berwick] (AP 11299).

Pleise a nostre seignur le Rey granter a son lige Robert de Tughall' le hamlet de Ederington' et vne pescherye en lewe de Twede qe est apelle Edirmouth a terme de sa vie, en alouance de costages et trauailes qil ad fet en sa ville de Berewyck', et pleise a Luy sauer qe le dit Robert iad demore peuse qe la ville fust rendu, et ad troue a ses costages de meme ouyt homes armez et quatre hoblurs pur les queux il ne prist vnke rens saf' pur les ouyt par ouyt semayms, et de ore prent il recorde de touz les gardeyns qe ont este et de Chanceler, Chamberlein et Mayoir.

Endorsed: seit enquise des choses contenues en ceste peticion la verite, et le Roy ent certifie si quil peusse outre commander sa volunte.

1335. On 9 October 1335 the chamberlain of Berwick was ordered to hold an enquiry into the value of the town[ship] of Edrington and other estates forfeited to the King. This enquiry, which was held on 20 January 1336, found that the lands belonged to Berwick castle, Edrington being worth 20 marks in time of peace but then waste, and the fishery of *Edirmouth* being worth 40 marks. It was also found that Tughale had kept eight armed men in Berwick at his own cost, except for wages received for eight weeks, in recompense for which the King had given him the town of East Nisbet, in the King's hands by the forfeiture of William de Estnesbit. When, however, William came into the King's peace this land had been restored to him according to the conditions granted to the earl of Athol (*Cal Inq Misc* ii, 351, 354).

54

Christopher de Colloyne, burgess of Berwick and born in Germany, petitions the King and Council that whereas he was imprisoned in Newcastle upon Tyne and has been for a year and more, contrary to the conditions laid down between the King and those of Berwick, without cause or offence, he requests his release, because he has done no trespass and spent all his means, and so can no longer endure this hardship (AP 10341).

A nostre seignur le Roy et a son consail Moustre si lui plest Cristofre de Colloyne, Burgeis de Berewik' et nee de Almaygne, qe comme il est emprisone et arestu son corps en la ville de Noefchastell' sur Tyne, et ensy ad este par vn an et plus encontre les condiciouns t[ai]lez parentre vostre treshaute seignurie et ceux de la dite ville de Berewik' sanz cause ou nulle manere de trespas: Dount il pri pur dieu et pur regard de pite de vostre grace especial endroit de sa delyuerance auoir: Desicomme il nad de rien trespasse a son eient, et sur ceo le dit Cristofre ad despendu quank' qe il auoit si ⟨qe⟩ rien lui remaynt dont il purra celle penance plus longment endurer.

No endorsement

c. 1335. On 10 October 1335 the mayor and bailiffs of Newcastle were ordered to allow various men of Berwick, including Christopher de Coloigne, to go anywhere in the realm to trade except to Berwick or to Scotland. They had been sent to Newcastle upon suspicion but were allowed to go at large within that town on bail (*Rot Scot* i, 381).

55

The burgesses of Berwick petition the archbishop of Canterbury, chancellor of England, that whereas they surrendered with the town according to conditions granted by the King, they have been imprisoned in Newcastle upon Tyne, where they have been for a year and more without cause or justification or any kind of wrongdoing. They request help before the King for their deliverance, as they have done no wrong and spent all they have, so that they can no longer endure this hardship (AP 10346).

A lur treshonurable seignur Lerceuesqe de Cantorbirs et Chancellier Dengleterre, Moustrent si lui plest les Burgeis de Berewik qe se rendirent ouesqes meisme la ville ala pees sur bones condicions taillez a nostre seignur le Roy, qe come ils sount emprisonez et arestuz lur corps en la ville de Noefchastell' sur Tyne et ount este passe ad vn an et plus, sanz cause et desert ou aucoun manere de trespas: Dount il prient pur dieu a vostre treshaute seignurie de vostre bone eyde et consail devers nostre dit seignur le Roy endroit de lur delyuerance auoir: Desicomme il nount de rien trespasse, et sur ceo si ount il despendu quank' qe ils auoynt, si qe il ne purront celle penance plus longment endurer.

Endorsed: Les Escoce qe demorent a Noef chastel eient cunge de marchander deinz Le roialme Dengleterre et sils voelt venir a Berewik pur leur condicions demander soient responduz par les deputez.

1335 John Stratford, archbishop of Canterbury, was appointed a second time as chancellor of England on 6 June 1335, and the order for release under safeguards was made on 10 October 1335 (*Rot Scot* i, 381; *HBC*, p. 84). Cf. no. 54 above.

56

His clerk and servant William de Emeldon petitions the King for a grant to him and his heirs of the lands lately held by Richard de Emeldon, uncle of William, in Berwick, they being unoccupied, of no value, and owing no rent to the King: paying to the King and his heirs the same rent as Richard paid for the same (AP 11310).

Emelden'

A nostre seignur le Roi pri le soen clerk' et seruant William de Emeldon' qe lui pleise granter a lui les places de terre quele Richard de Emeldon qest adonqes comande, vn[cl]e le dit William, tenoit en la ville de Berewyk', la quele terre nest mie enhabite ne rien vaut' ne rent au dit nostre seignur le Roi, a auoir au dit William et a ses heirs a touz iours, rendant au dit nostre seignur le Roi et a ses heirs tant come le dit Richard rendist pur meisme la terre.

Endorsed: Eit les places et les face en habiter, et Rendant ascune chose au Roi.

c. 1335. On 29 January 1336 a grant was made to William de Emeldon, King's clerk, for good service to the late King, of two places in Briggate in Berwick lately of Richard de Emeldon deceased, uncle of William, which came to the King by the forfeiture of Stephen Forbour, owing a rent of 12d for all services (*Rot Scot* i, 400). Richard de Emeldon is probably to be identified with the mayor of Newcastle killed at the battle of Halidon Hill, 19 July 1333. William was deputy of Robert de Burton as keeper of the St. Mary Magdalen Hospital, Berwick (Scott, p. 347) and chancellor to Edward de Balliol between 1346 and 1347 (Bain iii, 272).

57

William de Brunton, merchant of Newcastle upon Tyne, petitions the King and Council that whereas the King and Council appointed him mayor of Berwick after its conquest and made him attend solely to this office, whereby from the time of accepting office he lost the profits of all the merchandising he was wont to practise throughout England, and he has spent of his own to uphold the office to the King's benefit, which expense he can no longer sustain without the King's aid: he requests the King and Council to make some certain allowance to maintain his office without too much personal loss, having regard to previous expenses and the great loss to his aforesaid trading (AP 4599).

A nostre seignur le Roi et son counseil moustre William de Brunton' Marchant de Noef Chastelle sur Tyne qe come . . . nostre dit seignur le Roi et son conseil lui eussent ordeinez destre Maire de la ville de Berwyk sur Twede apres le Conquest dycelle et de entendre seulement a cel office, parmi quele entendance il ad perdu tanque encea les auantages et profit de tutes ses marchandises qil soleit vser parmi le roialme Dengleterre, et estre cea du temps qil receust loffice auantdit . . . [ad perdist] grantment de soen, qant a son menuz estat, par reson de mesme loffice garder et meintenir al oeps et auantages [nostre dit] seignur le Roi, queles despens il ne poet mais meintenir sanz leide nostre dit seignur le Roi: Dount pri lauandit William qil pleise au nostre dit seignur le Roi et son conseil ordeiner pur lui ascune certeine dont il purra le dit office garder ... come il ad fait tanqe encea, saunz trop perdre de soen, eant regard a les despens auantdites et a la grande perde qil ad eu en le meem temps de ses marchandises auantdites.

Endorsed: Eit .x. li' quex les Meirs soleient auant ces houres prendre pur leur fee; et autres .x. du doun le Roi, et soit bref mande au Chaumberloin illoqes de lui paier.

1335. On 12 October 1335 the treasurer and barons of the exchequer and the chamberlains were ordered to pay William de Burnton £40 in recompense for expenses incurred by him as mayor of Berwick in defence of the town. If this money gift could not be raised they were to make him a competent assignment where he could have quick satisfaction (*Rot Scot* i, 382). Burnton was indeed a prominent wool merchant who figures on the customs rolls of Newcastle and Berwick (PRO, Customs Accts 105/9, 193/8 passim). He served as one of the four bailiffs of Newcastle in 1314, 1316–18, 1321, 1323–25, and 1328–29, and as mayor in 1330, when he also represented that town in parliament (*Early Newcastle Deeds* (Surtees Soc., 137; 1924), pp. 210–12; *AA*[4] XVIII, 1940, p. 4). Despite his complaint that his duties in Berwick prevented him engaging in trade he paid customs in Berwick in 1335/6 on 54 sacks 25 stone of wool, 840 wool-fells and 6 dickers of hides (PRO, Customs Accts 193/8 passim).

58

William de Burnton petitions the King that whereas he held office in Berwick by the King's command since the town's surrender and is overworked and so ill that he cannot sustain such office without danger to himself, that the King may allow him to relinquish the office, and from the time he recovers his health he will be ready in peace and war to serve loyally as much as in him is in this or another office wherever ordered. He requests the King to grant him acquittance from customs dues throughout the King's power for life, in consideration of his work and expenses in the King's service, past and to come (AP 10343).

A nostre seignour le roi pri si ly plest le soen lige William de Burneton' qe comme par il ad demore en office dedeinz sa ville de Berewyk sur Twede par soen comandement puys qe la ville fust rendu en cea: Et le dit William ia est [moult] trauaille et si a mal ese qil ne purra sanz peril de soen corps tel office al honour et profit du dit nostre seignur le Roi meintenir, qe li pleise graunter de sa bone grace qe le dit William pusse estre allege et assouz du dit office: Et de quel houre qe dieu li durra recouerir de saunte il serra prest, en pees et en guerre, a seruir et faire loialment et bonement quantqe en li est en cel office ou autre, quiel lieu qe li plerra comander. Et pleise a nostre seignur le roi granter al dit William qil sait quite de Costume ⟨par tot le pouer le Roi⟩ pur terme de sa vie pur les trauayles et costages qil ad mis en son seruise et prest serra a fer quiel hour qil serra a ese de corps.

Endorsed: Soit parle oue lui qil demoerte en loffice, et endreit de son trauail il plest au Roi et a son conseil qil seit regarde couenablement.

?c. 1335. See no. 57 above, and compare the complaint of John de Burdon as chamberlain of Berwick, 1340–43, no. 39 above.

59

The poor nuns of Berwick petition the King to grant a charter of confirmation of 40 marks rent in Berwick which was their original endowment, and order his ministers at Berwick to allow them freely to enjoy their land and tenements and fisheries, both in the Tweed in Scotland and in other waters in his lordship in England and Scotland as they had previously. May he please to order his ministers to pay the nuns the money which the King granted for repair of their church and their other houses and the £20 granted them of his special grace, as more fully contained in his charter. They have received nothing since the battle but 20 marks, and by reason of the battle lost all their goods, grain, beasts and all they had (AP 1609).

Pleise a nostre seignur le Roi pur lamour de dieu et les almes ses auncestres grauntier as ces poures Nonayns de Berewyk' sa chartre de confirmacion de .xl. Marches de Rente en la dite ville de Berewyk' qe feust le comencement de lour fundacioen, et de comaunder a ses ministres de Berewyk par ses lettres qeles puissent franchemente enioier lour terre et tenementz et lour pescheries auxibien en Twede en Escoce come en altres Ewes qe sont deinz sa seignurie en Engleterre et en Escoce sicome eles auant ces houres ont eu. Et qe lui pleise comander a ses ditz ministres qe les ditz Noneyns soient serui del argent quel le dit Roi granta a eux pur redresser lour Esglise et lour altres maisons et les vint liures les queux il ad graunte de sa grace especiale sicome plus pleinement est contenu en sa chartre, qar eles ne eunt rien resceu de ceo puis la bataille fors tant solement vint Martz, de sicome eles furent destrutz de touz leur biens, bledz et bestes et quaunt qils auoient par reson de la bataille

Endorsed: Quant au conferment ...... tantqe le Roy soit serui de ses terres.

Quant au paiement soit mandez a Robert de Tughale, Chaumberlein de Berwyk', qe il fait la paie.

c. 1337. This Cistercian nunnery had been founded before 1153 by David I near Halidon Hill, where the battle was fought on 19 July 1333, and Edward III had granted on 28 July 1333 an annuity of £20 payable by the sheriff of Berwick from the issues of the town and county until lands of an equivalent value were found for them. He had also ordered the house to be rebuilt at his own expense, and ordered that an altar be erected there in honour of St Margaret the Virgin, on whose eve the victory had been obtained (*Rot Scot* i, 257; Cowan/Easson, p. 145). Tughale, who was to pay in accordance with the endorsement, does not appear as chamberlain of Berwick before 1337.

SECTION II

CUMBERLAND

This section does not present a full range of petitions from the northwest of England, lacking as it does all reference to the rebellion of Sir Andrew de Harcla. It does, however, reinforce the picture of misery caused in the north of England by the Scottish wars in the fourteenth century. It also supports the view that Cumbria was normally so far from court and the King that neither could be expected to know what was happening in the other setting. Possibly because of this isolation the people of Cumbria often presented their grievances along with neighbouring counties on the theme of the 'cost of war'. These petitions form a separate section below (III), in which nos 101, 102, 108, 110–113 and 117–118 refer specifically to Cumbria.

Legal

Cumbria formed part of the common-law system in England, and despite the distance from Westminster its inhabitants were required to sue there, and serve on assizes and juries outside the county of Cumberland (nos 60, 62, 63). Isabel, widow of Sir Richard de Cleterne, pleaded against any flouting of a statute which limited the King's right of pardon in unworthy causes (no. 66).

While there were no problems arising from franchises within the area (cf. no. 67 for a complaint against the inhabitants of the franchise of North Tynedale), inevitably friction arose from feudal incidents, particularly marriage and wardship. Sir Hubert de Multon was divorced, with the resultant clash of claims as to the identity of his first-born (no. 61). Robert de Welle married a wealthy widow without a royal licence (no. 64). The widow of Thomas de Multon of Egremont was concerned over the match arranged for her son in wardship (no. 65).

Ancient Petitions E498, 1937, 2034, 2035, 3042, 3044, 8082, 12939.

60

Adam de Bowes petitions the King and Council that whereas
Gilbert de Querton, Henry de Threelqeld and William de
Goldington sued a writ against him for 30 acres with appurten-
ances in Newbiggin in Cumberland he had appointed as his
attorney William Pynkene for the morrow of Martinmas [12
November] 1306. Pynkene died at Pontefract on his way from
York to London to plead for him, and Adam, who was on the
King's service in Scotland as Robert de Swyneburne testifies, lost
his land on the day through default, he not knowing of his
attorney's death. He craves remedy for the default (AP E498).

A nostre seignur le Roy et a son consail mustre Adam de Bowes
qe come Gilbert de Querton, Henri de Threelqeld et Willam de
Goldington' auient porte bref sur luy de trent acres de terre oue les
apurtenances en Niwebygging en le Conte de Comberlaund,
mesme celi Adam auantdit vint en response par son aturne
Williame Pynkene et auient ior lendemain de seint Martyn lan du
nostre seignur le Roy trentisme quart, le vantdit Williame de
Pynkene enchemenant de Euerwyk' auer Londres pur pleider pur
le vantdit Adam murust a Pondfreit: nent sachant le vantdit Adam,
qe fut en seruiz nostre seignur en Escoce, tesmoinant par Roberd
de Swyneburne, perdit sa terre al ior auant nome par defaute: Dunt
le auantdit Adam prie grace et remedie, issi qe cel ior li seit sauue et
qe ne seit mie perdant pur cele defaute.

Endorsed: Sequatur quod habeat testimonium quod fuit in seruicio
Regis.

1306/7. The same plaintiffs sued a writ for land in Nateby near
Kirkby Stephen against Peter le Walsh in 1304 (*CCR 1302–7*, p.
208).

61

Margaret widow of Sir Hubert de Multon petitions the King and Council that whereas John their son and heir is not yet thirteen and in the wardship of the King because on the day of his death Sir Hubert held all his lands by knight service from the heir of Thomas de Multon of Gilsland, then under age and in the King's wardship, a bastard William le Brun, fathered by Sir Hubert on his cousin Ada la Brune who had been married while in knowledge of their kinship and been divorced on proof of this previous knowledge, as she can prove, sued to have seisin of Sir Hubert's lands, to the deception of the King and the rightful heir. She craves that no livery of seisin be made, and that the Chancellor be warned to take no action without notifying Margaret to show what she knows touching the estate of the King and the heir, who is under age and in his wardship. The estates are the manors of Isel in Cumberland and of Surlingham in Norfolk (AP 3042).

A nostre seignur le Rey e a sun consail Mustre Margarete qe fu femme sire Huberd de Multon' qe com Johan lur fiz e heir ne seit vncore qe de age de tresse aunz e en la garde nostre seignur le Rey, par la resune qe le dit sire Huberd tint tuz ces tenemenz en chef par seruices de chiualer le iour qe il morust del heyr Thomas de Multon' de Gilleslaund qe aloure fust dedenz age e en la garde nostre seignur le Rey, vn Willame le Brun, bastard qe le dit sire Huberd' engendra akun tens de vne sue cousine Ade la Brune, la quele il ont primes espuse sachaunz le cosinage e entreques deuorz fesist puys par proue fete de la dite sachaunce de cosinage auant les espusailles, com la dite Margarete set e poet suffisaument mustrer, seut endeceyte du Rey e du dreyt heir susdit de auer seisine de terres qels furent au dit sire Huberd': Dunt ele prie qe nule seysine liure luy seit, ke le Chaunceler seyt garni qe il ne liure nule seysine de dites terres saunz fere garnir la dite Margarete a mustrer ceo qe ele sauera dire pur le estat le Rey e le dit heyr qe est denz age e en sa garde. Endreit de tenemenz fet asauer, le Maner de Ishale en le Cunte de Cumberlaund' E le Maner de Surlingeham en le Cunte de Norffok'.

Endorsed: Non deliberetur sine speciali precepto domini Regis.

c. 1310. Custody of the lands of Hubert de Multon was granted to William Inge on 13 February 1308, while the heir's marriage was granted to Robert de Cardoill, the King's yeoman, on 12 March 1309 (*CPR 1307–13*, pp. 46, 105). On 9 March 1308 the escheator north of Trent was ordered to survey the manor of Isel and enquire into any waste which might have been done by Richard le Brun, who had been given custody by Neil Campbell. If it were found that waste had been committed the manor was to be seized into the King's hands (*CFR* ii, 19). On 18 February 1310 the escheator was ordered to enter the manor, which was held in cornage for 13s 4d a year payable to Thomas de Multon of Gilsland. As explanation it was noted that Hubert de Multon had been betrothed to Ada la Brune, who had lived with him for four years and borne him a son William, aged 14 at Hubert's death. After the divorce of Ada on the grounds of affinity Hubert had married Margaret de Boys, whose son John was aged 7 at Hubert's death. Edward I had granted the custody of the lands to Neil Campbell, who 'sublet' it to Richard le Brun, brother of Ada. Richard fraudulently allowed his nephew William to take possession, to the King's contempt and the disherison of John (*ibid.*, 57). Seisin was granted to John de Multon on 20 September 1314 on his proof of age, after which he and Sir William Inge entered into a bond for £20 to cover claims of waste committed by Inge as guardian (*CCR 1313–18*, pp. 114, 196).

62

The commons of Cumberland petition the King that whereas men are arrested in the kingdom by indictment and on suspicion, in accordance with the Statute of Winchester, in Cumberland no indictment is taken but only attachment on suspicion of a bailiff. They desire this custom to be ended and that they be ruled by common law and according to the Statute of Winchester (AP 2034).

Endorsed: Mandetur vicecomiti et Coronatoribus quod capiant inquisiciones super hiis que secundum legem et consuetudinem regni capiende sunt, sicut alibi in regno, et tam per inquisicionem quam per suspeccionem faciant quod secundum legem et consuetudinem regni et secundum formam statuti Wynton' fuerit faciendum.

temp Edward II, The Statute of Winchester (1285) was concerned with maintenance of law and order, especially where suspected felons evaded justice by crossing boundaries and those responsible for bringing them to justice preferred to turn a blind eye. The absence of the sheriff's tourn was noticed in Northumberland in the mid-thirteenth century and, by inference, later (J. Hodgson, *Northumberland* III, i, 101). The petition is printed in *Select Cases in the Court of King's Bench III* (Selden Soc., 58), p. cxvii.

63

His lieges of Cumberland petition the King to have regard to their loss and hardships in order to preserve his land and their lives, and grant that they may not be belaboured by summonses nor distresses to serve on assizes and juries outside the county except for the grand assize, for they are distant from his court at London and too poor to pay fines and charges.

They also petition the King to grant them a sheriff of their own choice as will be for the good of him and them, for whom they will answer, as they have suffered many grievances before now from the whims of sheriffs. This election would be annual by common assent of the county (AP 2035).

Endorsed: Prima petitio non potest fieri, set tamen concesse sunt inquisiciones de nisi prius.
Secunda peticio est contra Ordinaciones

1311–16. Edward I in 1300, among the *Articuli super cartas*, had granted that sheriffs be elected by the counties, but the traditional manner of appointment in the Exchequer was quickly reimposed, and the Ordinances of 1311 sought to exclude royal influence only to the extent of entrusting the appointment to the Chancellor, Treasurer, and such others of the Council present in the Exchequer. In the absence of the Chancellor, the Treasurer should act with the Barons of the Exchequer and the Justices of the Bench. This latter method was confirmed by the Statute of Lincoln in 1316 (J. Conway Davies, *The Baronial Opposition to Edward II* (1918), pp. 521–4). Cumberland sheriffs had, indeed, held office for many years at a time. Michael de Harcla was sheriff from 1285 to 1298, and he was succeeded by William de Mulecastre, who continued until 1303. Thereafter the sheriffs were changed virtually annually until Andrew de Harcla, who accounted from Easter 1312 to Michaelmas 1315, when he was succeeded by John de Castre, who served from Michaelmas 1315 until June 1318. Harcla returned from April 1319 until his disgrace in February 1323 (PRO, *Lists and Indexes* ix (Sheriffs), 26). This petition is printed in *Select Cases in the Court of King's Bench II* (Selden Soc., 57), p. cxlviii.

64

Robert de Welle petitions the King and Council that whereas he fined in Chancery for his trespass in wedding without the King's leave Maud widow of Sir Robert de Clifford, which was pardoned him, and the King issued a writ under his great seal to Sir Robert de Clydrowe, then escheator north of Trent, to deliver the lands with all their issues received since the time of seizure, yet Robert de Clidrowe has retained as much as 100 marks (AP 12939).

A nostre seignur le Roy et a son conseyl mustre Roberd de Welle qe come par fyne fece en la Chauncelerye pur le trespas qe il fit esposaunt Maud qe fut la femme monsieur Roberd de Clyfford' sauns le conge du Roy ceux trespas lui feust pardones, et sur ceo nostre seignur le Roy manda par Bref de son grant seal a sire Roberd de Clydrowe adunqes achetur desa Trente qe il ⟨lui⟩ deliuera terres oue touz les issues resuez de meismes les terres pus le temps qe ele esteyent saysies en la meyn le Roy, de quei le dit Roberd de Clidrowe detient deuer lui alamontanse de Cent Mars, dount il prie remedye.

Endorsed: Mandetur per breue de magno sigillo Thesaurario et Baronibus de scaccario quod venire faciant escaetorem coram eis ad respondendum predicto Roberto de Welle et ibi fiat partibus iusticie complementum etc, et mittatur ista peticio Thesaurario et Baronibus predictis.

c. 1316. Robert de Welle and Maud, widow of the late Robert de

Clifford, tenant in chief, received a pardon for marrying without royal licence on 3 October 1316 on payment of a fine of £100 (*CPR 1313–17*, p. 551). The same day Robert de Cliderhow was ordered to deliver them her dower lands with her goods there and issues received since their seizure for her marriage without the King's licence (*CCR 1313–18*, p. 367). This order was repeated on 7 June 1319 in respect of her dower in Skelton in Cumberland, as Cliderhow had been removed from office before he could execute the order (*CCR 1318–23*, p. 84, cf. p. 269). See also no. 182 below.

65

Eleanor widow of Thomas de Multon of Egremont petitions the King about his intention concerning the marriage between John her son and heir and Joan daughter of Sir Piers de Gavaston, late earl of Cornwall, discussed in the lifetime of Thomas her lord, and the custody of two parts of the lands of the same Thomas in Cumberland until the heir comes of age, paying the annual value as returned at the Chancery of £76 8s 1¾d. She also petitions the King that the houses within the castle are ruinous and she seeks custody in order to maintain the houses. *Deleted:* She petitions that she may have care of the child under the King, until he has signified his pleasure (AP 3044).

A nostre seignur le Roi prie la sue lige si lui plest Alianore qe fu la femme Thomas de Multon' de Egremound' qe lui pleise dire sa volunte du Mariage purparle en temps le dit Thomas soun seignur entre Johan soun fiz e soun heir e Johane la filie monsz Piers de Gauaston' ⟨nadguers Counte de Cornuaill'⟩ et qe de sa grace la voille granter la garde de deux parties des terres qe furent au dit Thomas soun seignur en le Counte de Cumberland' tanqe lage le heir, rendaunt par an lestente returne en la Chauncelrie qe amonte a .lxxvj. li' .viij. s. .i. d ⟨ob.⟩ qᵃ. Et voille nostre seignur le Roi si lui plest entendre qe les Mesouns en le Chastel sount ruinouses, et pur taunt voleit ele si lui plest auer la garde asusteiner les Mesouns. *Deleted:* Et sil plest a nostre seignur le Roi ele prie qele puise auoir la nurture de lenfaunt agarder al oeps nostre seignur le Roi taunt qil eit ordeine de lui ceo qe lui plest.

No endorsement

AP 13987 is a duplicate of this, endorsed Coram Rege Herlaston, *without the deletion of the last sentence and with the verbal difference of* 'en point de' *for* 'ruinouses'.

?1322. The agreement for the marriage of John de Multon to Joan, dated 26 May 1317, was in the form of a bond for 1000 marks, payable by the King out of the fine of 1500 marks due from Thomas de Wake for refusal to marry Joan at the King's pleasure (*CPR 1313–17*, p. 654; *1317–21*, pp. 43, 251–2). The inquisition post mortem on Thomas de Multon's estates was held in February 1322, and found that John was about 14 years of age. The assignment of the widow's dower was made on 4 April 1322 (*Cal Inq pm* vi, 198–199). On 25 May 1322 custody of Egremont castle with the lands of Coupland was granted to Robert de Leyburn, and re-assigned on 10 June 1323 to Antony de Lucy (*CFR* iii, 132, 212). On 5 May 1325 the two-thirds of the honour of Egremont were restored to John de Multon, although he was still under age (*CCR 1323–27*, p. 268). John's marriage was granted on 10 January 1327 to William de la Zouche (*CPR 1324–27*, p. 347).

66

Isabel, widow of Sir Richard de Cleterne, petitions the King and Council that whereas she was in her manor of Ellenborough in Cumberland at peace with God and the King, an Adam son of Gilbert de Culwen the uncle came by night with other evildoers, by force and arms against the King's peace, and seized Isabel against her will and beat the people with her, wounded and manhandled them, and threw her across a horse and so led her from her manor to *Aykehurst* castle, where she was held until rescued by the power and aid of Sir Antony de Lucy. These evildoers now have their advocates in court seeking charters of pardon, and she begs the King and Council for the love of God, the salvation of the King's soul, and for the honour of women, that this 'peace' be denied them, because charters of pardon are so commonly granted by the influence of those near the King, regardless of the statute lately made, whereby the law is no more feared and evildoers are more emboldened to do wrong and notably in the March abovesaid, because they can resort to Scotland after their crimes (AP 1937).

A nostre seignur le Roi et son conseil moustre Isabele qe fut la femme monsz Richard de Cleterne qe par la ou ele estoit en son Manoir de Alenburgh' en le Counte de Cumbr' en la pees dieu et de nostre seignur le Roi qui ore est, qe dieu garde, la vint vn Adam le fitz Gilbert de Culwen' le vnkel nuyttantre et autres plusours oue li meffesours a force et armes encontre la pees nostre dit seignur le Roi, et la dite Isabele contre son gre rauirent et ses gentz oue li trouetz batirent, naufrerunt et malement treterunt et puis la ietterunt sur vn chiual a trauers et en tiel manere hors de son Manoir la menerent tanqe au Chastel de Aykhurst' et illoqes la tindrent tanqe rescus la fut fait par le power et leide monsz Antoigne de Lucy, les queux meffesours ount ⟨ia⟩ lour procuraturs en court pur chartre de pardon: Dont ele prie houmblement a nostre dit seignur le Roi et son conseil, pur lamur de dieu et saluacion del alme le Roi et pur honur de femmes, qe la pees leu soit defendu, qar chartres de pardon sont grantez si communement par procurement de ceaux qe sount pres du Roi, nient eiaunt regard' a Lestatut' nadgueres fait, par qai qe la lai nest de rien dotee mes le meffesours dassez plus enbaudiz de meffaire et nomement en la Marche susdit, pur le resut qil ount Descoce apres lour felonies faites.

Endorsed: Il ne doit mie auoir pardoun.

1338 x 1343. In April 1338 Richard de Cletergh was still alive and holding the tenth of a knight's fee at Cleator, worth £15 (*CCR 1337–39*, p. 366). *Aykhurst* has been identified with Hayes Castle near Distington (J. Wilson, 'The original name of Hayes Castle', *Transactions* Cumb. & West. AA Soc. 2, xvi, 29–39). A statute to limit the King's power of indiscriminate pardon for felonies at the request of courtiers had been enacted in 1328 and confirmed in 1336 and 1340. Rights of feudal wardship may lie behind the outrage. Sir Antony de Lucy was dead by 10 June 1343 (GEC, *Complete Peerage* viii, 252).

67

The commons of the county of Cumberland petition the King's Council that whereas there was a truce between the kings of England and Scotland the men of Tynedale, of the lordship of the

Queen, came through Cumberland and did great damage in Scotland, plundering goods and chattels, and returned by night, by reason of which the common people of Cumberland have been distrained to make redress because the evil-doers cannot be pursued within the franchise of Tynedale (AP 8082).

A conseil nostre seignur le Roi moustront les comunes du Counte de Cumbr' qu par la ou trew fust pris parentre le Roi Dengleterre et le Roy de Scoce [y] veynent les gentz de Tyndal' quil sont de la Seignurie nostre Dame la Roine et passent parmy le dite C[ou]nte de Cumbr' et font grant damage en Escoce et robbent lours biens et Chateux et reuenient noctauntre par la dite Counte, pur quel[s] damages et robberies les ditz Communes du dite Counte de Cumbr' sont destreutz de faire redresces par cause qils ne [purrent] suer les maufesours susditz de arester denz les dits Franchies de Tyndal': Pur quoi ils priont remedie pur dieu et en [oeure de] Charite.

Endorsed: soit le Conseil ma dame le Royne appelle et si ele ne orde remedie desdits meffesours adonqe soit grante commission as seignurs du paiis ou tielx meffesours passent darester et prendre mesmes les meffesours.

c. 1342. On 28 January 1343 a commission was issued to Gilbert de Umfraville, earl of Angus and lord of Redesdale, or his deputy, following complaints from the people of Northumberland and Cumberland that many disturbers of the peace came daily from his lordship into their counties and into the liberties of Tynedale, Hexham and Durham, feigning to be Scots and making prisoners of many men and taking them to Scotland and elsewhere for ransom and killing and taking booty of their animals. All indicted or appealed of such felonies were to be taken and dealt with according to the law and custom of England. Similar commissions were issued to Queen Philippa in respect of North Tynedale, to the Archbishop of York in respect of Hexhamshire, and to the Bishop of Durham in respect of Durham (*CPR 1343–45*, pp. 67, cf. 88).

Financial

Despite its distance from the King's exchequer and destruction by the Scots Cumbria was expected to contribute to the national lay subsidies (nos 68, 69, 73). Nor was it sufficient for Michael de Harcla as sheriff of Cumberland to attribute his failure to bring the county rents to the Treasurer 'by reason of burnings and waste'. He had to be more specific before a special enquiry (no. 70, cf. 73). Similarly, the assessors having valued the goods of the inhabitants of Kendal, the collectors insisted on this sum although in the meantime the town had burnt down (no. 71).

For a change, Richard Champion wanted support for a mining venture (no. 72), and the inhabitants of Penrith complained bitterly about tanners contaminating the town's only supply of water (no. 74).

Ancient Petitions E506, E726, 25, 594, 2939, 5121, 6761.

68

Thomas de Colewen and Hugh de Muleton, commissioned to tax, levy and collect the fifteenth in Cumberland, petition the King and Council that they were put by the sheriffs of Cumberland and Westmorland on assizes and juries for the King's Bench [i.e. Common Pleas], which they were unable to attend, wherefore the sheriffs made return of their issues and now have been ordered to levy them. They crave the King to act, especially as they remained at home by command of the Treasurer (AP E726).

A nostre seignur le Roy e a soun conseil prunt Thomas de Colewen e Hughe de Muleton' ke la ou il furent assignez e chargez par comaundement le Tresorer de taxer Leuer e receiuer le Quinzime en le Cunte de Cumbr[elaund], en meimes ceus tens les viscuntes de Cumbrel[aund] e We[stmor]laund les mistrent en assises e iurees au Baunk nostre seingnur (*sic*) le Rey ou eus ne poeyent ateindre pur le seruise le Rey, par quer les viscuntes returnerent Lur issues e or est comaunde au vescuntes a leuer meimes les issues: Dunt eus prient nostre seignur le Rey ke disicum ifurent en sun seruise ke il l[ur] voyelle de ceste chosse sa grace fere e de sicom il demorerent a Messun par le comaundement le Tresorer.

Endorsed: Mittatur Thesaurario et faciat de eis sicut aliis qui sunt 'eiusdem condicionis' [*deleted*] in tali casu et computando annum et diem.

scire faciant de quibus exitibus sunt onerati et [ex] quo tempore et coram quibus Justiciariis: postea Rotulis de Banco scrutatis compertum est quod exitus Thome de Corewen sunt de banco de anno .xx.° et extendunt se ad. .xx. marcas et exitus Hugonis de Multone sunt de eodem Banco .xx.° extendunt se ad .x. li'. Et quod dicti ⟨Thomas et Hugo qui fuerunt⟩ Collectores ⟨antedicti in Comitatu Cumbr'⟩ fuerunt in Leuando ..... de anno .xx.°, et preceptum eis factum est per Thesaurarium et barones ex parte Regis ne extra Comitatum vbi collectores fuerunt se transferrent set dicte collectioni omni modo intendentes, ideo fiat eis billa Cancellarie ad eundem Collectores— *palimpsest follows.*

1297. A warrant for the acquittance of Colewen for 20 marks and of Muleton for £10 was issued on 12 February 1297 (*CCR 1296–1302*, p. 14). The fifteenth was granted in 1290 (Willard, p. 343).

69

John de Lucy and Walter de Bampton, assessers and collectors of the thirtieth and twentieth in Cumberland, petition the King and Council that whereas they were charged to levy this, they found no sheriff nor royal bailiff who could assist them because of preoccupation with the taking of grain, carts and other royal needs, as they allege; hence they have received only £30. They request that someone be nominated to receive this, and advice as to the residue (AP 2939).

A nostre seignur le Roy e a son counseil Mustrent Johan de Lucy e Wauter de Bampton' Taxours e Coillours del Trentisme e [del] vincisme en le Counte de Cumberland qe la ou il sunt chargez a leuer les auaunditz trentisme e vintisme, il ne trouent

viscount' ne autre baillif' le Roy qe a eux pust estre entendaunt
pur les prises de bleez e cariages e autries bosoygnes le Roy
sicom il dicunt: Par ⟨quai⟩ il ne vnt vncore resceu forsqe .xxx.
liuers, de quels il prient qe vous voilez assigner a qi il purrount
faire la paye en ceo pays, e priount sil vous plest vostre counseil
de ceo qe est a leuer.

Endorsed: Fiat breue vicecomiti Cumbreland quod capiat terras et
tenementa predictorum Taxatorum in manum domini Regis vna
cum omnibus bonis et catallis suis et salua custodiat donec etc.
Et similiter fiat eis breue quod reddant rotulos suos ad mediam
quadragesimam coram Thesaurario apud Karliol' ad soluendum
terciam partem Tricesime Regis in hac parte contingentem.

c. 1306. Lucy and Brampton were appointed to collect and levy
the thirtieth and twentieth in Cumberland on 22 July 1306
(*CPR 1301–7*, p. 456).

70

Michael de Hartcla petitions the King and Council that whereas
the King granted him in Parliament at Westminster in 1305 an
allowance for the arrears which he was unable to levy while he
was sheriff of Cumberland by reason of the burnings and waste
done by the Scots in the county, he cannot have allowance from
the Treasurer and Barons of the Exchequer unless they be certified of these damages and losses at the hands of the Scots in the
county. He again begs for auditors to enquire into the damage
and losses, to certify the Treasurer and Barons so that they may
make allowance as the King previously granted (AP 25).

A nostre seignur le Roi et a son consail mustre Michel de
Hartcla que par la ou le Roi luy aueit grante de sa grace a son
parlement a Westmuster lan de son regne trentisme tierce qil
vst allouaunce de ses arrerages les quelx il ne poeit leuer tant
come il fu viscunte en le Counte de Cumbreland pur arsuns et
destructions que les Escotz aueient fait en meisme le Counte, et
il ne poet allouaunce auoir si le Tresorer et les Barons del
Escheker ne soient certifiez de ses damages et ses pertes quil
aueit par les Escotz en le dit Counte, par quei il prie vncore la

grace le Roi et al consail quil eit auditurs denquer de ses damages et ses pertes et pur certifier le Tresorer et les Barons issint quil puisse allouaunce auoir: Come le Roi luy granta autrefoith' de sa grace.

Endorsed: Assignentur Johannes de Insula et Johannes de Kirkeby per breue de Cancellaria ad inquirendum super contentis in peticione. Irrotulatur

1307. The initial petition of 1305 is summarized on the parliamentary roll (*Rot Parl* i, 163), where Harcla also sought allocation for £38 owed him by the King for wool taken from him for the King's use by Henry de Menevill. According to the endorsement he was to have a chancery writ to the Treasurer and Barons for 'grace at their discretion', the wool to be allocated against his arrears. On 26 June 1307 a commission was issued to John de Insula and John de Kirkeby following his [above] petition in parliament at Carlisle, to hold an enquiry within the county as to what issues he had been prevented from levying (*CPR 1301–7*, p. 549).

71

The poor people of Kirkby in Kendal petition the King and Council that whereas the town with their goods was burnt, reducing them to poverty and beggary, the assessors came and wished to tax them according to their possessions at Michaelmas without regard to what befell them a month later. They crave that they be taxed according to their present goods (AP E506).

A nostre seignur le Rey e a sun consoil moustrent le pouers gentz de Kyrkeby en Kendale com la dite ville ensemblement oue lour biens e chateux fust ars, de quei il sount pouers e mendynauntz, venent les taxours e taxer les voillent solom les biens e chateux qil vrent a laseint Michel, nyent eyaunz regarde de la cheaunce qe lour aueint vn Moys apres laseint Michel, Dount il prient pur dieu qe il peussent estre taxes solom les biens e chateus qe il ount ore entermeynes.

Endorsed: Nichil fiat.

?temp. Edward I. This fire does not seem otherwise recorded.

72

Richard Champion shows the King and Council that he has found mines of lead and silver in many places [*lewes*] of Cumberland and Westmorland, from which the King will derive much profit if he will undertake the expense. He craves a grant of the tenth penny, and will certify the King what more it is worth (AP 5121).

A nostre seignur le Roi et a son Consayl moustre Richard Champion qil ad troue myn de plom et dargent en moltz des Lewes en le Counte de Comberlond et de Westmerelond dunt nostre seignur le Roi poet auer grant profit sil voit mettre costages, et si pleysir soit a nostre seignur le Roi qil voile graunter la chose pur le dysme dener, il trouera bien qe le prendereit pur meuz certifier a nostre seignur le Roi qoi il purra valler.

Endorsed: Soit moustre ceste peticion au Tresorrer et il enface ceo qest affaire pur profit le Roi.   Coram domino Rege

c. 1324. On 22 May 1324 a protection for one year was issued for Richard Champion and Thomas de Allemaigne, appointed to dig, purge, and examine the King's mine in the counties of Cumberland and Westmorland (*CPR 1321–24*, p. 414).

73

The poor people of Cumberland petition the King for the towns burnt and devastated by the Scots. Following their suit before the King's council a commission was sent to Sir Thomas de Lucy and others of the county to enquire as to which towns were burnt and devastated and so remit their biennial tax, granted for 1346. By virtue of this, inquests were taken and returned into Chancery, which found divers towns were burnt and devastated in part or wholly. May it please the King to grant letters of privy seal to the Chancellor ordering writs to be sent to the Treasurer and Barons of the Exchequer to discharge the collectors and men of such towns as are returned as burnt and destroyed (AP 594).

1346. On 10 March 1346 Thomas de Lucy and John de Orton were commissioned to enquire in Cumberland and certify the King of the truth in a petition from both churchmen and laity of the county setting forth that although, because very many manors, towns, hamlets, lands and places of the county, with the crops, animals and other goods in them, were almost entirely burned and destroyed by a hostile invasion of the Scots after Michaelmas last past, and they had no means wherewith to cultivate their lands or support themselves, nevertheless they were grievously distrained for the last tenth and fifteenth granted by the clergy and commonalty of the realm, this being the second year of payment. They requested remission of the amount. With the return of the enquiry a supersession and pardon for a tenth and fifteenth due from the clergy and laity of Cumberland was issued on 10 May 1346. An extension was granted on 18 April 1348, on condition that payment was made on chattels outside the areas of devastation and on goods rescued (*CPR 1345–48*, pp. 105–6; *CCR 1346–49*, pp. 30, 448–9). The petition is printed in *Rot Parl* ii, 176 under 21 Edward III [1347].

74

The King's tenants of the town of Penrith petition the King and his Council in parliament that whereas they have no water in the said town, inhabited by great numbers of the King's tenants, save a little rivulet, a tributary of another stream, the tanners living in the town come and steep their skins in the rivulet at all times of the year on payment to the King of 4s in new rent through the steward of the place: by which skins, and the vermin they attract, the water is contaminated so that the tenants and other countryfolk coming to the town's market are discommoded. May it please the Council to question the bishop of Carlisle, who is the King's farmer of the town, and ordain a remedy (AP 6761).

A nostre seignur le Roi et a son bon conseil de ceste presente parlement moustront les tenant' nostre seignur [le Roi] de la vile de Penreth' qe come il ad nulle eawe en la dite vile, qest enhabite od grante numbre des tenantz le Roi, forqe dune petit ryuol qest vne braunche tirrant du autre ⟨eawe⟩, la v[ient] tannours demorantz en la dite vile et mettent lour pealx en grant noumbre a giser en le [dit] ryuol checun temps del an ⟨et rendant ent par an au Roi .iiij. s. de nouele arente par le seneschal de lieu⟩, par queux pealx et diuers vermyne nurree par yceux leawe est confect qe les ditz tenant ne autres gentz du pays venantz au dite vile pur la marche ... ne pount auoir lour easement ne estre seruis dy cele pur la confectione suisdite: Sur quay pleise au dit conseil examiner leuesqe de Kardoill' qest fermer nostre dit seignur le Roi de la vile susdit et ent ordeigner remedy.

Endorsed: Soient certeines bones gentz et sufficeants assigne denquere de la matire comprise en la bille et de ent certifier en la Chauncellerie.

1376. A commission was issued on 8 July 1376 to Thomas de Sandford, Robert de Ormesheved and William de Stapelton to enquire in Cumberland touching this petition from the King's tenants of Penrith complaining that a certain water running to the town was polluted by some of the town exercising the mystery of tanning, who daily cast hides in the water whereby there was much sickness in the town (*CPR 1374–77*, pp. 327–8). Thomas Appleby, bishop of Carlisle (1363–95), who was appointed a Warden of the Western Marches in 1367, had received custody of Penrith and Sowerby from Edward III on 6 March 1371 (*CFR* viii, 110; J. F. Curwen, *Castles and Towers of Cumberland and Westmorland* (1913), p. 448).

Carlisle

The city was doubly hit in its trade during the fourteenth century. The Scottish wars brought direct destruction to property, and the needs of defence resulted in seizure of provisions for the garrison, taxation, and general scarcity (nos 75, 77–79, 83–84). The hospital of St. Nicholas outside the city wall was particularly vulnerable (no. 67). John de Morpath complained that his houses inside the walls had been demolished for their timber 'to make towers and brattices for the town's defence' without any compensation (no. 80). Later the townsmen presented a double grievance that they had received no payment for their services in defence of Carlisle and been supplied with bad provisions, which had to be bought dear and sold cheap (no. 81). Isabel de Vernoune had taken her goods from the country to the imagined safety of the city, only to have them confiscated with the other goods of her brother, Sir Andrew de Harcla (no. 82).

Ancient Petitions E417, E517, E522, E539, 2209, 3029, 5046, 10186, 10187, 12914.

75

Henry de Dalston petitions the King and Council for 10s as compensation for a skip of barley malt worth 6s, taken to Carlisle market on the Saturday before SS Philip and James 23 Edward I [30 April 1295] and seized by Richard à Latimer, purveyor of Sir William de Kardoyl (AP E522).

A nostre seynor le Roy et a son Consayl Mustre Henr' de Dalston' ky par la ou il amena vne skeppe de Bras' de Orge al marche de Kardoyl le samedy prochayn auaunt la fest Saynt filipp' et Jacob' pris de .vj. s. Lan du regne nostre seynor le Roy quy deu garde .xxiij. la vynt vne Syr William de Kardoyl cheualer et prist la vauntdyt scheppe de Bras' par vne Ricard alatymer purueur meme cesty Willam' en la pris' et apres la prys': Dunt meme cely Henr' se pleynt a nostre seynur le Roy et a son Consayl et prye remedy pur deu, pur ce damage amuntunt a .x. s.

Endorsed: Sequatur per communem legem.

?1295. On 4 March 1296 Robert de la Ferete and William de Karliol were appointed captains and keepers of the peace in Cumberland during the King's pleasure (*CPR 1291–1301*, p. 185). Sir William received a grant of free warren in his lands at Saxelingham in Norfolk and at Oughterby in Kirkbampton and at Crosby in Cumberland on 3 August 1291 (*CChR* ii, 403).

76

The poor brothers and sisters of the hospital of St Nicholas outside Carlisle petition the King and Council and constantly pray, for the love of God, that they may have the bishop of Carlisle as protector as he was from time immemorial since the first bishop 'Ewale', to whom King Henry II granted custody of the hospital in frankalmoign for the finding of a chaplain to sing for the souls of the king, his ancestors and successors. Ewale assigned this chaplain as warden under him of the possessions of the hospital, to direct its almsgiving, and so had each bishop thereafter until the present, when sir Hugh de Cressingham seized the hospital into the King's hand by *quo waranto*, because their charters of witness were burnt in the great fire of Carlisle, since when they had had no means of survival as their rents, houses, livelihood and other possessions and goods had been rendered worthless for lack of protection. They cannot survive without the King's aid, and seek speedy remedy, that the bishop have custody like his predecessors, and as the burnt charter testified (AP E517).

A nostre seignur le Roy e a son consail prient e requerent les poures chaitifs e meseysez freres e soers del Hospital de seint Nicholas hors de Kardoil, qui prient pur dit seignur le Roy noit e iour come pur leur lige seignur, e qi sount destruit par guerre e par arzouns, qe nostre seignur le Roy voille pur lamur dieu auoir merci de eux e graunter eux de sa grace quil puissent auoir lur gardeyn Leuesqe de Kardoil, come toutz iours ount eu del temps dount memoire ne court puis le temps qe le primer Euesqe de Kardoil Ewale par noun, a qi le Roy Henry le secund, auncestre nostre dit seignur, auoit graunte la garde del dit Hospital en pure e perpetuele aumoigne a lui e ses successours pur trouer vn chapeleyn chauntaunt pur les aumes le Roy Henry auauntnome e les almes de ses auncestres e ses successours a toutz iours, le quel Ewale assigna vn chapeleyn qi fust gardeyn ⟨desouz lui⟩ del dit Hospital e des possessions a meisme Lospital apurtenantz e de toutz les biens moebles e nient moebles e ⟨a⟩ la charite de la mesun sustenir, e issint chescun Euesqe apres autre de cel temps puis en cea, iesqe au temps Leuesqe qi ore est, e vncore puis son temps tant qe sire Hughe de Cressingham prist le auaunt-

dit Hospital en la mayn le Roy par le quo Waranto en eyre des
Justices, pur ceo qil nauoyent nul garaunt des choses auantdites,
kar lur chartres qe ceo tesmoignerent furent arses par la graunt
⟨arson de kardoil⟩, dunt vnqes puis ne teyerent ne lur sustenaunce
nauoient come auoir soloient mes lur rentes, mesons, gaignerie
e toutz lur autres possessions e biens sount anyentitz e destruitz
par defaute de garde: Par quoi il sount honiz aremenaunt sil neyent
eyde de nostre seignur le Roy, Dunt il prient pur lamur de dieu e
seint Nicholas qe hastif remedie lur soit graunte, e qe le Roy
voille comaunder qe leuesqe eit la garde, si come ses predecessors la soloient auoir e come la chartre qe est arse la
tesmoigne.

Endorsed: Coram Rege   Roy non habet consilium ad restituendum illud quod recuperauit in Itinere Justiciariorum.

1296–97. The hospital of St. Nicholas was founded as a leper
hospital before 1201. After the death of most of the original
lepers they were replaced by sick poor, benefactors often reserving
the right to nominate sick persons. The commonalty of Carlisle,
in return for the hospital admitting all the lepers in the city,
granted that each Sunday a pottle of ale be due from each brew-
house in the city and a loaf of bread from each baker exposing
bread for sale on the Saturday. In 1292 the bishop of Carlisle
claimed the right of institution, on the nomination of a chaplain
by the brethren of the hospital. The Crown denied any such
rights and claimed sole patronage: and at the eyre that year
judgment was given in the King's favour. The existing master
resigned and Hugh de Cressingham (1293–97) was appointed in
his place. As the hospital was situated outside the city it was
without protection on the outbreak of the Scottish wars in
1296. The great fire of Carlisle took place in May 1292 (*VCH
Cumberland* ii, (1905), 31, 199–201).

77

The people of the city of Carlisle petition the King and
Council for respite from the new tax for which they are rated
at a tenth of their rents and a fifteenth of their goods. They are

straitly distrained for these and their house-doors sealed (AP 10187).

A nostre seignour le Roi e a son conseil prient ses gentz de la Cite de Kardoil qe par la ou il sount taxes de lour rentes al disme dener e de lour moebles al quinzime dener pur les queux deners il sount ore greuousment destreintz e les Huss de lour meisouns ensealles: dount il vous prient de la nouele taxacion estre relesse ou mis en respiste.

No endorsement

1312. On the reasonable assumption that the 'new tax' was not the lay subsidy of a tenth and fifteenth levied in 1332 (from which the men of Carlisle were exempted on 4 February 1333 (*CPR 1330–34*, p. 402) but a tallage, as rents are specified, which were not normally liable, the rates applicable would date the petition to 1312 (Stubbs ii, 349 n4).

78

The poor people of Carlisle petition the King and Council for grant of a murage for repair of the town wall, supplying a brattice and recutting the moat and strengthening the gates and draw-bridges (AP 10186).

A nostre seignur le Roi et a son conseil prient ses pouers gens de Cardoill' qil lour voille grantier Murage a sa volunte a dorer pur reparailler le Mure de la ville qest descheu de nouel, et pur bretager meisme le Mure et pur les fosses redrescer, et pur le portes et les pontz treticz sustener et meintenir, desicome la ville est en greignour qele ne fu.

No endorsement

1314 or 1336. Leave to collect a murage for three years was granted on 14 March 1314. It was re-granted for five years on 16 January 1336 (*CPR 1313–17*, p. 93: *1334–38*, p. 194).

79

John de Dysorford, householder of Carlisle, petitions the King's Council to send money and victuals to the city and castle in accordance with the King's letter, as the householders are in such straits that they can scarcely abide there (AP E539).

Au conseil nostre seignur le Roi pri Johan de Dysorford' messager de Karlel qil voillent ordener pur la dite ville de Karlel e pur le Chastel de mesme la vile solunc ceo qe le Roi comaunda par sa lettre e cestes choses voilletz hastiuement faire, kar la dite vile e le Chastel sunt en graunt peril par defaut' de deners e de vitaille e les messagers sunt a si graunt meschef qil ne poent mes demurer par defaut.

No endorsement

?1316. On 30 March 1316 John de Pokford of Dishforth was given protection for one year, prior to his mission to carry 200 marks to the keeper of Carlisle (*CPR 1313–17*, p. 446; *CCR 1313–18*, p. 279). On 1 March 1334 John de Disceford was granted the office of bailiff of Birdforth wapentake in North Yorkshire for his good service in provisioning Edinburgh in the time of Edward II (*CFR* iv, 395).

80

John de Morpeth petitions the King and Council that whereas he had houses within the walls of Carlisle the Scots came and besieged the town for twelve days and assailed it day and night with towers and other engines; and Sir Andrew de Harcla and Sir Robert de Swyneburn came with the common people of the town and broke down those houses, worth 5 marks a year, and removed the timber to make towers and brattices for the town's defence and made no reparation (AP 3029).

A nostre seignur le Roi et soen counseil moustre Johan de Morpath' qe come il auoit ces Mesones en la vile de Cardoill' dedenz les Mures, vindrent nos Enemys Descoce et assegerent la dite vile par .xij. iours et lassailerent de iour et de nuyt par Ber-

frays et autres engines, la vindrent monsieur Andreu de Harcla
et monsieur Robert de Swyneburn' ensemblement oue la Comune
de la dite vile et abatirent les dites mesones qe valoint par an .v.
mars et emporterent le Merin pur faire Berfrays et bretages en
defense de la dite vile, et vnkes le dit Johan ne auoit restoraunce
dount il pri remedi pur dieu.

Endorsed: Soient certeins gentz assignez en Chauncellerie denquere
par quele cause sa meson fust abatu et de totes autres articles
necessaires etc. et returne lenqueste en Chauncellerie,
          le Roi se auise et face reson.

c. 1316. On 2 November 1316 the city of Carlisle was pardoned
£80 in arrears of its farm, against the costs of repairing and
strengthening the walls and ditches and constructing engines
(*CPR 1313–17*, p. 559). The siege lasted from 22 July to 1 August
1316. The petition is calendared in Bain iii, 88.

                              81

   Their liegemen of Carlisle petition the King and Council that
whereas they have garrisoned the town for seven whole years
and suffered hunger, thirst and much other evil, all for want of
wages, and have lost horses, armour and whatever they could
spend, all for want of pay, for the provision-keepers kept moving
and would never settle accounts with them, to their great un-
doing, as well as other evil practices whereby the victuallers supplied them with wine and other victuals of little value, such as
bad wine at 9 marks the tun, which would scarcely sell at 2
marks, and similarly grain, and thereby they are brought to
poverty: and now the King at Northampton ordered them to be
issued with clothes and money and no one can meet this because
of all the mischief which has befallen (AP E417).

   A nostre seignur le Roi et a son conseil moustrent vos liges
gentz de la ville Cardoill' qi vnt demorrez en la garneison dela
dite ville .vij. aunz entierement, vnt soeffert leyntz feym, seif et
mult dautre cheytiuete et tout par defaute des gages, et a ceo vnt
il perduz et engage chiuauz, armures et autres choses quantqil
porreient fyner et tout par defaute de paiement, car les vitaillers
qe vnt demorrez illoeqes vnt estie souent remue et vnt ale auaunt

et ne voeleient nyent acompter oduesqes eaux, et tieu chose les
vnt mult mis a meschief od autres mauueises seruises qe les
vitaillers les vnt serui, car vyns et autres vitailles qil vnt eau et
qe vnt estie de petite value, il vnt mis si haut vn tonel de
mauueys vyn a Noef mars qil nel porreient vendre a peyne por
.ij. marcs et en tieu manere de ble qil pristrent, et tieux
paiementz les ad mult od autres mauueys paiementz mis en
pouerte, le Roi a Norhampton' comanda qil deussent estre serui
de Robes et dargent et vnqes nul homme les voleit de riens
regarder por tout le meschief qil vnt eau et vnt; de quei il prient
por dieu qe remedie lour seit fait, issint qe por lour long'
seruice ne moergent en defaute.

Endorsed: Coram Rege   *Deleted:* Coram Rege et consilio

1307–18. The references to seven years of fighting around Carlisle
suggest the reign of Edward II, who held assemblies at
Northampton in both 1307 and 1318.

82

Isabel de Vernoune petitions the King and Council that like
other people she removed her goods to Carlisle castle and its town
for safety from the Scots, namely 2 sacks of wool priced at
20 marks, a silver cup at 40s, a habergeon at 100s, a saddle for
a knight's palfrey at 2 marks, half a tan-coloured cloth at 40s,
and a varlet's bed consisting of a mattress and sacking at 10s, a
silk horse-trapper at 20s, an Irish-scarlet mantle at 10s, an aketon
at 20s, a saddle with lining at 10s, a bacinet and aventail at one
mark, a hauberk at 50s, and a shod-courser at £20, a shod-sumpter
at 4 marks, and a shod-rouncey at 12 marks. And when Sir
Andrew de Harcla was declared forfeit, all these things were taken
into the King's hands by Sir Antony de Lucy, Sir Hugh de
Louther, Sir Robert de Barton, Thomas de Fethirstanhalght and
William de Haltecle and John Dounay. Later, when Sir Humphrey
de Waldin and William de Aykeleued were commissioned to
inquire into the goods of Sir Andrew, it was found that these
items belonged to Isabel, and she vouches the record of their
inquest and craves remedy (AP 12914).

A nostre seignur le Roi et a soun consoille prie Isabelle de Vernoune qe come ele amoua ses biens al Chastell' de Cardoille et a la ville pur sauuement garder pur les enemyes Descoce come autres gent fesoient, cest asauoir deux sakes de leynes prise de .xx. mars et vne coupe dargent prise de .xl. s. et vne Jupell' prise de .c. s. et vne seal a pallefre pur chiualer prise de .ij. mars et vne demy drape de tanne prise de .xl. s. et vne lyet pur vallet cest asauoir vn matresce vne caneuesce de yndecarde pris de .x. s. vne huce vne tapite de la suyt pris de .xx. s. vne Maunteill' vermeille Dirlaund' pris de .x. s. vne Aketon' pris de. .xx. s. vne Paneloun et vne spozeyn pris de .x. s. vne bacinet et vne Auentayille pris de vn mark vn Hauberk prise de .L. s. et vne Coursour ferraunt pris de .xx. li' et vne someer ferraunt pris de .iiij. mars et vne Rouncie ferraunt pris de .xij. mars. Et quant sire Andreu de Harcla se forfist deuers nostre seignur le Roi totes cestes choses furent pris en la mayne nostre seignur le Roi parmy les mayns sire Antoyn de Lucy sire Hugh' de Louther' sire Robert de Banton' (sic) Thomas de Fethirstanhalght et William de Haltecle et Johan Dounay. Et puis quant sire Wmfray de Waldin et William de Aykeleued' furent assigne denquerrer de les chateux le dit Andreu [si] troue fut qe les ⟨auan⟩dit chateux troue en la ville et en le Chastell' furont al dite Isabelle et ceo vouche ele recorde del enquest pris par les ⟨ditz⟩ Vmfray et William par quoy de cestes choses ele prie remedie.

Herl[aston']

Endorsed: Soit mande bref a sire Antoin etc qil certifie de la cause de la prise des biens nomez en la petition en la main le Roi et queux biens etc de quele value et a qi il furent etc, cestes certificacion retorne en Chauncellerie, soit illoeqes face droit.

Et aussint soit mande a Humfree qil certefie de ce qe fust troue deuant li par enqueste.

post 1323. On 10 September 1323 Humphrey de Waleden, William de Aykeheved and John de Kyngeston were appointed to survey the King's lands in Westmorland and Cumberland and to enquire into the goods of the late Andrew de Harcla and other rebels. They were also to investigate complaints against the King's officers and purchases of victuals (*CPR 1321–24*, p. 375). Isabel de

Vernoun may be identified with the sister of Andrew de Harcla, who married Richard de Vernoun about 1292. As Richard is known to have survived until 1330 he may at the date of the petition have been a prisoner in the hands of the Scots. Cf. F. W. Ragg, 'Maud's Meaburn and Newby: de Veteripont, le Franceys and de Vernon' *Transactions*, Cumb. & West. AA Soc., 2 xii, 326, 333–334.

83

Bennet de Eglefeld petitions the King and Council that whereas he owes the King £15 for victuals bought of the King's father at Holme Cultram in Cumberland, the King owes him £15 in an assignment on the Exchequer made by Thomas de Bourgh, clerk, being the remainder of a debt due for victuals bought at Brigham for the garrison of Carlisle castle and for the town, that an order be made to the Treasurer and Barons of the Exchequer to offset the one against the other, as he is a poor man from the Borders, and the victuals were bought to relieve him from want arising from frequent enemy incursions (AP 2209).

A nostre seignur le Roi et son conseil prie Benet de Eglefeld qe come il soit tenuz au Roi en .xv. li' pur vitailles achatez du Roi le pier a Holmcoltran en counte de Cumberland' et le dit Roys luy soit tenuz en .xv. li' dune dette qe luy est due en Lescheqer dun assignement a luy fait par Thomas de Bourgh' clerk' dun surplusage qe mesme celuy Thomas y auoyt dune dette qe le dit Roi le pier luy deuoyt pur vitailles de luy achatez a Brigham pur la garnison du chastel et de la ville de Cardoil', plese au dit nostre seignur le Roi et son conseil pur dieu comander al Tresorer et as Barons del Escheqer qe Lune dette soit deschargee pur lautre, eyauntz regard si leur plest qe le dit Benet est vn pouers homme de la Marche Descoce et qe les dites vitailles furent achatez pur sa soustenaunce pur grant defaut et meschief qil ad soeff[er]t par les soueneres venues des enemys en celes parties.

Endorsed: Soit bref mande as Tresorer et Barons de lescheqer compernant leffect de la peticion qe si troue soit qe le surplusage feust assigne au dit Benet par assent des ditz Tresorer et Barons qils lui allowent lune dette en lautre.

?c. 1327. Thomas de Burgh occurs as parson of Brigham in July
1323. He was escheator north of Trent pre-1324, and an executor
of the will of Master John Walwayn about 1324 (*CCR 1323–27*,
pp. 128, 162, 231). Cf. no. 100 below.

84

The poor citizens of Carlisle petition the lords of parliament that
whereas they have incurred great expenses in repair of the gates,
walls and ditches of the city, and in watching by night and day on
the city walls and their safe-keeping, and whereas by the good
counsel of Lord Neville, the warden, new great works have been
begun and not completed, such as turnpikes and great garrets on
the walls and new ditches, and whereas they are charged annually
at the King's Exchequer with £80 for tolls, mills and fisheries,
which with the greater part of the city are wholly burnt and
destroyed by the Scots, and subsequently all land, tenements,
grain, goods and chattels in all parts of the city have been burnt,
wasted and destroyed by the enemy, French and Scots, lying in
wait before the city since the Assumption last past [15 August], by
cause of which losses, impoverishment and the assaults on the city
walls every day a great part of the common people have fled the
city, and many others wish to flee unless they receive your help.
May it please your gracious lordships to consider these mischiefs,
and the fact that the tolls, mills and fisheries are wholly destroyed
by the enemy, and the great works started but not finished, and
provide a remedy, namely that they be discharged at the
Exchequer for three or four years until the tolls, mills and fisheries
and defence works be in order (AP 5046).

As tressages seignures de ceste Parlement Moustront les poures
Citezeins de Cardoill' qe come il ont ewe et vncore ont grandes
trauailles et costages entour la reparacioun et amendement des
portes, mures et fosses du dite Citee et des continuelles agates de
noet et iour sur les mures du dite Citee et la sauue garde dycelle, et
come par le bon auys le seignur de Neuille illeoqes gardeyn grandes
oueraignes a de nouelle sont commencez et nient performez come
en Turnepikes et grandes garettes sur les mures et nouelles fosses: et
come ils sont chagez (*sic*) al Escheker nostre seignur le Roi
annuelment de paier qatrevintz liures pur Tonealx, Molyns et

Pescheries, dont les ditz Tolnealx, Molyns et Pescheries ensemble oue le greindre partie de lour Citee sont toutoutrement arcez et destruitz par les enemys Descoce et ensement ore tarde toutz les terres et tenementz ensemble oue bles, biens et chatealx de toutz parties du dite Citee sont arcez, gastez et destrutz par les enemys de France et Descoce engisantz deuant la dite Citee al Assumpcioun de nostre dame darrayn passez, pur cause des queux perdes, enpouerissementz et nomement des grandes agaites sur les mures du dite [Cit]ee par eux toutz iours continuez grande partie des communes du dite Citee ont disgerpez la dite Citee et vncore plusours veullient, si ne soient voz tresgraciouses [secours]: Pur qoi plese a voz tresgraciouses seignures considerier les ditz meschiefs, enpouerissementz et les grandes agaites et qe le Tolnealx, Molyns et Pescheries [sont tou]toutrement destrutz par les enemys auantditz et grandes oueraignez commense et nient performez, et ent ordiner remedie: Cest assauoir destre descharges [de ferme]...... e al Escheqer par qatre ans ou trois tanqe les ditz Tolnealx, Molyns, Pescheries et oueraignes soient leuez et performez, por dieu et en oeure de [charite].

No endorsement

1385. On 1 December 1385 an order was sent to the Treasurer and Barons of the Exchequer following a petition from John Thirlwealle, late sheriff of Cumberland, for allowance in his account for issues, farms and rents arising from the great number of royal demesne lands and other lands, serjeanties, assarts and small farms in Cumberland wasted by the King's enemies, and from the cost of ditches lately made for the defence of Carlisle against their attacks. The truth of these allegations is testified by John de Nevylle of Raby before the King in Chancery. A similar order on behalf of Amand Mounceux, sheriff of Cumberland, was issued on the testimony of John and Richard Lescrope (*CCR 1385–89*, pp. 25–6). This petition could have been presented at the October parliament of 1385, although the lack of any endorsement directing enrolment makes it understandable that it is absent from the parliamentary roll.

Holme Cultram

The Cistercian abbey of Holme Cultram suffered the same difficulties as its lay neighbours. The King's forest adjoined their lands (no. 85), their grain was seized by the King's purveyers (no. 86), the Scots drove off their livestock (no. 87), and they were unable to pay for surplus victuals sold them by the King because of their losses (no. 88).

Ancient Petitions E516, 2583, 2588, 2592.

85

The abbot and convent of Holme Cultram petition the King and Council for relief from forest encroachments and rents taken from their common land, or for leave to hold the land at fee, as they have better right to it than any other (AP E516).

A nostre seignur le Roy e son conseille prient ses Moignes le Abbe e le Couent de Holmcoltram qe les purprestures e les arentementz qe sunt prises en la foreste denz lour commune a lours grauns greuaunces e dammages en diuerses lyus seynt ostez de tut en tut, ou kil les puyssent auer a fee, rendaunt la ferme au Roy, desicom il deyuent de (?)drait ester plus pres qe nul autre de prendre de lur commune demayne.

Endorsed: Quia parliamentum iam finitum est, nichil potest fieri hac vice.

?c. 1302. On 10 August 1302 Robert de Clifford, justice of the Forest north of Trent, was ordered to permit the abbot and convent of Holme Cultram to have in peace common of pasture between Caldew and Ellen in accordance with the charter of Richard I, and to remove any hindrances (*CCR 1296–1302*, p. 547).

86

The same petition the King and Council for allowance to offset 68½ quarters of wheat at 5s 8d a quarter, taken for the King's use at

Carnarvon in 1297, against the tenth owed by them to the King (AP 2583).

A nostre seignur le Roy e a soun consail priunt ses Moygnes Lalbe e le Couent de Holmcoltram ke si com en lan de soun Regne .xxv. furent aprisez e pris a karnaruan al hus nostre seygnur le Roy .lxviij. quarters e demie de furment de lauantdit Albe, pris del quarter .v. s. .viij. d. dount lalbe ad taille du pris, en quel pris le Roy est vnkor tenuz. Dount lalbe e le Counent priunt alowance de la dette ou ke meme la dette les fait alow en la dime kil sount tenuz au Roy.

Endorsed: Johannes de Kyrkeby examinet tallias et ad cuius comodum frumentum deuenit et quis debet inde onerari et certificet Consilium.   Irrotulatur

1306–7. By an order dated 26 February 1307 the Treasurer and Barons of the Exchequer were instructed to inspect the rolls of Hugh de Leominstre, who was the King's chamberlain at Caernavon in 1297. The abbot of Holme Cultram claimed to have received from him a tally for £19 8s 2d for the 68½ quarters of wheat taken by him for the King's use. If found accurate, the abbot was to have allowance in any debts due from him at the Exchequer or to have an assignment (*CCR 1302–7*, p. 487).

87

The same petition the King for the advowson of the church of Brough under Stainmore in Westmorland, within his gift, and for leave to appropriate it, in view of their poverty arising from the Scottish war and recent burning and looting and driving of beasts, horses, oxen and cows to the number of 500 and more, whereby they are empoverished so that they can no longer live together in the service of God without great aid (AP 2592).

A nostre seignur le Roi prient ses pouers Chapeleyns Labbe et Couent de sa Meson de Holmcoltran qe come eus seient destrutz en plusors maneres par la guerre Descoce et ia de nouele ars et desrobez en plusors lieus et leur bestes fraiez, Cheuaux boefs et vaches .v.ᶜ et plus, et si sunt il enpoueriz par tant qil ne pount viuer ensemble a dieu seruir sanz grant aide: Par quoi il prient a nostre seignur le Roi leur auoue, qil voille pur dieu auer regarde de leur grandes pertes en temps son pier qe dieux assoile et en son temps, et qil les voille graunter de sa grace la voesone del Esglise de Burgh' desoutz Estaynesmore en le Counte de Westmorland dunt il est verrai Patroun, et qil la puissent approprier en amendement de leur pouer estate.

Endorsed: Dominus Rex intellexit quod dominus Robertus de Clifford' dum vixit posuit clamorem in aduocacione illa, et heres ipsius Robertus est infra etatem et in custodia Regis, propter quod ante legitimam etatem eiusdem heredis nichil inde fieri potest.

1315–16. As an alternative they requested Kirkby Thore in recompense (*VCH, Cumberland* ii, 166). A licence for them in mortmain for £10 was granted on 2 November 1316 (*CPR 1313–17*, p. 563).

88

The same petition the King for pardon of 20 marks owed to the King for victuals in view of their destruction through the Scottish wars and now in the last warfare previous to the battle of Berwick, when the Scots ravaged in those parts and drove away their goods. These victuals of the King were and are stored on their premises and much of them carted by them to the King's profit (AP 2588).

A nostre seignur le Roi prient ses po[ures Ch]apeleins Labbe et le Couent de Holmcoltran qe come ils ount este tut outragement destruitz par les gueres Descoce et a ore en la dreine guerre deuaunt la bataille de Berewik' quant les enemis Descoce ..... rent et destruerent en celes parties et les biens enchacez hors du pais Les ditz Abbe et Couent en lour graunt meschef ..... lement pur lur viure achaterent des vitailles nostre dit seignur le Roi a la summe de .xx. mars, queux il deuient a lour treshautisme seignur auauntdit: qil pleise a sa seignurie reale, de sa bone grace et pur les almes de ses auncestres, eyant regard a leur graunt destruition et pouerte et a ceo qils sunt de sa propre fundacion et a ceo qe totes les vitailles nostre seignur le Roi furent et sount en celes parties herbergez en leur meisouns et graunt partie des ditz vitailles par eux car[riee] en

profit de lur treshonurable seignur auauntdit, pardoner a eux les.
.xx. mars auauntditz en amendement de leur poure estat pur
oeure de charite.

Endorsed: Coram Rege et magno consilio
Eient respit tanqe a la seint Michel prochein auenir et endemettres suent deuers le Roi dauer grace.

1334. By an order of 4 March 1334 the Treasurer and Barons were
ordered to cause the abbot and convent of Holme Cultram to have
respite until Michaelmas following for 20 marks owed for victuals
bought of the King at Carlisle, in consideration of the damage
sustained by them through frequent incursions of the Scots in those
parts (*CCR 1333–37*, p. 306).

The Liberty of Cockermouth

Following the death in 1293 of Isabel de Forz, countess of
Aumale, the honour of Cockermouth escheated to the Crown for
want of heirs and was held by a series of royal keepers including
John de St. John, Piers Gaveston, Robert de Leybourne, Andrew
de Harcla and finally Antony de Lucy (J. F. Curwen, *The Castles
and Towers of Cumberland and Westmorland*, pp. 128–9, 492–4). This
meant not only attempts by the keepers to uphold their rights but
also attempts by the King and his creditors to exploit a temporary
windfall. The burgesses of Cockermouth emphasised that their
borough was now royal and needed royal aid (no. 93), and John de
Warthole asked for a newly created bailiffship (no. 97). The near
presence of the forest of Inglewood was viewed with hope by
Richard de Denton, who wanted the office of master forester (no.
98), but with concern by John de St. John and Thomas de Lucy,
who were alarmed by the licences given by the King to make
assarts and so restrict their rights of common pasture in the
woodland (nos 91, 92, 95, 96). Other petitions were for restoration
of lands forfeited for adherence to the Scots, many of whom had
intermarried with local Cumbrian families (nos 89, 94, 99). Finally,
the keeper of Cockermouth required a pardon for letting a
prisoner escape from the castle (no. 90).

Ancient Petitions E66, E92, E372, E375, 22, 24, 48, 49, 2210, 3967,
3976, 6779.

89

William du Gardyn petitions the King for a grant of his own land in *Louthwait* in Cumberland, seized during the first Scottish war in accordance with a letter to every English sheriff to seize Scottish lands in their shrievalties, as it was held of the earl of Buchan, although he had never borne arms against the King (AP E66).

[A nos]tre seigneur le Rey prie William du Gardyn quil voille de sa grace grantier quil eit sa terre de Louthwait en le [Conte] de Cumbreland, la quele terre fu seisi en la Mein nostre seigneur le Rey en la primer guere descoce, pur ceo [ches]kun vescont dengleterre auoit Lectre aseisir Lour terres descoce en lour vescontiez, et il adunc par ..... tenuz par le Conte de Bouchan, ne vnques armes ne porta contre le Rey, mes touz iours puis ..... le Rey et vnquor est prest afair, par quai il prie la grace le Rey.

Endorsed: Consimilis peticio est coram Rege   Rem'

?c. 1299.

90

John de St. John, keeper of the castle and honour of Cockermouth, in the King's wardship, petitions that whereas Adam de Kereseye, his bailiff, and John Burghman, his castle gaoler, had received in ward a prisoner named Simon Fot to keep safe, and Simon had broken the castle prison and escaped and they had raised the pursuit and taken and beheaded him, the King may pardon the escape as pursuit was made, in order that they be not challenged by the justices in eyre or later (AP 3976).

A nostre seignour le Roy e a son consail mustre Johan de seint Johan, gardeyn du Chastel e del honeur de Cokermuth' du baille Roy, qe come Adam de Kereseye son Baillif e Johan Burghman seon Gaoler de mesme le Chastel eussent receu en leur garde vn prison qi ont a noun Simon Fot a sauuement garder en la prison de mesme le Chastel, E mesme cely Simon eust

debrise la prisoun de mesme le Chastel e eschape hors de lur garde
e eux tantost leue la menee e le sywrrent tanqe ateint fust e
descole, par quey il prie le Rey de sa grace les voille pardoner
cel eschap desicome il porta Juyse par leur siwte, isse qil nen
soient chalangez en Eyre de Justices ne allyours en temps auenir.
Wygeton'

Endorsed: Si ita sit Rex concedit quod quieti sint de escapio illo
nec occasionentur in Itinere Justiciariorum.

1302. On the authority of this endorsement, approved by Council
in parliament in 1302, an enquiry was taken by the sheriff and
coroners of Cumberland which confirmed that Fot escaped from
Cockermouth castle while it was in the custody of John de St.
John, that he was pursued with hue and cry, and taken and beheaded as a fugitive. Subsequently a pardon was issued on 13 July
1305 to St. John's heirs and to Adam de Kereseye and John
Burghman (*CPR 1301–7*, p. 373).

91

John de St. John and Thomas de Lucy petition the King and
Council that whereas they hold jointly Allerdale wood in the
forest of Inglewood, the King wishes to make intakes in the wood
to John's damage and Thomas's disinheritance. The right of
Thomas was investigated by Chancery writ when the King
and Thomas held the wood in common, when it was found that
Thomas should have a writ against the King's assarters, to desist
until further orders. Now they have returned and make intakes
as before, and the petitioners crave remedy (AP 3967).

A nostre seigneur Le Rey e asoen conseil Mustrent Johan de
Seint Johan e thomas de Lucy qe desicom eus tenent Le Boys
de Allerdale denz la foreste denglewode en commun issi qe nul
ne fet son seueral, la vient nostre seigneur le Rey e sei voet
apruer en le dit Boys a grant damage lauantdit Johan de seintio-
han e a la desheritaunce le dit Thomas, pur ceo qe le dreit
Thomas fust enquis par brief de la Chauncelerie quant nostre
seigneur le Rey e le dit Thomas tindrent le dit Boys en commun e lenquest returne en la chauncelerie, parunt Thomas auoit

brief as approuours le Rey quil sessasent de appruer tanqe usent autre Maundement; E or venent de nouel e fount les apprumenz sicom auant fesoient, dunt il prient remedie.

Endorsed: Rex uult ponere in sufferenciam approuamentum suum, quamdiu dictus Johannes tenuerit Manerium de Cokermue de concessione Regis.   .C.   Irrotulatur

?1302. John de St. John was appointed captain and King's lieutenant in the counties of Cumberland, Westmorland and Lancashire, the vale of Annan and the marches as far as Roxburgh on 25 September 1300, for the defence of the realm and the harassing of the Scots (*CPR 1292–1301*, p. 537). Earlier, on 14 January 1300, Robert de Clifford, justice north of Trent, Master Richard de Abyndon and Michael de Harcla were authorized to arrent the King's wastes in Allerdale wood in the forest of Inglewood and elsewhere in the forest, and to commit them by number of acres to tenants, to hold in fee simple or otherwise at a yearly rent at the Exchequer, and send the details to Chancery to enable charters to be made out for the lessees. They were also to sell wood, both green and dry, from these 'wastes', by view of the foresters, and to answer at the Exchequer for the money arising therefrom (*ibid.*, p. 486).

92

John de St. John and Thomas de Lucy petition the King that whereas they hold Allerdale wood and great part of Inglewood wood in common as belonging to the manor of Cockermouth, with the appurtenant agistment, pannage and estovers, so that only the soil belongs to the King, and the wood is outside the forest, many local people by authority of the King's officers have encroached on and enclosed a great part of their wood with ditch and fence, through which they have lost their agistment, attachments, pannage and other things. They ask the King to allow them to rent the soil, as they are nearest, because the wood and verdure is theirs, all but the soil (AP E92).

A nostre seignur Le Rei Moustre Johan de seint Johan et Thomas de Lucy que com il tyngnent Le Boys de Alredale et grant partie

du Boys de Engelwode en commun apurtenaunt au Maner de
Cokermuthe et la gistement et pannage et attachemenz de mort
Boys appent a eus, issi que au Rei rien demoert fors que le
soil, et cel Boys est desaforeste, plurous gens du pays par auctorite
et soffraunce de Ministre Le Rei purpernent et enclount graunt
partie del Boys des auantdyz Johan et Thomas de Fosse et de
Palys, par quei il perdent agistement et attachemenz et pannage
et autres choses que a eus appendent, dunt il prient que si nostre
seignur Le Rei se voille apprower de sun soil que il Lour grante
de arrenter cel Wast et respoundre au Rei parmi Lours Mains
de cel aprowement, pur coe que il deiuent estre plus procheins,
par la resun que le Boys et le couert est lour et quant que i appent
sauue le Soil.   Cumbreland

Endorsed: responsum est huic petitioni sicut peticioni domini
Johannis de sancto Johanne   Rem'   irrotulatur

1300–03. See no. 91 above. John de St. John held Cockermouth
Castle from 26 September 1300 until his death (*CPR 1292–1301*,
p. 537; *1301–7*, p. 110).

93

The burgesses of Cockermouth in Cumberland petition the
King for a grant at pleasure of a pontage to repair the three
bridges washed away by a great flood of water before Christmas
past: resulting from which the borough, which is the King's, and
the market and all the King's rents are greatly harmed and the
countryside much damaged (AP 22).

A nostre seygnur Le Rey prient ses Burgeys de Cokermuth'
en Le Counte de Cumbreland qe come les treys pountz de mesme
le Burgh' feussent en portez auaunt le Nowel dreyn passe par
la grant cretine de ewe qadonts feu: Par quey le dist Burgh',
qe est Burgh' le Rey, e le Marche e totes les fermes le Rey
illeuqes sount grauntement enpirez e le pays en viroun moult en
damage: qe le Rey de sa grace lour voille grauntier pountage
a durer taunt come il luy plest pur refayre mesme les pountz.

Endorsed: fiat per quinquennium   Irrotulatur

1304. Pontage for five years was granted on 22 January 1305 (*CPR 1301–7*, p. 412). The reply to this petition is printed in *Rot Parl* i, 160.

94

Thomas son of Thomas de la Moriley petitions the King for his land in the King's hands in the townships of Ellenborough, Little Broughton, Gutterby and Picket How in Cumberland, seized because his father, whose heir he is, was against the King in the first Scottish war and subsequently came into his peace and remained in it and died in his fealty. He is of full age and holds nothing else of the King (AP 24).

Cumbreland:

Thomas le fiz Thomas de la Moriley prie a nostre seygnur le Ray ⟨sa Grace⟩ de sa tere ke est en la mayne le Ray en les viles de Alneburgh', Petit Brouthton', Godrykby e Pykhou en le Counte de Cumbreland par la resoune ke Thomas de la Moriley soun pere ky hayre il est fue encountre le Ray en la prime Gere de Escoce e en meymes la primere ⟨gere⟩ vint a la pese le Ray e tute sa vie se tint a la pese e morust a la fay le Ray, E fet aremembrere ke il est de playn age e ne tient neent enchef du Ray.

Endorsed: Coram Consilio   ... [*second endorsement erased?*]
Inquiratur per breue de Cancellaria de modo et causa captionis earumdem terrarum in manum Regis Et de aliis circumstanciis etc: Et si petens semper fuerit ad pacem Regis necne: Et Rex super hoc certioretur etc.

1304. The petition is summarized in *Rot Parl* i, 162. The original enquiry into Moriley's lands was held in August 1298 (*Cal Inq pm* iii, 378: cf. vi, 363).

95

Thomas de Lucy petitions the King and Council that whereas he held Allerdale wood in common, so that the soil belongs to the King but half the wood belongs to Thomas, the King's men

came and felled most of the wood to enclose Holme Cultram
and build the King's peel at Dumfries, for which he craves remedy
(AP 49).

A nostre seignur le Roi e a son conseil moustre Thomas de
Lucy qe la ou le Roi e meisme celui Thomas tiegnent le boys
de Allerdale en comun, issi qe le soyl est au Roy e la moyte de
meisme le boys a meisme cesti Thomas, La viegnent les gentz
le Roi e ount abatu tut le pluis de meisme cel boys pur Lenclosture
de Holmcoltram e ensement pur le piel nostre seignur le Roi de
Dunfres, par quei le dit Thomas prie remedye.

Endorsed: Robertus de Clifford vel eius locum tenens et Johannes
de Insula videant boscam et ibidem inquirant de dampnis infra
contentis per breue de Cancellaria et certificent consilium.

c. 1305. Cf. nos 91 and 92 above, and 96 below.

96

The same to the King and Council that whereas the King
and he had Allerdale wood in common, so that the soil belongs
to the King and the verdure is in common, the King has felled
most of the wood for his peels at Dumfries and Holme Cultram,
for which he claims recompense (AP 48).

A nostre seignur le Roy e a soen consail Mustre Thomas de
Lucy qe la ou nostre seignur le Roy e luy tenent le boyz de Allerdale en commune, issi qe le soile est a nostre seignur le Roy e
le couert en commune, la ad nostre seignur ⟨abatu tut le plus
de⟩ le Boyz pur soen peel de Dunfres e soen peel de Holmcoltram: Dunt il prie a nostre seignur le Roy, qil luy voil faire
ascun rewarde e alouwaunce de sa grace.

Endorsed: Robertus de Clyfford' vel eius locum tenens et Johannes
de Insula videant boscum et ibidem inquirant de dampnis infra
contentis per breue de Cancellaria et certificent consilium.

Irrotulatur

1305. The reply to this petition is printed in *Rot Parl* i, 196.

97

John de Warthole, liege varlet, petitions the King and Council that whereas he stayed with the King throughout his war in Scotland and has been taken and ransomed thrice and suffered much damage through destruction of his lands, goods and chattels, he may receive a bailiffship in Derwentfells for life, which has not previously been leased and is supposed to be worth 40s a year (AP E372).

A nostre seignur le Roy et a son conseil prie soen lige vallet Johan de Warthole qad demorez ouesqe nostre dit seignur le Roy en tote sa guerre descoce et ad este pris et raunczonez par les enemis trois foiz et grant meschief suffert en diuerses maneres par quoi ses ⟨terres⟩ biens et ses chateux sont tut destruitz: quil lui voille de sa grace granter en eide de sa sustenance vne petite baillie en Derewent' felles ⟨a terme de sa vie⟩ que nul homme ne tient quant ore ne riens ne rent a nostre dit seignur le Roy, la quele baillie il entent que lui purroit valer entour .xl. s. par an.

pur Johan de Warthole

Endorsed: coram Rege et magno consilio

temp Edward I. Derwentfells was within the honour of Cockermouth and 'Warthole' is now Warthall in Plumbland.

98

Richard de Denton petitions the King for a grant of the mastership of Inglewood forest for life, in view of his service and the fact he was twice taken by the Scots in the King's service and his lands are now wholly waste (AP E375).

A nostre seignur le Roy prie Richard de Denton' qe ly pleize de sa grace graunter a ly en regerdoun de son seruiz la mestre forestrie Denglewode a terme de sa vie et qil voille auoyr garde, a ceo qe le dit Richard' ad este ia deux foitz pris par les enemis de scoce en le seruicz nostre seignur le Roy et ses teres ore tuttes destrutes.

Endorsed: Coram Rege

?1296–1322.

99

Thomas de Redman and John the hunter of Camerton, cousins and heirs of Alan of Camerton, petition the King and Council for restoration of the dower lands of Mary, widow of Alan, who held a third of Alan's lands in Cumberland which are part of their inheritance. Because Mary in life held with the Scots from the start of the Scottish war, the sheriff of Cumberland seized these dower lands and still retains them although she died three years previously (AP 6779).

A nostre seignur le Roi ⟨et a son conseil⟩ mustrent Thomas de Redman et Johan le Venur de Camberton', Cosyns et heirs Alayn de Camberton', qe com Marie qe fust la femme le dit Aleyn de Camberton' tynt en dower la tierce partie des terres que furent al dit Aleyn iadys son barun en le Cunte de Cumber' del heritage les auantditz Thomas et Johan, Lauantdite Marie tant come ele vesquyt' puis le comencement de la guerre Descoce tynt oue les Escotz encontre nostre seignur le Roy, dunt le viscunte del Cunte de Cumberl' seisi le dites terres qele tynt en dower en la mayn le Roi, dunt le Roi vncore est seisi: Par quei les auantditz Thomas et Johan prient pur dieu granter remedie desicome la dite Marie Morust treis anz passez.

Endorsed: Petrus Malorre et Johannes de Insula Capiant istam Inquisicionem.   Irrotulatur

1307. The petition is summarized on the parliamentary roll (*Rot Parl* i, 196, cf. 210).

100

Bennet de Eglesfeld petitions the King and Council that whereas he bought the manor of Clifton, held of the honour of Cockermouth and within the King's hands but not Crown land, the escheator came and seized the manor, contrary to the Great Charter, because he had purchased it without royal licence, and Bennet craves a writ to the escheator to release it (AP 2210).

A nostre seignur le Roi et a son counseil prie Beneit de Eglesfeld qe com il eit purchace le Maner de Clifton', qest tenuz del Honour de Cokermouth', qe est en la meyn nostre seignur le Roi et nient de la Coroune, la vient Leschetour et ad seisi le dit Maner countre la fourme de la graunde chartre, pur ceo qe le dit Benet ad purchace le dit Maner saunz counge nostre seignur le Roi, sur quei le dit Benet prie brief al Eschetour qil ouste la meyn.

Endorsed: Sequatur in Cancellaria   Irrotulatur

1320. This is noted on the parliamentary roll for October 1320 (*Rot Parl* i, 375). The pardon for acquiring 18 acres of land in Little Broughton from John de Eglesfeld, who held them in chief of the honour of Cockermouth, and for acquiring the manor of Clifton from Adam de Eglesfeld, who similarly held it in chief of the same honour, was issued to Bennet on 22 July 1322. The lands were entailed with remainders to Joan de Rybton, Bennet's sister, and her heirs, and to William de Eglesfeld and his heirs, with final reversion to Adam and his heirs. A fine of one mark was paid for this (*CPR 1321–24*, p. 194). Cf. no. 83 above.

SECTION III

COSTS OF WAR

The scheme of grouping petitions according to their place of origin posed a problem where they were submitted from several counties or ecclesiastical districts jointly: the common theme of complaint, however, was the burden of the state of war endemic between England and Scotland during the fourteenth century, which affected every aspect of life.

The northerners presented a lurid picture of burnt and looted houses and churches (nos 105–106, 109, 111, 113, 118–20). They wrote of extortions practised not only by the Scots but also by the English castellans against their compatriots (nos 112, 113). They referred to murrain among the cattle (no. 102). Antony de Lucy complained about the loss of two prisoners, probably claimed by the King in accordance with the custom of restricting liberty to ransom where the prisoners were of political or military importance (no. 110). (Such a clause was to be found in the service-indenture of Thomas de Fishburn in December 1315 [CPR 1313–17, p. 373, cf. p. 687], and formed the basis of the quarrel between Harry Hotspur and Henry IV.)

The King and his Treasurer, nevertheless, required a precise quantification of losses, where and when. To the bishop of Carlisle, claiming expenses on an embassy to treat with the Scots at Newcastle, it was coldly answered that the business was to the immediate profit of his diocese, and 'he did not go so far from his bishopric' (no. 103). The respite on collection of taxes in Cumberland, Westmorland and Northumberland granted in 1321 was intended to be of temporary duration (no. 102). The response to Lord Greystoke's request for aid towards payment of his ransom was an order for an enquiry into the preliminary circumstances (no. 117). Some petitions received no answer at all (nos 115, 120).

Ancient Petitions E391, 871, 2936, 4086, 4147, 4221, 5037, 5117,

5206, 5208, 5225, 5624, 6477, 6776, 8179, 8625, 8864, 8870, 10289, 10868, 15295.

101

The clergy of the bishopric of Carlisle and the archdeaconry of Richmond petition the King and Council that whereas they have often been devastated by the coming of the Scots and so much impoverished that previously a new tax-assessment of their benefices was made for the levying of clerical aids, and now the Pope has granted the King a tenth from the clergy of England as aid: may it please the King to consider their poverty and hardships of long standing, and order this tenth to be levied according to the last assessment, as they cannot bear the other as their condition is not yet recovered, and many benefices are highly assessed where no one can take anything through devastation. They request a writ similar to that granted to those of the bishopric of Durham (AP 871).

A nostre seygnur le Roy et a son counseil prie le Clerge de leuesche de Carduill' et del Ercedekene de Richemundshire, qe come il ount este souentfeat destrutz par la venue des enemys Descoce et de ceo sunt moult enpoueritz, parquoi autrefeat en diuers eides qe lui furunt grauntez de leur benefices le dit nostre seygnur le Roy fit taxer de nouel par son bref mesme ceux benefices, et solunk' cel tax ensi fete de nouel fit leuer les eydes, et ore eit le Pape graunte au dit nostre seygnur le Roy la disme du clerge Dengleterre en eyde de luy, qil plese au dit nostre seygnur le Roy par charite auer regard' a leur pouerte et meschefs qil ount et longement ount eu, et comaunder a leuer de eux cest disme solunk' le dit drener tax qe fut feit par son comandement, quar de autre ne pount il vnquore estre chargez, purceo qe lour estat nest de riens vnquore releue, et plusors benefitz sount taxez a graunt value, des queux home ne pout rien prendre, pur la destruccion .... fet sur eux. Et qil pount sur ceo auer bref' sicome graunte est a ceux de leuesche de Duresme.

Endorsed: Fiat ista vice de gracia, saluo iure Regis in aduentu.

Irrotulatur

1318–19. On 28 October 1318 John Sandall, bishop of Winchester, principal collector of the papal tenth, was ordered to supersede the assessment and collection according to the old assessment in the diocese of Carlisle, and to levy it according to current values, the bishop of Carlisle having been ordered to enquire into the matter because of the devastation by the Scots of benefices and their temporalities (*CCR 1318–23*, p. 24). Earlier, on 16 July 1317, an enquiry was ordered into the current value of benefices in the archdeaconry of Richmond (*CPR 1317–21*, p. 13). In 1327 the clergy of the diocese of Carlisle were pardoned any arrears still outstanding. Cf. *Rot Parl* ii, 433; *Rotuli Parliamentorum Anglie Hactenus Inediti*, (Camden Soc., 3rd Ser. LI, 1935), 153. See no 157 below for the Durham respite.

102

The King's liegemen of Cumberland, Westmorland and Northumberland petition the King that whereas they are devastated by war and a sudden murrain of beasts so that they have no means of sustenance nor of tillage, they may be pardoned all manner of debts demanded by summons of the Exchequer or otherwise as annual rent for the coming three years or until they have recovered. This debt was respited until All Saints next [1 November], for which they greatly thank him (AP 4086).

Item, A nostre seignur le Roi prient ses lieges gentz des Countez de Cumbr' Westmerl' et Northumbr' qe come il soyent destrutz par la gere et par sodeyn morin de[s b]estes issint qil nount dount viure ne lour terres gayner, qil voille pur lour grant meschief pardoner a eux totes maners des dettes qe vienent en demand sur eaux par somouns hors del Escheker ou qe en altre maner est demande de rent annuele, tanqe en cea pur terres et altres choses, et pur treis aunz a venir ou tanke qils soint releuez par layde de dieu et de luy, la quele dette il ad mis en respit tanke qe a la feste de touz seintz prochein a venir, dount eux luy mercient moult.

Endorsed: Pur ce qe triene estre, le Roi voet qe ses dettes se leuent apres le respit passer.

c. 1321. On 1 June 1321 the Barons of the Exchequer were ordered to relax any distresses for debts other than certain farms in Cumberland and Northumberland until All Saints (PRO, QR Mem Roll 94, p. 43d). A brief respite had earlier been granted to the men of Northumberland on 8 May 1321 (*ibid.*, m 47d). A further respite of a year was granted on 3 November 1322, and successively extended until an indefinite respite was granted to the men of Northumberland and Westmorland on 10 December 1325 (*ibid.* 96 mm 17d, 20: 97 mm 34d, 79d, 87d: 102 mm 32d, 44, 57, 65).

103

The King's chaplain, John bishop of Carlisle, petitions the King that whereas the King ordered him to journey to Newcastle with other magnates on embassy at Candlemas [2 February 1321] to treat with the Scots on certain heads, and he stayed 9 weeks and was put to great expense, he requests that on account of his great losses he be granted an allowance for expenses (AP 5117).

A nostre seignur le Roi prie ⟨son chappleyn⟩ Johan Euesqe de Cardoil qe come nostre seignur le Roi ly comanda de tourner a Noef Chastel sur Tyne en message od autres grantz de la terre a la Purificacion lan de son regne .xiiij.^me de treter de les Escoce sur certeynes poyntz, en queu message il demura .ix. symeyns et myst grantz custages, plese au dit nostre seignur en eiaunt regard de sa grant destruccion, comander qe alowance ly soit fait de ses despenses pur le temps auantdit.

Endorsed: Il semble au Roi et a tut son counseil qe depuis qe il ala pur commune profit du Roi et du Roialme et de sa Euesche et qil ne ala mie si loinz ⟨hors de Leuesche⟩, qil se put suffrir.
Irrotulatur   Coram Rege

1321–24. The commission to John of Halton, bishop of Carlisle, was issued on 19 January 1321 and surrendered unused ten months later on 30 November (*CPR 1317–21*, p. 554: *1321–24*, p. 37). Halton died on 1 November 1324 (*HBC*, p. 213).

104

John de Denum petitions the King that whereas he has a castle in Cumberland called Melmerby Tower, which could be kept by a dozen men at arms, he has kept it until now and has often been assailed by the Scots to their great loss, and John's lands are so devastated there and elsewhere that he can no longer bear the expense. He craves help in the form of wages or otherwise until times change, because all the country around would suffer great peril and loss if it were taken through lack of garrison (AP 5208).

A nostre seignur le Roi si lui plest, prie Johan de Denum qe la ou il ad vne forterece (*sic*) on le Countee de Cumberland qest appelle la To[urr]e de Melmorby, la quele poet estre garde par duz hommes darmes: E il la dite Tourre toutz iours ad garde iesqes encea e souent ad este assailly par les enemys Descoce e toutz iours bien defendu par la grace de dieu tanqe a ore, a grauntz damages de ditz enemys e pert de lour gentz, e ia soient les terres le dit Johan si destruytz la e ailliours par tout qil nad poer de trouer les coustages: Par quoi pleise a nostre seignur le Roi qil lui voille aider en ascune manere a cele garde faire, ou de gages ou dautres choses a la value, tanqe le secle se chaunge deuers teles parties, qar graunt peril et graunt pert serroit a tout le pays entour si ele feust pris e perdu, qe dieu defende, par defaut de garde.

Endorsed: Se auis daucun Mariage, garde ou ferme et en certifie le Roi, et il par bon conseil lui fera aucun regard' par qoi il ⟨le⟩ puisse du mielz garder, a saluacion du pais.   Denum

1320–26. The owner of Melmerby was Margaret, heiress of John de Wigeton. Wigeton was dead by April 1315, when routine enquiries as to the identity of the heir necessitated consultation with the Bishop of London as to whether Margaret's parents were lawfully married or subsequently divorced. This was not settled in Margaret's favour before 7 July 1320 (*Cal Inq pm* v, 87, 297–300). John de Denum had married the heiress by July 1322 when a settlement was made of the estates of Wigton, Kirkbride and their members on himself and his wife, with remainder to

Margaret's right heirs. In September 1323 he was summoned to answer for issues arising from the time John de Wigeton was keeper of the lands in Liddell lately of Thomas Wake (PRO, QR Mem Roll 97 m 236; *CPR 1321–23* p. 175 cf. p. 362). Denum may be identified with the King's yeomen who in December 1323 was given custody of Horston Castle and other lands in Derbyshire (*CFR* iii, 253, 333). As he was dead before 13 October 1326 he must be differentiated from the King's serjeant at law of the same name (*Cal of Memoranda Rolls 1326–1327*, pp. 171, 201). The petition is calendared in Bain iii, 163.

105

The Prior of St. Oswald [Nostell] petitions the King and Council that whereas his house is impoverished through recent bad years and the church of Bamburgh is largely wasted, which should be a great support, and he must consider ordering the canons to disperse: he requests the removal of brother John of Hexham, a canon of Jedburgh, entrusted to him by the King for the past two years (AP E391).

A nostre seignur le Roy e a son conseil moustre le .. Prieur de Seint Oswald qe sa meison dount il est gardeyn est molt a desouz et enpouery par la reson des mauuaysez anneez qe ount estetz e de sa Eglise de bamburgh' qe solait estre la grayndre soustenaunce de sa meison, qe nettement est destrut', Dount il lui coueynt ses chanoignes en dispersion maunder: E le vauntdite .. Prieur de vn frere Johan de Hexceldesham, chanoigne de Gedeworth, sez deux auntz par nostre seignur le Roy ad este charge, Dount le vauntdite Prieur pri pur dieu qil poet estre descharge e le ⟨dite⟩ chanoigne remue.

Endorsed: Coram magno consilio

1315–26. During the years of attempted dominance Edward I and his son had recruited English monks and canons for Scottish monasteries. In turn, with Scottish revival under Robert de Brus these English religious were ejected and forced to find alternative houses in England. Both Guisborough and Thornton-on-Humber were required to provide accommodation for them

(Bain iii, 162–63; *North'd Pet*, pp. 30–1). The link between Nostell Priory in West Yorkshire and Bamburgh in Northumberland can be traced at least to the date of the foundation of St. Oswald's about 1121, when Henry I gave the canons the church with the implied intention that it form the financial basis of a dependent monastic cell. A small community of canons was established by 1228, and in 1292 the revenue of Bamburgh was estimated at £400 a year. The nearness of the cell to the Border, however, resulted in heavy losses. The parish church may have been destroyed by fire about 1297, and in the 'new taxation' of 1318 Bamburgh was described as 'devastated and entirely destroyed'. The Scots again laid the parish waste about 1328, when Nostell was already in debt through rebuilding its own choir, and there was a further harrying in 1342/3 (*NCH* i, 73–90).

106

A clerk of Northumberland called John de Roubiry petitions the King and Council that whereas he is ruined by the Scottish enemy and his parents killed in earlier warfare, he may have the King's letters to the Abbot and Convent of Thornton-on-Humber to receive him as a canon in their house and clothe him at their expense: for he has nothing to support himself (AP 6776).

A nostre seignur le Roi et a son conseil pri vn Clerk' de Northumbreland quest apelle Johan de Roubiry, le quel est destruit oue les enemis Descoce et ses parentz octiz par les guerres qont estee, pur lamour nostre seignur le Roi quil lui pleise granter de sa grace ses lettres al Abbe et le Couent de Thorneton' sur Humbre qil voille receiure le dit Clerk' en Chanoyn de lour Meson pur dieu seruir et prier pur nostre dit seignur le Rois (*sic*) et pur ses auncestres et lui trouer abite a lour custages, qar le dit Clerk' nad riens dont il meismes le purra trouer.

Endorsed: Coram Rege Herl[aston]

temp Edward II. The Augustinian abbey of Thornton had at least 30 canons into the fourteenth century (Knowles & Hadcock, p. 176). It was used regularly by the Edwards as a source of pensions for old servants (cf. *Cal Chancery Warrants* i, 467, 478; *CPR 1333–37*, p. 333).

107

The King's bachelors Richard de Denton and John de Orrete petition the King and Council that they have heard there are certain Scotsmen of the King's enmity wishing to become his lieges, and they will be more willing when they hear that Richard and John have power from the King to receive them into his peace. They request a commission, for the King's profit and the confusion of his enemies (AP 5225).

Pleyse a nostre seignur le Roi et a soun counseil pur ceo qe ses liges Bachelurs Richard de Denton et Johan de Orrete ount entenduz qil y soynt ascunes gentz descoce qe sount del enemite nostre seignur le Roi et voillynt estre a sa fay, et le plus volentz sil entendisent qe Richard et Johan auaunt nomes eussunt poer de nostre seignur le Roi de les retceiure a sa pees, qil lui plese son commission granter pur le profist nostre seignur le Roi et en artrissement de ses enemys.

Endorsed: E[iant] semblable commission qe monsieur Antoigne de Lucy en ad, issint tot foitz qe par cele cause la commission le dit monsieur Antoigne ne soit defeite.

1327. This authority was granted to Richard de Denton and John de Orreton on 28 September 1327 (*CPR 1327–30*, p. 168).

108

The King's serjeant John de Denum petitions the King and Council for an order to sir Robert de Wodehous, keeper of the Wardrobe, to account with him for the time he was on the King's business in northern parts in company with the archbishop of York and others, and for a bill under his seal for payment (AP 5206).

A nostre seignur le Roi et son conseil prie son lige sergeant Johan de Denum qe lui pleise commander a sire Robert de

Wodehous, gardein de la Garderobe, qil acompte od lui de temps qil estoit en uostre message es parties du North' en la compaignie Lerceuesqe Deuerwyk' et autres, et qil lui en face bille desouz son seal en paiement.

Endorsed: Soit fait.

1327–28. Wodehouse was Keeper of the King's Wardrobe between October 1323 and August 1328, and William Melton archbishop of York from 1316 to 1340 (*HBC*, pp. 78, 264). While Denum had been accredited to go on embassy to Scotland in June 1326, this was not with the archbishop of York (*CPR 1324–27*, p. 278). In April 1327, however, he is mentioned as one of the archbishop's entourage (*CPR 1327–30*, p. 95).

109

The clergy of the bishopric of Durham, the counties of Northumberland, Westmorland and Cumberland, and the archdeaconries of Richmond, Cleveland, York and the East Riding, with the franchise of St. Cuthbert of [North] Allerton, Allertonshire and Crayke, both secular and religious, petition the King and Council that whereas the Scottish war, which has lasted 34 years, has devastated their goods, their churches and manors are burnt, their books, chalices and church ornaments looted and carried off, and they are so impoverished that they can scarcely maintain their functions and in several places—, nevertheless despite their poverty and devastation they are ready to pay the tenth granted for four years, but at the true current value of their benefices. The collectors, however, are compelling them to pay according to the ancient assessment, and the clergy aforesaid sued their petition before the King at a Council at Nottingham: and the King sent a writ, the copy of which is attached, to Master John Souereyn, collector of the tenth, to refrain from levying on benefices assessed either at the new rate or where there was no new assessment until the present parliament, and all the said clergy crave a remedy (AP 8625).

A nostre seignur le Roi et a son conseil moustre la Clergie del Euesche de Duresme, des Countez de Northumbr', Westmerl'

et Cumbr', et des Ercedekenez de Richemund', Clyueland',
Euerwyk', Estrithyng et de la franchise de seint Cuthbert de
Aluerton', Aluertonshire et Creyk auxibien seculers come
religious, qe par la ou par la guerre Descoce qe lour dura .xxxiiij.
auns il ont este destruitz en biens et en possessions, lour eglises
et lour Manoirs ars, et lour liures et lour chalices et les
ornementz de seinte eglise desrobbez et emportez de .... soit
issint enpouerez qil ne suffisent a grant peyne a la sustenance de
lour Ministres, et en plusurs lieux vnqore ne .... mie, et nient
contreesteant lour pouerte et lour destruccion si sont il prestz de
paier la disme de quatre aunz nadgaire .... la verroie value de lour
benifices quant aore, et pur ce qe les coillours de la dite disme firent
compulsion par escouiengement et .... de seinte eglise a la dite
Clegie a paier selonc lanciene taxacion, ceux de la Clergie del
Euesche de Doresme, [des Countez] de Northumbr' Westmerl'
et Cumbr', et des Ercedeknez de Richemund' et de Clyueland'
suyrent par lour peticion d[evant] ... le Roi ore a cest conseil
qe dreyn feut a Notingham et prierent remedie, par quei le Roi
manda par son bref, le transescrit est cosu a ceste peticion, a Mestre
Johan Souereyn, coillour de ladite disme, qil ne deueroit rien leuer
des benifices es dites .... selonc le nouel tax tanqe a cest parlement et qe des benifices en mesme les parties qe ne feurent mie
de nouel tax .. .. roit de tot et rien demander tanqe au dit
parlement, dont tute la Clergie auantdite prie qe remedie lour soit
fait.

Endorsed: Seit [mande a Mestre Johan Sovereyn] pro ascun grant
le Roi qil veigne deuant le conseil pur la cause auantdite.
  Et puis .... Mestre Johan par la comandement nostre seignur
le Roi et sun conseil est deuant eux en parlement, purce qe le
Roi de sa grace auoit grante a la dite Clergie qil paieront la [moite]
de la dite disme reserue a son oeps selonc le nouel taxe, et qe
les benifices et temporaltez ens bien susdites, qe ne feurent mie
einz ces heures taxe, soient de nouel taxe e dont lour value a ore, e
selonc le dit taxe paierent la dite moite de la disme a nostre
seignur le Roi: granta a la reuerence nostre seignur le Roi e son
conseil qil de ceste chose escriuest a nostre seint piere le Pape as
aident sa volunte de lautre moite reserue a son oeure, e tanqe il
serra par le Pape de ceo certifie, qil leuera rien des ditz benifices e
temporaltes forsqe selonc le nouel taxe, e dautre benifices e

temporaltez de nouel nient taxe il surserra endemettres. Et purce soit lettre mande au dit Mestre Johan qil face leuer la dite disme endemettres en la fourme auantdite.

1330. A Council was summoned at Nottingham for 15 October 1330 (*HBC*, p. 518). On 15 December 1330 Master Itherio de Concoreto, the papal collector of the tenth imposed for four years by the pope on the clergy of England, Ireland and Wales, of which half was granted to the King, was reminded of a royal order resulting from this petition, to supersede the collection until the current parliament met. There, with the assent of Itherio, it was agreed that payment be based on the new assessment, which was to cover benefices and temporalities not previously revalued. Itherio was to inform the pope that his share would be half the new total. The tenth might now be collected according to this new valuation (*CCR 1330–33*, pp. 77–8). The writ referred to is missing.

110

Antony de Lucy petitions the King and Council that they decree that justice be done over William de Douglas and William Bard', his prisoners taken in war in Scotland, who were removed from him in the fashion previously explained to the King and Council. Although the King ordered often previously that they be delivered to him, nothing has yet been done (AP 2936).

A nostre seignur le Roi et a son conseil pri Antoigne de Lucy qil lour pleise ordeyner qe reson ly soit fait de William de Douglas William Bard' ses prisons pris de guere en Escoce, les queux ly feuront tolletz ⟨en la Manere⟩ qe nostre dit seignur le Roi et son conseil ount bien entendou auant ces heures, qar tout eit nostre seignur le Roy comaunde auant ces heures souent qe les ditz prisons ly fuissent liueretz, vnqore rien en est fait.

Endorsed: Coram Rege et magno consilio
Enfourme le conseil des nouns de ceux qi pristrent les prisons de lui qe mettent chalange en eux, et adonqes eit bref a eux qil soient deuant le Roi a Noef Chastel sur Tyne lendemayne

de la Trinite a faire et recey[ure] ce qe le Roi ordenera et son conseil, et soit le dit Antoigne illoqes a mesme le iour.

c. 1333. On 28 March 1333 Ranulph Dacre, constable of Carlisle castle, was ordered to keep in irons William Douglas of *Polerte* and William Bard, prisoners of war, and not deliver them without a special royal order (*CCR 1333–37*, p. 101).

III

The lieges of Cumberland petition the King's council that whereas Sir Antony de Lucy was ordered by writ to parliament on the quindene of Michaelmas, whereas he was a Warden in the counties of Cumberland, Northumberland and Westmorland, on which day or before the Scots with all their power were about to enter England to destroy, wherefore they besought Sir Antony to stay with them to do his best for the safety of the country, as there was no other magnate in those parts to whom the people of the country might attach themselves so completely nor so willingly be in his company for good or ill, according to the chances of war. Therefore they humbly crave that he be excused from parliament, and request their lordships to give credence to the knights of parliament, bearers of these letters, in the matters they show more plainly by word of mouth touching the mishaps and perils of the said march (AP 10289).

Au counsaile nostre seignur le Roy moustrent ces lieges gentz du Counte de Cumbr' qe come monsieur Auntoigne de Lucy soit maundee au parlement par brief a la quinzeyn de la seynt Michel tote soit il assignee vn des gardeyns en les Countes de Cumbr', Northumbr' et Westmerland: a queu iour ou deuaunt les Enemys Descoce oue tote lour poer sount prestes a entrer la terre Dengleterre et destruer. Par quey par nostre grant request auoms priee monsieur Auntoigne qil voile demurrer entre nous a ceste foith, a faire le bien qil purra pur la saluete du paies, desicome il ny ad nulle altre grant vers ces parties a qi toes les gentz du paies se attrerunt si entierment, ne de si bon volente a prendre en sa compaigne le bien et le male solom les auentures de guerre come a luy. Par quey sires nous vous prioms humblement qe a ceo parlement luy voilliet auoir excuse. Et vous requerroms

sires qe vous voillietz doner foy et credence a nos chyualers du parlement porteurs de cestes, des choses qils vous moustrount plus playnement par bouches touchauntz les meschiefs et les periles de la marche susdite.
Traces of red wax on dorse representing two oval seals and one small round seal.

1339. Antony de Lucy was appointed warden of the Marches in 1336 and received a personal summons to parliament from 1321 to 1342. (C. H. Hunter Blair, *AA*[4] XXVIII, 1950, pp. 41–2). A parliament was summoned for Westminster on 13 October [quindene of Michaelmas] 1339 (*HBC*, p. 510).

112

The King's poor lieges of Cumberland and Westmorland petition the King and Council [that whereas it was] ordered that no lord nor constable nor castellan nor keeper charge them for giving them refuge in castles while the enemy is in power, nevertheless the keepers etc. exact such outrageous sums from them that they would prefer to evacuate the land for the time being rather than seek such security. [They charge] for two or three nights 5s and sometimes a half mark, regardless of the fact that the same people are willing to expend life and limb and what they have to defend the castles at their own expense, in return for their accommodation. They crave remedy, that it may not be necessary to evacuate their land and that there be an order that those returning shall answer any plea according to the law of the land when the King appoints investigators (AP 4147).

A nostre seignur le Roi et son conseil mostrent ses poures liges gentz des Countez de Cumberlaund et de Westmerlaund qe ia soit .. .. air ordeyne feut par nostre seignur le Roi et son conseil qe nul seignur ne Conestable de chastel ne Chastelleyn ne Gardyn n .... des dites gentz pur socurs de Chasteux durant le poeir des Enemys, Iadumeyns Gardeyns, Chastelleyns, Conest-[ables] .. .. s parnent si outragouses raunceons de eux qe plus lor vaudroit de voider la terre pur le temps qe tiel socurs quere .. .. s pur deux nuytees ou treis .v. s. et daucuns demy marc, nemye eant regard a ce qe mesmes ceux gentz se voelen .. ..

de vie et de membre et de quant qils ount pur defendre et sauuer les chasteux a lor custages demeyn pur lor demoer .... ils prient pur dieu remedi par si reale mandement, qil ne lor coueigne mye voider lor terre et qe mote soit el mandement qe les en revenantz respoignent deuant enquerors a chescuny pleynte solom lei de terre quant nostre seignur le Roi les voudra assigner denq[uerer] de cestes choses.

Endorsed: Seit maunde etc par brief' des choses contenues, et tutes autres acordez en tieu cas a suifere de faire greuaunce contre laccord: auxint seit comande de crier et publier ceo qe feut acorde et .... ceux qe contre lacord desore vodrent faire.

temp Edward II–III. On 23 March 1333 the sheriffs of Cumberland and Westmorland were ordered to proclaim that all wishing to leave the counties with their goods and animals on account of the Scottish wars might travel south through the King's forests, pastures and wastes, and live there and pasture their animals freely (*CPR 1333–37*, p. 101).

113

The commons of Northumberland, Cumberland and Westmorland petition the King touching the oppressions they have suffered under colour of a truce which is more damaging than open war.

Firstly, the Scots have overrun the lands both of the King and of his lieges in the counties of Berwick, Roxburgh, Dumfries, —, valued at £30,000 and more.

Item, during this truce they have killed more than 700 persons and mounted forays into the King's lordships in Scotland as well as England—, and in Northumberland and Cumberland [seized] 700 ploughs and more, and [taken] any able-bodied persons who could harm them.

Item, the town of Berwick pays certain tribute in money, wine and victuals to the earl of the Scottish March, although the King gave 1000 marks—

Item, Tweedmouth, adjoining that town, paid 10 marks this year.

Item, Wark castle paid 20 marks this year.

Item, the King's lieges in Roxburghshire paid 100 marks this year.

Item, the men of Redesdale paid 50 marks a year.

Item, divers lieges in Cumberland and Dumfriesshire pay £100 a year.

Item, all those ransomed by the Scots are in such state that they dare not support their neighbours when the Scots ride among them to harry the King's lieges nor make rescues when the Scots return with their booty.

Item, the castle of Lochmaben, 20 leagues within Scotland, is in such a strait that neither men, victuals nor provisions can enter without special licence from Sir Archibald de Douglas.

Item, the King's lieges are ransomed or held imprisoned, contrary to the express terms of truce. For these causes the Wardens have admitted their impotence, and the country lies desolate, and the true lieges of the King evacuate their lands and, seeking their livelihood elsewhere, will abandon the country to the Scots if remedy be not ordained in the present parliament.

Item, apart from all these articles, there are the arrears of 8,000 marks and 4,000 marks due at Midsummer, being the ransom of the King of Scotland lately dead, of which sum the kingdom has great need (AP 6477).

A lour tresredoulte et tressouereyn seignur le Roy moustrent les Comunes des Countees de Northumbr', Cumbr' et Westmerland les .... ables greuaunces qils s[oeffert] .... desoutz Colour dune trieu, la quelle est a eux plus damageant qe ne serroit ouerte guerre.

A de primes ount les Escoces acrochez les possessions sibien de Roi come de pluses de ses lieges les Counteez de Berwik', Roxbergh', Drumfreez, ... a la somme de trent Mille liures et plus.

Item ils ount dedeins ceste trieu tuez plus de sept Cent persone et (?)serarde chiualcheez dedeins les seignuries du Roi sibien en Escoce come en Engleterre ... [l]es Countez de Northumbr' et Cumbr' susditz sept Cent Charues et plus, et si ascuns persones defensables qe lour purra greuer soient par eux pr[is] ...

Item la ville de Berwyk paie certein tribute sibien en deniers, vyn, come en autres vitailles al Counte de la Marche descoce: Nientcountreesteant qe le Roi doun Mille Marcs ....

Item Twedemouthe, qest aieynaunt a la dite ville, paie cest an .x. marcz.

Item la Chastell' de Werk ad paie ceste an .xx. marcz.

Item les lieges du Roy dedeins le viscounte de Roxburgh' paient ceste an .C. marcz.

Item les gentz de Ridesdail' par an .l. marcz.

Item diuerses lieges du Roi deins les Counteez de Cumbr' et Drumfreez paient par an .C. li'.

Item, est assauoir qe touz les desusditz qe ensi soit raunceonez par les Escoces sont de tiel condicion qils nosent Suppouaillier lour veisins quant les Escoces chiualchent parmy eux pur mesfaire enuers les lieges du Roy, ne faite rescous quant les Escoces ratourn-ent ouesqe la mesfaite.

Item, le Chastell' de loghmaban, qest assye vint leuez dedeins Escoce, est en tiel distresce qe homme, vitaille ne puruoiance y poet entrier sanz especial licence de Monsieur Archibaud de [Douglas].

Item, les lieges du Roi sont plusours raunceonez come prisoners et les autres detenuz en vile prison countre les expresses parolles des trieux: Pur quelles greuaunces desusditz les ... Gardeins se ount retreatz a cause de nounpouair, et ensi est tout la paijs desolate, et coment les vrays lieges du Roi voidier lour terres et heritages et quere lour viures aillours .... abaundonier les paijs as Escoces si remedie ne soie ordeignez en ceste present parlement.

Item, outre tous ces articles desusditz y sont aderiers nient paiez oitz Mille marcz et quatre Mille marcz al seint Johan le Baptistre proschein venant ..... Marcz de la raunceon du Roi descoce qe darrein morust, de quelle somme la roialme en ad des graunt mestier.

No endorsement

1379/80. At the time of the death of David II on 22 February 1371 there was a truce between England and Scotland. This was prolonged, and the new King Robert II agreed to continue to pay the arrears of the ransom of his predecessor. The last payment was made at Midsummer 1377. At the rate of 4,000 marks a year, arrears of 8,000 marks as noted would suggest that the petition should be dated between Midsummer 1379 and Midsummer 1380, and was presumably presented at the Westminster parliament of

16 January 1380. There was fierce Border fighting in 1372 and 1377: and in both 1378 and 1384 Berwick was briefly recaptured by the Scots (Ridpath, pp. 346–55; cf. Bain iv, 265). The position of Lochmaben had long been precarious. On 25 August 1364 Sir Archibald de Douglas, warden of the Western March of Scotland and lieutenant of the King of Scotland, entered into an indenture with Sir John de Multon, lieutenant of the Earl of Hereford, for a year's assurance for lands, woods, fishings, etc appurtenant to the lands of the earl in Annandale and to the castle and garrison of Lochmaben. The Scots captured the castle in February 1384 (Bain iv, 23–24, 73).

114

The lieges of Cumberland, Northumberland and Westmorland petition the King that whereas they are the nearest counties to the Scottish march and their sovereign security is the safe-keeping of the city and castles of Carlisle, Newcastle upon Tyne, Roxburgh and Berwick, which towns and castles are so ruinous and weak that without repair they cannot resist their enemies, as the march-dwellers in this parliament can testify, the King should order both the overhaul of the towns and castles and that adequate constables stay therein (AP 5037).

1377. This petition is entered on the roll for the parliament of October 1377 (*Rot Parl* iii, 30).

115

Ralph, lord Greystoke, petitions the King of Castile and Leon and Duke of Lancaster that whereas he was commissioned a Warden of the March with the Earl of Northumberland and was ordered by the King and Council to have custody of Roxburgh castle, on his way to assume custody he was captured inside England by the earl of the Scottish March and put to a great ransom beyond his power to repay without complete destitution for life unless he be aided. May his lordship help him, having regard to his capture within England, doing nothing contrary to the ordinance of truce, and without ever having harmed the Scots either in Scotland or England (AP 4221).

A son tresgracieus tresnoble et tresdoute Seignour le Roi de Chastell' de Lyoune et Duk' de Lancastre moustre Rauff' Baroun de Graistok qe come il fuist ordeigne par commission vn des gardeignes de la Marche oue le Counte de Northumbr' et auxi il fuist ordeigne par le Roi et soun conseil dauoir la garde del Chastell' de Rokesburgh' et sur ceo en chyminaunt deuers le dit Chastell' de prendre la garde dycell' solonc ceo qil auoit en comaundement il fuist pris deinz le Roialme Dengleterre par le Count de la Marche Descoce et mys a grant somme de Raunceoun, la quelle somme il nest point de poiar depaier si noun qil seit toutoutrement destruyt par terme de sa vie saunz releuer: Par quay plese a vostre tresgracious Seignourie, pur dieu et en oeps de charite, de luy eaider qil ne soit outrement defait, eiant regarde tresnoble Seignour pur ceo qil fuist pris deinz le Roialme Dengleterre rien fesaunt encountre lordynaunce de la grant trieu, ne vnqes ne fist male alescoces deinz lour Roialme Descoce ne deinz le Reialme Dengleterre nyent plus.

No endorsement

1380. The duke of Lancaster was then the King's lieutenant in the Marches towards Scotland. Ralph, lord Greystoke, had been commissioned joint warden of the East Marches in Northumberland on 29 May 1380 (*Rot Scot* ii, 24), and was apparently captured with his companions by George Dunbar, earl of March, at Horse Rigg on the Border line to the west of Glendale in the last week of June 1380 (G.E.C., *Complete Peerage* vi, 195). The incident was part of a reprisal for the capture of two ships sailing to Scotland laden with Scotsmen's goods and merchandise valued at £10,000, and the disposal thereof by Sir William de Hilton and other lieges of Northumberland, Yorkshire, Lincolnshire and Norfolk, for which reason the Scots had captured many animals and goods as well as persons on the Marches, and were retaining them until restitution or satisfaction was made. An enquiry into this was ordered on 5 December 1381, when a commission was issued to John, duke of Lancaster, Alexander, archbishop of York, John de Neville of Raby, Roger de Clifford, Henry Lescrope, John Marmyon and Roger de Fulthorp (*CPR 1381–85*, p. 84). Help towards the cost of Greystoke's ransom was approved and William Helmesale, a Grimsby merchant, was allowed to sell 200 quarters

of malt to a Scottish friar for delivery in Scotland as part of this
sum. Unfortunately the transaction was misunderstood, and a
distress order was issued against Helmesale by the Exchequer,
directed to the sheriff of Lincoln. This was to be superseded on
the testimony of Sir John de Neville of Raby, a Warden of the
March (*CCR 1381–85*, p. 417). A fellow-prisoner, John of
Creswell, was allowed on 6 November 1382 to have delivery
of confiscated Scottish goods, captured at sea by the lieges of
Newcastle, to the total value of 40 marks towards his ransom
of £40 (*CPR 1381–85*, p. 182). The petition is calendared in Bain
iv, 69.

116

The King's lieges, Lord Greystoke, William de Aton, [and]
Robert de Hilton, the bearer of the present letter, petition the
King on their own behalf and for other knights, squires and archers
to the number of 120 and more, taken by the earl of the Scottish
March while within England on their way to Roxburgh castle.
The earl holds them because of goods in a Scottish ship taken
by Sir William de Hilton and now mostly detained by
men of Newcastle, Hull and Lynn. They request that writs be
sent to these towns to release the goods by indenture, to answer
on the March Day, which could assist the release of the petitioners:
considering that they were taken on the King's service (AP 8864).

A nostre tresredoute et tressouereign' Seignour le Roi Supplient
vos lieges le Baroun de Greystok', William de Aton', Robert de
Hilton' portur des presentz pur eux et autres chiualers esquiers
et archiers al nombre de .vj.ˣˣ et plus qe furent pris par le Count
de la Marche Descoce dedeinz vostre Roialme Dengleterre alant
vers le Chastiell' de Rokesburgh' pur la salue garde dicelle sanz
ascun mal faire, et le quel Count les tient en prison a cause des
biens prisez en vn Nief Descoce par monsieur William de Hilton'
et les biens vnquore pur la plus graunt partie sont a force ocupiez
par les gentz de Noef Chastell' sur Tune, Kyngeston' sur Hull'
et Lyne: Qe pleise a vostre Roialte graunter briefz as ditz villes
de deliuerer les biens par eux ocupiez com desus par endenture
pur ent respondre au graunt iour de Marche, qe moult purra valoir

al deliuerance des ditz suppliantz, et ceo vous pleise graciousement faire, considerez qils furent pris en vostre seruise.

Traces of red seal on face

Endorsed: Soient lerceuesqe Deuerwik', le Count de Northumbr', le Baron de Greystok', monsieur Rauf de Euere, monsieur William de Skipwith', monsieur Johan Conestable de Halsham et monsieur Walter' de Petwardyn coniuntz a resceuire les ditz biens et briefs faitz a ceo deliuerer par eux et lour deputez.

? 1381. See no. 114 above.
AP 8870 is a duplicate of above, even to the endorsement.

117

Ralph, lord Greystoke, petitions the King and Council in parliament that whereas he was commissioned by the King and Council to guard Roxburgh castle, and was captured with others of his men by the earl of the Scottish March within England on their way to the castle, as reprisal for Scottish ships with several merchants aboard which a Sir William, lord Hilton, with divers men of Northumberland and other Englishmen took, he was put to ransom for 1000 marks. He craves an order from the King and Council that Sir William and all his company be arrested wherever found in England until an agreement be reached over Ralph's ransom, and the rest [of the plunder] (AP 5624).

A nostre tresredoute seignur le Roi et soun tresage (*sic*) consail en cest present parlement moustre Rauf Baroun de Graystok' qe come il fuist assigne par les ditz nostre seignur le Roi et conseil de garder le Chastell' de Rokesburgh', sur qoi le Cont del March' desescoces lui prist et autres plusours de ses gentz dedeinz la roialme Dengleterre enalant a dit Chastell' a cause dune punde pur Niefs descoce od plusours Marchandis en ycels, quels Niefs vn monsz William Baroun de Hilton' oue diuerses gentz de Northumbr' et autres Engleis pristerent, le quel Rauf est mys a Raunsoun de Mille marcz: qe plese a nostre dit tresredoute seignur le Roi et son sage consail comander qe le dit monsz William, et touz autres de sa compaignie qy furent, soient arrestuz en qeconqe partie dengleterre qils puissent estre trouez, tanqe gree soit fait a dit Rauf pur soun dit Raunsoun et du remenant gree soit fait a nostre dit seignur le Roi.

Endorsed: Soit commission faite as certains suffisantes et indifferentes persones denquere et de eulx enfourmer viis et modis des niefs et les biens en y celles dont ceste bille fait mencion et as queux mains ceulx sont deuenuz et de quele value ceulx sont, et de arester touz ceulx en qi mains les biens serront trouez et de les tenir en arest tanqz ils verront faire et aueront fait surtee suffisante de respondre au Roi de la value de mesmes les biens a lour mains issint deuenuz. Et si par cas aucun vorra trauerser lenqueste prise en ce cas, soit lessez aler a large par suffisante meinprise de respondre au Roi des ditz biens ou de la value si soit trouez encontre lui.

1381. It was probably in response to this petition, presented in the ?November parliament, that the commission of December 1381 was issued. See no. 115 above.

118

A petition to the King's council for commissions to certain lords, knights or squires of Northumberland, Cumberland and Westmorland to enquire into the towns burnt and destroyed by the Scots in the said counties and certify the Treasurer and Barons of the Exchequer in order that the collectors of tenths and fifteenths due to account can be discharged of the tenths and fifteenths assessed on towns so destroyed.

May it please the Treasurer that the following names should be on the commission:—the bishop of Carlisle, John Lord Roos, Ralph Lord Neville, Sir John de Irby, Sir John de Derwentwatre, Sir Christopher de Moresby, in Cumberland and Westmorland [Sir Richard Lescrope, *added*].

The Earl Marshal, Sir Mathew de Redman, Sir Ralph de Eure, Sir Thomas Umfraville, John de Mitford in Northumberland. *noted* from the Treasurer to the Chancellor (AP 8179).

Pleise a consell' nostre seignure le Roi dordeigner commissions as certeignez seignurs, Chiualers ou Esquiers dez Counteez de

Northumbr', Cumbr' et Westmerl' denquerrer queux sont lez
villez arsez et destruyt par les Escoce es Countez susditz et de
ent certifier as Tresorer et Barouns de lescheqer par tant que lez
Coilliours des dismez et quinzismes que sont acompter poient estre
descharger dez dismez et quinzismez assys sur lez villes issint
destruyt.

Sil plest a monsieur le Tresorer, sez sont lez nouns deux as quex
lez commissions serront direct ou as deux eux

    leuesque de kardoill' Johan sieur de Ros Rauf sieur de Neuill'
Monsieur Johan de Irby Chiualer Monsieur Johan de Derwentwatre Chiualer Monsieur Cristofer de Morisby Chiualer en lez
Counteez de Cumb' et Westmerl' ⟨Monsieur Richard
lescrop' *added*⟩

    le Conte Marsshall' Monsieur Maheu de Redmane Monsieur
Raufe de Eure Monsieur Thomas Vmfravill' Johan de
Mitford' En le Counte de Northumbr'

domino Cancellario   Per Thesaurarium

1389. On 26 May 1389 a commission was issued to Thomas, earl
marshal and earl of Nottingham, Matthew de Redman, Ralph
de Eure, Thomas Umfravill and John de Mitford to enquire in
Northumberland the names of places wholly or in part burnt by
the Scots, to enable the collectors of the tenth and fifteenth last
granted in parliament to be discharged. A similar commission was
given to Thomas, bishop of Carlisle, John Lord Roos, Ralph de
Nevill, Richard Lescrope, John de Irby, John de Derwentwatre
and Christopher de Morisby in Cumberland and Westmorland
(*CPR 1388–92*, p. 60).

<h2 style="text-align:center">119</h2>

The King's poor lieges and inhabitants of Northumberland and
Westmorland petition the King and Council that whereas they
dwell on the Scottish march and their possessions, goods and
chattels are burnt and destroyed by frequent forays of the Scots,
and the greater part have nothing on which to live, they are on
the point of abandoning the country if they are not relieved by
royal aid. They crave quittance of the fifteenth granted in the
last parliament at Cambridge, to amend their state of poverty
(AP 10868).

A tresexcellent et tresgracious seignour nostre seignour le Roi
et son bone conceille moustrent et ceux compleynent sez pouers
lieges et inhabitantz dez Contez de Northumbr' et Westmerl' qe
come voz ditz lieges et inhabitantz dez Countez auantditz sont
demurant sure la Marche descoce dont lour possessiouns, bienz
et chateux sont arsez et destrutz par souent chiuachez de vos
ennemys descoce et pur la greindre partie rienz nont dont viure,
issint qe voz ditz lieges et inhabitantz sont en poynt de guerpre
la paijs toute desolate, si par vostre tresgraciouse seignourie et eide
ne soient releuez; qe pleis a vostre hautesse et souerein seignourie
releser as ditz voz lieges la quinzisme grante en vostre darrein
parlement tenuz a Cantebr' en amendement de leur pouer' estate,
pur dieu et en oeure de charite.

Endorsed: Soient respite tanqe le mois de seint Michel et comiss'
ordeinez de inquiere dez terres degastez en le mesme temps
Pur Northumbreland' le count Mareschall' Monsieur Matheu de
 redman Monsieur Thomas dumframville John [*sic*] de Mitford
Pur Cumbeland leuesqe de kardoill' le sieur de roos le sieur de
 neuille Monsieur Johan de irby amand manceux
Pur Westmerland le sieur de clifford Monsieur richard de scrope
 Monsieur W Lancastre Willum Ormesheud'

1390. On 1 March 1390, following a petition in the Westminster
parliament, remission was granted of fines, issues, amercements
and arrears of farms and accountancy for tenths and fifteenths,
because of the seizure of goods and chattels, burning and
destruction by the French and Scots, so that many were compelled
to leave the country (*CPR 1388–92*, p. 203). See also above, no. 117.
The Cambridge parliament was summoned for 9 September 1388
(*HBC*, p. 527).

120

The King's poor lieges of Northumberland, Cumberland and
Westmorland petition the Duke of Bedford, lieutenant of
England, that whereas they have long been annually burnt,
despoiled and devastated by sudden inroads of the Scots they are
brought to nothing through great mortalities, as well as by many
other losses, damage and burdens by reason of great forays and

their resistance to the enemy: wherefore if any tax be put on them and levied they will be ruined and the counties deprived of inhabitants for ever. They crave the Duke to consider this and the fact that the countries are frontiers to the Scottish March and daily vexed and set to insupportable expense, and pardon them all manner of tenths and fifteenths and other taxes or tallages whatsoever granted to the King in this present parliament by the lieges, and to acquit and discharge them and the collectors at the King's Exchequer for the said causes (AP 15295).

A tressoueraigne et tresgracious seignur le duk de Bedford' lieutenant Dengleterre

Suppliont humblement les poueres liges nostre seignur le Roy des Contes de Northumbr' Cumbr' et Westmerland qe come ils ount este chescun an par longe temps deuant ces heures et soint a present par sodeyne inuasions des enemys descoce arsez, despoilez et destruitz, et auxint sibien par grantz mortalites des ditz liges illoeqes come par plusours autre perdes, damages et greuances, queux les di[tz lig]es par grantz chiuaches et resistence de la malice des enemys auantditz ount sustenuz et susteignent de iour en autre sount anientez, empeirez et empouerez qe si ascun charge, imposicion ou taxe soit mys sur les ditz liges et de eux leuez les ditz liges serrount anientez et destruitz, et les ditz Countes des enhabitantz en ycelles desolacz et destituitz pur touz iours: qe pleise a vostre tresgracious seignurie considerer les premisses, et come les ditz Countes sont les frountures sur les Marches descoce et chescun iour vexez et trauailez et mys a importables charges, et sur ceo pardoner et relesser a les ditz liges et a chescun de eux touz maneres des dismes et quinzismes et autres taxes ou taillages qeconqes grauntez a nostre seignur le Roy en cest present parlement par les loyes gentz et les ditz liges des ditz Countes, et les Collectours dycelles ent acquit et descharger en lescheqer nostre seignur le Roy par les causes prediz en oeuere de charite.

No endorsement

1415. John, duke of Bedford, was regent of England in the absence of Henry V in France between 11 August and 16 November 1415, and again between 23/25 July 1417 and 1/3 February 1421 (*HBC*, p. 37). A pardon of all tenths, fifteenths and taxes due in Cumberland, Westmorland and Northumberland was issued on 13

November 1415, following a grant in parliament on the previous day (12 November 1415). There had been earlier pardons on 13 June 1413 and 8 December 1414 (*Rot Parl* iv, 71; *CPR 1413–16*, pp. 28, 275, 371).

SECTION IV

DURHAM

The number of petitions directed to the King and his Council from Durham may seem surprising to those taught to regard the area as a palatinate, proud of its independence from royal administration. On the one hand the Bishop himself as petitioner might demonstrate his role of sole channel of communication between the local inhabitants and the Crown. On the other hand it might confirm, for opponents of the theory of effective autonomy, the illusory nature of the Bishop's independence.

The Durham petitions on the whole support the contention that this process was a last resort, where the Common Law was unable to provide a remedy. No amount of litigation in the Bishop's temporal courts would have induced a foreign power, be he the Count of Flanders or the King of Scotland, to restore property or compensate for personal injuries (nos 125, 126). Durham merchants had to pay royal customs even within the palatinate at Hartlepool, despite the pretensions and protests of Bishop Bek (*Bek*, pp. 86, 191, 199, 204, 206). The Bishops of Durham waged for centuries an unequal trade-war with Newcastle upon Tyne for control of the south bank of the Tyne, which was partly their own demesne land and all within their franchise, finally conceding defeat when in 1555 Bishop Tunstall leased the Saltmeadows and tolls of Gateshead to the corporation of Newcastle for 450 years at the nominal rent of £6 10s 8d (R. Welford, *History of Newcastle and Gateshead*, (1885), ii, 312–15) (nos 122, 127). The King's army was liable to live off the countryside as much in England as in Scotland (no 137), and Durham inhabitants in their need were as liable as other northern inhabitants to seize the opportunity to buy surplus army stores at Newcastle, only to find themselves unable to settle when the day of reckoning came (nos 131, 134, 138).

The action taken by the 'commons of Durham' to buy a truce with the Scots in 1315 (nos 128, 130), while supporting Lapsley's theory of a Durham assembly capable of imposing local taxation, can be paralleled from other counties. In Cumberland, despite royal protests, not only was a truce bought in 1314 but royal auditors were appointed to check that the money had been properly applied, without peculation (*CPR 1313–17*, p. 240). The fact of Durham's special legal status, considered more fully in Section IV e (nos 163–176), was recognized only to the extent that remedies for Durham grievances were often delegated to the Bishop of Durham for execution (nos 128, 130).

Whatever inhibitions might be felt by the laity, the clergy had no hesitation in approaching the King to rectify double presentations to churches in the diocese, especially where the King was the offending party (nos 140, 141, 144, 147, 148). The petitions, indeed, give the impression of hungry clerks waiting impatiently for incumbents to die and so provide a vacancy. Robert of Warcop had the different problem of being overtaxed for papal subsidies (no. 143). Thomas del Chaumbre was caught by an act against the farming of English church revenues by papal nominees (no. 146), while John Kyllome and John Herle had both been caught by the second Statute of Provisors of 1390 (nos 149, 150).

The clergy were also concerned with petitions in the 'finance' section. The Prior and Convent of Durham wanted an order to the sheriffs of York and Northumberland to restore such of their goods as had been dispersed within their bailiwicks (no. 152), while the Prior pursued the interminable suit for execution of the royal grant of an annuity of £40 payable at Berwick, made in the enthusiasm of Scottish conquest and dishonoured thereafter (nos 145, 153, 154, 158). Another petition was presented for non-payment of a rent in wheat for the use of the monks on Farne Island (no. 156). The Durham monks, like the monks of Holme Cultram, sought relief from repayment of money for victuals (nos 88, 158), and disingenuously suggested that they should benefit from the general pardon to the men of Northumberland for such debts (no. 160). Even lay petitions had a clerical flavour: Robert de Barton claimed his expenses for extra time spent collecting the King's issues resultant from the vacancy after the death of Bishop Bek (no. 155), and Nicholas de Ellerker, a Newcastle wool-merchant, protested against a worthless assignment made on the Prior of Durham as collector of money received from the sale of surplus war-supplies (no. 161). The final petition in this section is Bishop Hatfield's hapless tale of how he was brazenly defrauded by Alice Perrers, whose aid he had sought to obtain repayment of some of his tallies on the Exchequer (no. 162).

The division of material between the legal and prerogative sections is almost necessarily arbitrary, as the most practical aspect of the powers of the Bishop of Durham as Count Palatine was his right to have a chancery issuing legal writs, and his possession of law courts staffed by his own officers. The criterion for inclusion in the legal section is that the petition involved the use of the Bishop's court or chancery, rightly or wrongly. Useful light is shed on the question whether the Bishop of Durham could lawfully issue writs created after the last known eyre in Durham in 1279 (nos 169–173. 175; cf. J. Scammell, 'The Origin and Limitations of the Liberty of Durham') English Historical Review LXXXI, 1966, pp. 461–73). Interestingly, it was testified in 1293 at the proceedings of quo waranto in Newcastle, which itself ranked as an eyre, that Bishop Robert of Holy Island had failed to crave the articles of eyre from the royal justices in 1278/9 although he summoned his own eyre in Durham and Sadberge (PRO, Assize Rolls 225, 650 m 39). There is no record of any eyre being summoned by Bishop Bek in 1293, parallel to the royal eyre in Northumberland, but this does not necessarily prove its non-existence, as the Durham chancery records are very incomplete before the time of Bishop Bury.

The final section deals with petitions illustrating the special temporal authority or prerogative of the Bishop in Durham. Most of these arise from his claim to forfeiture of lands where the holder was found guilty of treason. The fact that both John de Balliol and Robert de Brus were holders of land within the Bishopric meant that the King of England was highly interested in the claim and inclined to dispute it. Other notable 'traitors' were John Eure, Robert Holland and Walter Selby, all implicated with Thomas of Lancaster and the Scots. In addition to these matters the Bishops of Durham were also concerned to maintain other rights from royal encroachment. Bishop Beaumont wished to have a liberal interpretation of his claim to have his own coinage, stamped by dies supplied from the King's Exchange (no. 186). He or his successor also wanted to collect the profits arising from the establishment of the home wool-staples in 1333 (no. 195), as of the fines levied from distraint of knighthood (no. 201).

Bishop Bury wanted his own officers to enforce the embargo on export of bullion and plate (no. 202). Bishop Hatfield wanted exemption for the palatinate from national taxes (no. 203).

These Durham petitions illustrate very clearly that while many of the medieval Kings were genuinely willing to recognise the special liberties of St. Cuthbert, neither the Bishop nor his 'subjects' could be wholly independent of royal supervision because so many of their activities had repercussions outside the palatinate.

Trade

As Durham failed to achieve independence from the national customs system, and its merchants were involved also in international trade, petitions to the King were natural. In addition, the King automatically assumed control during vacancies of the see of Durham, giving rise to such abuses of power as the tallaging of the Bishop's boroughs (no. 124).

Ancient Petitions 1962, 2149, 2163, 4982, 5767, 7522, 12493.

121

John de Cotes and William de Cotes, merchants of the town of Durham, petition the King that whereas they brought their wool to Kingston on Hull in the first year of the present King [1327], from which the King borrowed a mark a sack, and Robert de Burton and John de Barton, then customs collectors of the town, received the money and rendered their account at the Exchequer and paid the money over: John and William request a letter of privy seal to the Treasurer and Barons of the Exchequer to search the rolls of Robert and John. What is found due to John and William should be repaid them by the Treasurer and Chamberlains of the Exchequer or allowance made, notwithstanding any orders or ordinances made previously (AP 4982).

A nostre seignur le Roy priount Johan de Cotes et William de Cotes, Merchauntz de la ville de Duresme, qe come les auauntditz Johan et William amenerunt lour leyns a le Porte de

Kyngiston' sour Hull' en lan du regne nostre seignur le Roy qore
est primer, dount nostre dit seignur le Roy apromta de eux de
chesqun sak' de layne vn Marc', et Robert de Burton' et Johan
de Barton' furont a tiele houre Custoumers de la dite ville et
resceuront les ditz deniers et ount rendu lour acompte en Lescheker
et paie les deniers: Dount priont le dit Johan et William qil pount
auer lettre de priue seal a Tresorer et as Barouns de Lescheker
pur ensercher les Roules del acompte les ditz Robert et Johan,
et ceo qe serra troue due audit Johan et William qe le Tresorer
et Chaumberleyns del Escheker luy facent paiement ou couenable
assignement de les ditz deniers, nient countresteaunt quecumqes
mandementz ou ordenaunce faitz auaunt ces heures.

Endorsed: Soit mande as Tresorer et Barouns de lescheker qe
ils veues les lettres dont la peticioun fait mencioun, sils troeffent
qe la dette seit clere et vnqore due, adonqe facent paiement ou
couenable assignement, Resceuiantz etc.

c. 1330. The relevant order was sent on 20 December 1330 to
the Treasurer and Barons of the Exchequer and the Chamberlains.
This stated that John de Cotes and William de Cotes had shown
by petition before King and Council that the King owed them
£40 19s 6d, lent to him under the cocket seal, and they prayed
repayment or allowance in their next customs dues on wool etc.
sent by them out of the realm. This sum if due was to be paid
from the Treasury or allowed them in their next customs (*CCR
1330–33*, p. 87).

William and John de Cotes were general merchants. John de
Cotes can be traced from the customs accounts of Newcastle and
Hartlepool from 1326 in a fairly big way of business (PRO,
Customs Accts 49/4: 105/9, 12). In 1328 he bought wool
from the bursar of Durham Priory. He also supplied the monks
between 1329 and 1337 with almonds, sugar, wax, cloth and wine
(Durham, Bursars Accts passim). His wool was caught in the
Dordrecht seizure of 1337/8 (PRO, Enrolled Wool Accts:
E101/457/9 m 1d).

122

John Belle of Hartlepool petitions the King and Council that
whereas the King assigned him as controller of Hartlepool and

ordered the Treasurer and Barons of the Exchequer to pay him the customary wage, they replied that they could not pay customary wages as there was not a controller before him, and they must have a precise figure. He craves wages similar to other controllers at Newcastle or Hull or Boston or other ports (AP 7522).

A nostre seignur le Roi et a son conseil prie Johan Belle de Hertilpole qe come nostre seignur le Roi li auoit assigne destre contrelour al port de Hertilpol [et co]manda as Tresorer et barons del Escheqer qils li feissent auoir gages acustumez, a queu mandement les ditz Tresorer et Barons respondu qils ne poent gages acustumez paier a li pur ce qe vnqes contrelour ne fust en cel port deuant le dit Johan, issint [qe ne] voillent rien paier si ses gages ne soient mys en certein; qe pleise a nostre dit seignur le Roi comander qil preigne tiels gages come ils allow[ent] les autres contreroulours de Noef Chastel, ou de Kyngeston', ou de seint Botulf ou aillors en autres portz ou autrement ... ce qil prenda pur ses ditz gages.

Endorsed: Soit mande as Tresorer et Barons del escheker qe en regarde a ce qe autres Contreroulours en autres portz pernent pur lour gages, facent paier au dit Johan ses gages pur le temps qil ad demore selonc lour descrecions.

c. 1332. Belle had been appointed on 27 January 1332 to replace Roger de Gosewyk as fellow collector with Nicholas de Bruntoft of the King's wool customs at Hartlepool (*CFR 1327–37*, pp. 296–297). Despite the allegation of the Exchequer there had certainly been a second customs-official at Hartlepool since 1305, when Andrew de Brumtoft and Peter del Mareys were ordered to return the old cocket seal to the Exchequer, where they would receive a new seal for wools and fells (PRO, QR Mem Roll 78 m 4d: cf. 83 mm 105r-d: 85 m 4).

123

The lieges of Hartlepool petition the King and Council that whereas his ancestors, King John and King Henry his son, granted them by charters the privilege of being free burgesses with laws and customs like the burgesses of Newcastle upon Tyne, the burgesses of Newcastle have been granted freedom from tonnage, murage, pavage, pontage, passage, stallage, lastage, hidage, quayage, strandage, terrage, pickage, anchorage, and all such customs throughout England. They crave a similar freedom throughout the King's realm and all seaports, including the Cinque Ports, in consideration of their great destruction and travail by reason of the wars of his ancestors and his own, by confirmation of their charters with the clause *licet* (AP 5767).

[A nostre seignur le Roi et] a son conseil prient ses liges gentz de la ville de Hertilpole qe come le progenitours nostre seignur le Roi qore est, cest a sauer le Roi Johan et le Roy Henri son fitz, eont grantee as les ditz gentz de Hertilpole par lour Chartres qils seient frankes Burgeis e auoient meismes les fraunchises, leis et coustumes come les Burgeis de Noef Chaustel sure Tyne eont, et les ditz Burgeis de Noef Chaustel sont quittes de coustumes de tonneu, morage, pauage, pontage, passage, stallage, lastage, hidage, kayage, strandage, terrage, pikage, ankerrage et de toutz tielz coustumes par tout le Roialme Dengleterre, qe lour pleise auoir regarde a lour graunt destructioun et a lour graunt trauailes qils ont eu en la gere de ses progenitours et en sa gere demeigne, et en regerdon de toutz lour grantz trauails granter as ditz gentz de Hertilpole, lour heirs et lour successours qils puissent estre quittes des coustumes de tonneu, morage, pauage, pountage, passage, stallage, lastage, hidage, kayage, strandage, terrage, pikage, ankerage et de toutz tiels coustumes par toutz le Roialme a poer nostre dit seignur le Roi et par toutz les portes de Meer auxi bien deinz les Cynk' portes come aillours a toutz iours, de confermer les chartres les Rois susdites de la clause de licet.

Endorsed: Soit vewe ses chartres en Chauncellerie et si riens ne soit compris qe soit preiudiciel au Roi, soit conferme par resonable fin, et auxint soit vewe la chartre de la ville de Noef Chastel et si troue soit qe la chartre de Hertilpol' soit tiele come la peticion suppose adonqe eient declaracion de tonnue Murage et autres tieles custumes contenues en la chartre de Noef Chastel par resonable fyn.

temp Edward III (probably 1331 x 1365). Henry III granted to the free burgesses of Hartlepool the laws and liberties of Newcastle upon Tyne on 2 July 1234, thereby confirming liberties previously conferred by Peter de Brus in the twelfth century, by King John in 1201, and by Bishop Richard Poor and his chapter in 1230 (*CChR* v, 191, 370; Surtees, iii, 386–87). The earliest charters to Newcastle contain no specific grants of exemption from tolls. Tolls, however, are explicitly mentioned in the grant of 1318 and in subsequent confirmations of this charter in 1331 and 1357 (*CChR* iii, 392: iv, 214: v, 154). When the Hartlepool borough charter was confirmed on 28 January 1365 no reference was made to exemption from tolls (*Ibid.* v, 191). The petition may be compared with the direct request for information as to the customs of Newcastle made to the mayor by the mayor, bailiff and burgesses of Stockton in 1344 (M. H. Dodds, 'The Bishops' Boroughs', *AA*[3] XII, (1915), 121–22).

124

The burgesses of Durham, Darlington, Auckland, Gateshead and Stockton in the franchise of Durham petition the King and Council that whereas they are free burgesses of free condition and not liable to tallage, and never were tallaged nor were their ancestors, neither *sede plena* nor *sede vacante* except in the time of King Edward, the present King's grandfather, and then by extortion of the keepers of the temporalities during the vacancy, and now after the death of Louis, lately bishop of Durham, this extortion has continued and they have been tallaged more than £60, wherefore they crave the King that such money paid be not treated as a precedent (AP 2149).

A nostre seignur le Roi et a son conseil mustrent les Burgeys de Duresme, Derlyngton', Aukland', Gatesheued et Stocton' en la franchise de Duresme qe come ils sount francs Burgeys et de franc estat et nient taillables par le ... de ... vnqes taillez ne furent eux ne lour auncestres en nul temps le see pleni ne le see vacaunt mes de temps [le Roi. E. ael] nostre dit seignur le Roi, et puis encea par extorcioun des gardeinz des temporaltes, le see vacaunt, et ore e[ncea] ... apres Loys nadgares Euesqe de Dureme cele extorsioun fut continue sur eux et tailles a plus qu .Lx. li', les queux [deners] ils eunt paiez; par quei les ditz Burgeys prient au dit nostre seignur le Roi qe lui plest pur les ditz deners qils eunt paiez, issint qad este fait deuant ces houres encountre eux, mes ne soit tret en ensaumple.

Endorsed: Seit maunde as Tresorer et Barons par bref du grant seal de sercher les roules et remembrances del escheker touchantz ceste chose, qils certifient en Chancellerie de queu temps cels taillages comencerent et par quele cause et, quant ceste chose serra returne en Chancellerie, le Chanceller apellez a lui les Justices et autres du conseil, face ouir droit.

In a bad state

post 1333. An order to search the Exchequer records for tallage precedents had been previously ordered on 11 June 1312. Then it was found that a tallage of £14 had been raised from Durham city during the vacancy after the death of Bishop Robert of Holy Island. Only one earlier detailed account survives, for 1196, but a general reference to tallage levied on the bishopric, or 'common aid', was of regular occurrence in the rolls of keepers during the vacancies (PRO, QR Mem Roll 86 mm 34, 80d; *Boldon Buke* pp. vi–vii; *Reg Pal Dun* ii, 863, 920, 935). The tallage exacted after the death of Bishop Bek amounted to £597 2s. After Bishop Beaumont's death in 1333 £352 10s 4d was collected as 'tallage', but was said specifically to be derived from 'bondsmen' (PRO, Ministers Accts 1144/18 m 1; *Reg Pal Dun* iv, 91).

125

The King's merchants, Robert Cokside of Durham and Robert de Gretewych' of Durham, petition the King and Council that whereas in time of peace between the King and Flanders they sent to Flanders by their servants, William Cokside and Richard de Lyndeseye, 30 sarplers of wool to trade, the count of Flanders suddenly and without cause arrested these servants and the wool worth £300 and still holds them under arrest, to the great impoverishment of the merchants. Also whereas the servants had bought in Flanders 28 coloured cloths at 70s, and 25 striped cloths at 4 marks, and 1000 pieces of canvas priced £9, and a pipe of spicery and silks priced £40, the Count on the allegation by Simon

Fauvale that the King owed Simon a sum of money, arrested the cloth, canvas, spices and mercery priced £213 13s 4d and still holds it under arrest, to their detriment (AP 1962).

A nostre seignur le Roi et a son conseil prient ses Marchauntz Robert Cokside de Duresme et Robert de Gretewych' de Duresme qe come les ditz Robert et Robert en temps de pees entre nostre dit seignur le Roi et ceux de Flaundres eussent enuoiez en Flaundres par lour seruantz, William Cokside et Richarde de Lyndeseye, xxx. sarplers de leyne a marchander et faire ent lour profit, le Counte de Flaundres fist par ses Ministres sodeynement et sanz cause arester les corps des ditz seruantz et auxint les dites leynes pris de .ccc. li' et vncore les detient en arest a graunt enpouerissement des ditz Marchauntz. Et auxint par la ou les ditz seruantz les ditz Marchantz auoient acthate en les dites parties de Flaundres .xxviij. draps de colour pris de chescun drap .lxx. s. et vynt et cynk' draps de Raye pris de chescun drap' .iiij. Marcs, et Mille de Caneuace pris de .ix. li' et vne pipe despicerie et Mercerie pris de .xl. li', le dit Counte a la sute Simon Fauuale fesant suggestion au dit Counte qe nostre seignur le Roi feust tenu au dit Simon en vne summe dargent, fist arester les ditz draps, Caneuace, espicerie et Mercerie pris de .ccxiij. li' .xiij. s. .iiij. d. et vnqore les detient souz areste en anientissement de lour estat, dont ils prient pur dieu qe remedie lour soit fait.

Endorsed: Coram Rege et magno consilio
Soit mande a Leuesqe de Duresme par bref contenant leffect de ceste peticion qil face enquere auxibien par serment des marchantz come des autres si larest feust fait come la peticion suppose, et par queux et de qi poair ils sont, et queux biens et marchandies des ditz marchantz feurent arestuz, et de quele value et des autres articles et quant lenquest serra retourne et larest serra troue fait, et le passage de la Meer soit clos come il est aore, adonqes eient arest sur les piers et communers de ceux qi firent la dit arest, issint qe larest ne se estend' mie as biens et marchandies des marchantz demorantz en Engleterre ne qi ont fraunk' tenementz en Engleterre, et si le passage soit ouert quant lenquest serra retourne, adonqes soit mande a les seignurs de faire droit, et soit outre tenuz launcien cours.

1337. The enquiry was held at Durham on Monday, 19 May 1337, when it was testified that the sarplers were worth £360, from which the servants, Cokside and Lyndeseye, had deducted £20 as expenses. They had bought 39 coloured cloths worth £104: 14 striped cloths, worth £32 13s 4d: 1000 pieces of canvas, worth £9: three mazers worth 6s 3d: and a pipe of spices and mercery worth £40. The goods were arrested by the burgomaster and échevins of Bruges on Thursday, 26 September 1336 (*Cal Inq Misc* ii, 390–91).

Cockside and Gretewych may have been in partnership, as they were jointly granted lands in Moorsley by Peter de Brackenbury and Cecily his wife in 1337. This may have been as security, as the Brackenburys had apparently regained possession by 1339 (Durham, Misc Charters 5367, 6479–82).

Robert Cockside between February and September 1332 shipped 70 sacks of wool from Hartlepool and between January and June 1334 shipped from Newcastle 26 sacks of wool and a last of hides. In 1339 he bought from the convent of Durham tithes and bark in Bearpark wood for tanning, while supplying them with cloth for liveries and with groceries. He was collector of customs at Hartlepool and Yarm from 1 May 1341 to 13 September 1342 (PRO, Customs Accts 49/4; 105/6; Enrolled Accts 4 m 9d; Durham, Bursars Accts 1339–44 passim).

Robert Gretewych occurs as a Hartlepool shipper. From 1334 he supplied the Durham monks with sugar, malt, cloth for liveries, and wine. He farmed their grain tithes of Shadforth in 1341 (Durham, Bursars Accts 1334–41 passim).

126

The King's poor merchants, William de Duresme of Darlington and John his brother, petition the King and Council that whereas in time of peace between England and the men of Flanders they sent from England 19 sarplers and a pocket of wool worth £237 to trade there and make their profit, the count of Flanders and his officers came and seized the merchandise and retain it to their great hardship (AP 2163).

A nostre seignur le Roi et a son conseil mostrent ses poures Marchantz William de Duresme de Derlyngton et Johan son frere

qe come ils en temps de pees entre nous et les gentz de Flaundres
auoient amenez hors du roialme dengleterre .xix. sarplers et vn
poket de leine a la vaillance de .ccxxxvij. li' a les dites parties
de Flaundres pur marchander illoqes et ent faire lour profit, la
vyndrent le Counte de Flaundres et ses Ministres illoeqes et
aresterent les dites marchandises et ent firent lour volunte et vnqore
les detenent a grant empouerissement de lour estat, de qoi ils prient
remedie.

Endorsed: Coram Rege et magno consilio
Soient certeines genz assignez denquere auxibien par serement
des marchantz come des autres si larest feut fait come la peticion
suppose et a qi sute et par qi il feut fait et par quele cause, et
quant lenquest serra retourne si troue soit qe la peticion contient
verite, adonqes si le passage soit clos come il est aore, eient arest
sur les piers et communers issi tote foiz qe larest ne se estend'
mie as biens et marchandies des genz demorantz en Engleterre
ne qe ont frank' tenement' en Engleterre, et si le passage soit ouert
adonqes suent par launcien cours cea en arere vse.

1337. An enquiry held at Durham on Monday, 16 June 1337,
found that the brothers had had 17 sarplers of wool worth £12
each and two sarplers and a poke worth £30 seized at Bruges
by the count of Flanders and the burgomasters and échevins of
Bruges on the previous 26 September (*Cal Inq Misc* ii, 382). On
22 May 1338 they were given allowances in the port of Hartlepool
totalling £312 17s 7d (*CCR 1337–39*, p. 432).
The brothers were responsible for the export from Newcastle
in 1333/4 of 108 sacks of wool and a last of hides. William was
a leading supplier to the monks of Durham of cattle, cloth and
wine. He also purchased from them wool and corn-tithes between
1330 and 1338 (PRO, Customs Accts 105/6; Durham, Bursars
Accts 1330–38 passim).

127

John, bishop of Durham, petitions the King that whereas by
a statute of King Edward III in parliament at York in 1335 it
was ordained that all merchants and others wishing to buy or sell

any merchandise from any quarter might freely sell in city, borough, town, seaport, fair, market or other place within the realm, within or outside franchises, and that none be prevented from buying freely in those places and carrying them wherever they would where it was to the general profit, notwithstanding any liberties granted to the contrary or usage, custom or judgment given, and whereas the bishop's predecessors used to have great annual profit from the coal in their soil within the bishopric and royal franchise of Durham and specially by loading and shipping in ships and vessels seeking it in the water of Tyne, which profit represented a large part of the revenue of the church of Durham: the men of Newcastle upon Tyne, contrary to the tenor of the said statute and to the great prejudice of the church and the diminution of the profits of the petitioner, have hindered and do hinder him and those wishing to buy coals. And especially whereas the petitioner, by confirmation of the King's ancestors, ought to have access for ships and other vessels to his part of the water, the men of Newcastle and their officers prevent vessels arriving and loading coal and other commodities, and will not allow the bishop to have his own vessels on the water for receiving his coals: and also the men of Newcastle without royal warrant and for their own profit put grievous imposts on each chaldron of coal laden on that water, and have demanded the same for the bishop's coal from men wishing to ship it, which is prejudicial to the said church. For these causes the bishop has had no profit from his coal during his time, and he craves consideration of these things and suitable remedy, with a charter to ensure peace and prevent the grievous harassment, so that merchants and others well-disposed can come with their ships and other vessels into the bishopric and royal franchise of Durham wherever they wish in the water of Tyne, and load and unload coal and other merchandise and carry it where they will without impediment from the men of Newcastle and elsewhere, and that the bishop and his successors can have their own vessels wherever they wish on the water to discharge their coal, load and despatch wherever they want, or sell it to merchants and others wishing to buy, and that the same merchants can ship and send it wherever they want, without impediment or impost or other charge or levy on the coal or other things by the men of Newcastle or elsewhere on the water, notwithstanding any charter, franchise, usage, custom or other alleged cause, contrary to the intent of the said statute (AP 12493).

A nostre tresredote et tresgracieux seignur le Roy Supplie vostre humble Chapellein et oratour Johan Euesqe de duresme qe comme par vn estatuit qe feut fait en le temps du Roi Edward vostre aiel, qe dieux assoille, en son parlement tenuz a Euerwyk lan de son Regne noefisme, ordenez soit et establiz qe touz marchantz, aliens et denizeins, et tous autres de quel estat ou condicion qils soient qi achater ou vendre vuillent queconques marchandises ou autres choses vendables de queu part qils viegnent, par foreins ou par denizeins, a quel lieu qe ce soit Citee, burgh, ville, port de mier, feire, marchee, ou autre lieu deinz le Roiaume dedeinz franchise ou dehors, les puissent franchement et sanz destouber vendre a qi qe leur plest, et qe nul alien ne denizein ne soit destourbez qil ne puisse franchement achater les diz marchandises et autres choses vendables en les lieux susdiz et carier la ou li plerra a son oeps demesne ou au profit du Roi et des grantz et du poeple du dit Roiaume, nient contreesteant chartre de franchise a ascune Citee, burgh', ville, port de mier ou autre lieu deinz le dit Roiaume grantez au contraire, ne vsage, ne custume, ne Juggementz renduz sur leur chartres, vsages ou custumes qils purront allegger, sicomme en mesme lestatuit est contenuz plus a plein: et soit ensi qe la ou les predecessores du dit Euesqe soloient auoir grand profit annuel de leur charbons esteanz en leur soil deinz leur paiis appellez leueschee et franchise Roiale de duresme et nomeement par la deliuerance et passage qils en auoient par niefs et vesseux qe les venoient querre en leawe de Tyne, liquel profit estoit vne grande parcelle du profit de leglise et Eveschee de duresme, les gentz de la ville de Noefchastel sur Tyne pur leur singuler profit, encontre le purport de lestatuit auandit et en grand preiudice de la dite eglise et en grand grief et subtraccion du profit du dit suppliant, ont destourbez et destourbent mesme le suppliant et ceux qe ses ditz charbons volroient achater, en tiele manere qe le dit suppliant nen poet auoir ascune deliuerance ne profit sicomme il deuoit par vertue de lestatut auandit: et en especial la ou le dit suppliant par grant et confermement de voz nobles progenitures Rois dengleterre faitz a ses ditz predecessures doit auoir arriuail des niefs et autres vesseux de la partie du dit paiis appellez leueschee en leawe susdit, les dites genz de Noefchastel et leur Ministres

destourbent qe nul vessel ne poet arriuer ne se charger des ditz
charbons ne dautres choses de la dite partie du dit Eueschee en
leawe auandite, et ne volont soeffrir le dit Euesqe a ce qil est garniz
auoir nuls vesselx du sien propre en mesme leawe pur li seruir
a la deliuerance de ses ditz charbons, et auxi les dites genz de
Noefchastel, sanz grant ou auttorite Roiale, ont pur leur singuler
profit mys et mettent greuouses imposicions et charges de deniers
aprendre sur chescum chaldre de charboun qe sera chargez en la
dite eawe, et mesmes les imposicions et charges ont demandez
et demandent des charbons du dit Euesqe des genz qe les volroient
auoir eskippez, la quele chose est auxi en grand preiudice et damage
dudit suppliant et de leglise auandite: pur lesqueles causes le dit
Euesqe nauoit onqes puis son temps ascun profit de ses charbons
susditz: Il plese a vostre hautesse considerez les choses susdites
puruoir sur ce de remede couenable pur le dit Euesqe et pur ses
dites eglise et Eueschee, et par especial qil vous plese de vostre
benignite Roiale granter au dit suppliant et a ses successures a
touz Jours par vostre chartre pur pees et quiete de mesmes les
eglise et Eueschee, et pur ouster perpetuelement la greuouse
destourbance auandite, qe les marchanz et autres queconques amys
de vostre Roiaume qe volront, puissent peisiblement et quiete-
ment ouesqe leur niefs et autres vesselx queconques arriuer sur
la partie du dit paiie appellez leueschee et franchise Roiale de
duresme en quel lieu qe leur plerra en la dite eawe de Tyne, et
illeoqes charger et descharger charbons et autres merchandises et
choses queconques qils y volront charger et descharger de mesme
la partie, et les ditz charbons et autres choses queux ils ensi
chargeront amener la ou leur plerra, sanz destourbance des dites
genz de Noefchastel ne dautres queconques, et qe le dit Euesqe
et ses successures puissent auoir leur vesselx propres en toute la
dite eawe, queu part qe leur plerra pur eux seruir a la deliuerance
de leur ditz charbons, et faire charger et enuoier leur ditz charbons
queu part qe leur plerra, ou les vendre a les marchantz et autres
qi achater les volront, et qe les ditz marchantz et autres les puissent
eskipper et amesner la ou leur plerra, sanz ansune destourbance
ou ascune imposicion ou autre charge queconque estre pris ou
leuez de mesmes les charbons ou autres choses auandites par les
gentz de la dite ville de Noefchastel ne par autre queconques nulle
part en leawe auandite, queconque chartre, franchise, vsage,
custume ou autre cause qe purra estre alleggez contre le purport

du dit Estatuit nyent contreesteantz.

No endorsement. Slits for closure, but no trace of wax.

1383. This petition by John Fordham, bishop of Durham (1382–1388), formerly enclosed in chancery warrant 1/483/3073, gave rise to the grant on 28 December 1383 by Richard II to the Bishop of Durham of permission to load and unload ships on the south bank of the Tyne, notwithstanding the liberties of Newcastle and providing that customs dues were met and nothing was shipped to the King's enemies (*CChR* v, 290–91). The victory was short-lived, cf. *North'd Pet.*, pp. 258–9.

War Claims

When it came to warfare Durham was as subject as the neighbouring counties of Northumberland and Cumberland to Scottish inroads, and its inhabitants' petitions for royal compensation were no different.

Ancient Petitions E360, 2159–60, 2237–38, 2537, 3778, 5312, 5938, 6512, 7419, 13516, 15562.

128

John de Wessington petitions the King that whereas the commons of the bishopric of Durham sent him as hostage to Sir Robert de Brus for money due for a truce, he was held for two years because 36 marks remained owing, which he himself paid to have his release. And he cannot have for this money remedy or recompense from the commons, and craves from the King a letter to the bishop or his deputy (AP 7419).

A nostre seigneur le Roy Mustre Johan de Wessington' qe come la comunalte del Euesche de Duresme luy mist en hostage por [suretz] del dit Eueschie a sire Robert de Bruys por vne soume denar' dieue au dit sire Robert por suffraunce de guerre a certein Jour a paier, outre quel Jour il fust detenuz illoqes par deux aunz por ceo qe .xxxvj. Mars' furent vncore despayez, de quels deners ii mesmes prest la paye por sa deliueraunce auoir. E des quels deners il ne peot vers la ditte comunalte remedie ne resone auoir, sour quei il pri au dit nostre seigneur le Roi de sa lettre al Euesqe ou a son leu tenant qe remedi e resone sur ceo a luy soit fait.

Endorsed: Mandetur Episcopo quod audita querela super contentis in peticione fieri faciat iusticiam Ita quod Rex non audiat amplius inde querelam.   Irrotulatur

1317. While truces were bought by the commons of Durham from the Scots on at least eight occasions between 1311 and 1327, the truce for 1314 specifically required hostages as pledges for payment in full (J. Scammell, 'Robert I and the North of England', *EHR* LXXIV (1958), pp. 393 n2, 394). The second payment of 400 marks fell due on 8 January 1315, which allowing the two years in prison would date the petition to 1317 (*Scrip Tres* p. cxiii).

129

Joan, widow of John de la Chaumbre, petitions the King and Council that whereas the King ordered the Bishop of Durham to provide suitable maintenance according to her station in Sherburn Hospital because her husband was killed in the King's service in defence of Berwick castle in the company of Roger de Horsleye, the Bishop replied that the hospital was so burdened that she could not be accommodated. She craves that the King grant her a portion of victuals from Newcastle upon Tyne for her subsistence, as she has spent all her livelihood on this suit (AP E360).

A nostre seignour le Roi e soun counseil Moustre Johane qe fu la femme Johan de la Chaumbre qe par la ou nostre seignur le Roi auoit maunde a leueske de Durem qil feist auer a mesme cele Johane couenable sustenaunce solum son estat en la Maisone de Shireburne, pur ceo qe le dit Johan soun baroun fu occis en le seruice nostre seignour le Roi en defens du Chastel de Berewyk en la compaignie Roger de Horsleye, La ad Leueske respondu qe la Mesone est taunt charge qele ne puet illoqes estre serui: Par quei la dite Johane prie a nostre seignour le Roi qil de sa grace la voille granter vne partie des vitailles dont ele puet viuere, aprendre a Noefchastel sur Tyne, qar le poi qele ⟨auoit⟩ dont viuere ad ele despendu enfesant ceste suyte, par quei ele prie la grace le Roi.

Endorsed: Coram Rege

c. 1318. Roger Horsley was successively constable of Bamburgh castle, Berwick (1317–18) and Bamburgh again (*North'd Pet*, p. 62). Sherburn hospital had been founded by Bishop Puiset about 1181 for 65 lepers. From the numerous references to these in the foundation charter as 'brothers and sisters' it has been suggested that they were to be monks and nuns drawn from houses in the north of England (Knowles & Hadcock, p. 391; Surtees i, 285). This may be doubted, as preference was to be shown for lepers from the lands of the bishops of Durham. The King's order to Bishop Beaumont to provide maintenance was dated at York on 2 October 1318 (*CCR 1318–23*, p. 101).

130

William de Kellawe of Thornley petitions the King and Council that whereas lately by common assent of the bishopric of Durham he took from the money of William de Heberne in Durham £70 to pay to Sir Robert de Brus for the safety of the bishopric, this money was later recovered against him together with damages of 100s before sir Robert de Sapy, sir Adam de Brom and Adam de Bowes, then the King's justices during the last vacancy in the bishopric. By them he was committed to prison for the money, where he still remains. He craves the King, because it was done jointly and for the common profit, that the Bishop of Durham be ordered to levy the money from the community so that he may be acquitted and that he be not destroyed, and that in the meantime he may be bailed (AP 5938).

A nostre seignur le Roi et a son conseil moustre William de Kellawe de Thornlawe qe la ou nadgeres par commun assent del euesche de Dorrem il prist de les deniers William de Heberme en Dorrem .lxx. li' qe feuront paiez por la sauuete la dite euesche a sire Robert de Brus par commun assent de tut le pais: les queux deners le dit William de Heberme apres en la darayne vacacion del euesche auantdite recouera vers le dit William de Kellawe et ses damages a .c. s. deuant sire Robert de Sapy, sire Adam de Brom et Adam de Bowes adonqes Justices nostre seignur le Roi, deuant queux il feust commande ala prisone pur les ditz deners et vnqore demoer en prisone: par qei il prie a nostre seignur le Roi, desicome ceo fust fait de commun et por commun profit, qil voille mander al euesqe de Dorrem qil face leuer les deners auantditz de la communalte auantdite, issint qil soit acquite et qe il ne soit destruit pur son benfait et sen le meen temps son corps puisse estre par meynprise.

Endorsed: Mandetur per breue Episcopo vel eius locum tenenti quod vocatis coram eo hominibus parcium illarum qui saluacionem habuerunt per solucionum huiusmodi denariorum et Willelmo de Kellawe, si invenerit quod idem Willelmus denarios infra contentos de communi assensu hominum parcium illarum cepit et eos pro saluacione parcium illarum posuit vt supponitur in peticione, tunc eidem Willelmo faciat indilate iusticie complementum: Ita quod querela amplius inde non veniat ad Regem.

c. 1318. The vacancy after the death of Bishop Kellawe lasted from 9 October 1316 until 4 May 1317. During this time Sapy acted as Keeper, Brome as Chancellor of Durham, and Bowes as Sheriff (*Reg Pal Dun* iv, 146, 148–49; *CPR 1313–17*, pp. 555, 644). Subsequently Kellawe sued before the King and a writ of certiorari, sent to Adam de Brome on 22 October 1319, resulted in the delivery of the record that on 11 January 1317 before Brome at Durham Kellawe had been charged with breaking into Heberme's house in the Durham Bailey on 25 November 1315, forcing open a chest and abstracting £70. The jurors testified that the Scots had entered the bishopric, and the commons assembled in Durham entered into a bond for the general good to make an immediate fine of 1600 marks with the enemy. As the money was not to hand, it was ordained that some should go from house to house in the Bailey seeking money deposited and where it was found seizing it to speed the payment of the fine until such time as a levy from the commons could be made, when satisfaction would be made to those whose money had been seized. William de Kellawe and David de Rothebiry were acting as searchers when they took Heberme's money. As it was taken, however, without

Heberme's personal consent, the court awarded Heberme recovery of his money, with 100s damages, and Kellawe was committed to gaol. Following Kellawe's allegations of legal error Heberme was ordered through Bishop Beaumont to appear before the King on the fortnight after Michaelmas 1319, and despite Heberme's default Kellawe was invited to demonstrate these errors. He argued that as the commons had agreed to the interim forced levy Heberme was bound thereby, and furthermore that the justices should not have allowed Heberme to sue Kellawe in particular but only the commons in general. These arguments were accepted, and Kellawe's release from gaol was ordered, with restitution of any money levied on his land or chattels on Heberme's behalf (*Reg Pal Dun* iv, 159–65; cf. J. Scammell, *EHR* LXXIV (1958), pp. 399–40).

Two receipts for 'blackmail money' payable in 1317 by Kellawe survive in the Durham Dean and Chapter Muniments (Misc Charters 3506, 3589; cf. 4912—an expense allowance for £20 from Kellawe for carrying money to Scotland).

131

The King's lieges, the mayor and commons of Hartlepool, petition the King that whereas Sir Robert de Brus had granted a truce to the whole bishopric of Durham except Hartlepool, which he intended to burn and destroy because of a ship they captured at sea charged with his armaments and victuals, the mayor and commons enclosed a great part of the town and are building the wall to the best of their power. They crave a grant of 100 marks which are owed the King for victuals bought of the King's father by a Robert de Musgrave, whose term for repayment is a year come next Easter (AP 2537).

A nostre seignur le Roi priount ses liges gentz le Mair e la communalte de Hertilpoll' qe come sire Roberd de Brus ad graunte vne trewe a tout Leueschee de Duresme forpris la ville de Hertilpoll', quele il est en volunte arder e destruer pur vne neef qils pristerount en la Meer chargee de ses armeours e de ses vitales, par quoi les ditz Mair e la communalte ount enclos graunte partie de la ville e sont defesauntz le Muyre tancome lour poer purra suffir, qil pleise graunter a eux Cent marz qe duez lui sont de vitales achatez de son pier par vn Roberd' de Musgraue, dont le terme du paiement serra a la Pask' qe vendra a vn an.

Endorsed: Fiat in auxilium operis murorum   [*erased*]
   Assignentur denarii Burg' etc in auxilium operis etc, ita quod cum festinacione app[lic]entur circa reparacionem quod periculum non eueniat etc.

1319. The wall-building had started after the royal grant of a murage for three years on 1 September 1315 (*CPR 1313–17*, p. 347). The ship was captured early in 1319, and on 17 March 1319 Bishop Beaumont was ordered to deliver it to royal officers. The July following it was apparently sailed to York, after payment of a reward of 200 marks to the captors, including John Bille, William Jetour, Nicholas de Bruntoft and John de Hawkeslaw (*CPR 1317–21*, pp. 62, 67, 90, 354). Robert de Musgrave was alleged to have been involved in the capture of a wine-ship off the mouth of the Humber in 1313, but his appearance in the King's court to answer the charge in 1317/18 was excused on the grounds that he was needed for the defence of Newcastle (*CCR 1313–18*, p. 497; *CPR 1317–21*, p. 600). In November 1315 he received a royal safe-conduct on going to France to buy corn and other victuals for Newcastle upon Tyne (*CPR 1313–17*, p. 370). He was an exporter of wool from Newcastle in 1326 and 1334 (PRO, Customs Accts 105/5, 6). The petition is calendared in Bain iii, 114.

132

Ralph de Neville petitions the King that whereas Sir Robert de Neville his brother was killed by the Scots and Sir Alexander de Neville and John de Neville his brothers and himself captured on the same day, and his two brothers were held until they paid a great ransom, and himself was ransomed for 2000 marks, for which his hostages are held until the money be paid or he surrenders himself again: he craves aid from the King towards his ransom, with a wardship, marriage or other money-paying asset towards this. And may he give leave to Sir Randulph de Neville his father, whose heir he is, to enfeoff him with his manor of Houghton in Norfolk, which is held of the King, towards the ransom and his maintenance, for the said Sir Randulph is so impoverished through ransoms paid for his sons that he has nothing with which to help Ralph save by giving him his land (AP 6512).

A nostre seignur le Roi moustre Rauf de Neuille qe com monsieur Robert de Neuille son frer fut tue par les enemys Descotz e sire Alexandre de Neuille e Johan de Neuille ses freres e il mesmes pris a mesme la iorne e ses deus freres detenuz tanqe il vrrunt grante ransone paye: E il mesmes est mys aransone de deus Mile mars, pur queus ses ostages demorunt tanqe les deners soent payez ou qe son corps seit reentre: Dount il pri a nostre seignur le Roy siluy pleise qil luy voille de sa grace eider deuers sa ransone de asqune garde, mariage ou autre chose de qei il pust deners prendre en eide de sa ransone. E qil voille doner le conge a sire Randolf' de Neuille son pier qi heir il est de feffer luy de son Maner de Houton' en Norffolk, qest tenue de nostre seignur le Roy, en eide de la ransone le dit Rauf' e de sa sustenaunce, car le dit sire Randolf est si enpouery par ransones qil ad paye pur ses fiz qil nad rien dount il pust eider le dit Rauf forqe a doner luy de sa tere.

Endorsed: Le Roi en voet auer auis.
Le Roi ad grantez le conge del feffement.

c. 1320. Robert de Neville, 'Peacock of the North', having killed his kinsman Richard Marmaduke on Framwellgate Bridge, Durham, in 1318, undertook war-service against the Scots to avoid standing trial but was killed outside Berwick the following year (GEC, *Complete Peerage* ix, 498–99). Ralph was of the King's household and steward to Edward III from October 1330 to March 1336 (*HBC*, p. 75). The licence for Ranulph, son and heir of Mary de Neville, to enfeof Ralph with his manor of Houghton is dated 28 October 1320 (*CPR 1317–21*, p. 514). The petition is calendared in Bain iii, 101.

133

The prior and convent of Durham petition the King and Council that whereas they are destroyed by the Scottish war, which has lasted long, and by incursions of the enemy, who often have burnt and devastated them, and by other oppressions and notably by their last coming with the connivance of certain of the King's enemies, whereby these Scottish enemies stayed from the Friday after St. Hilary until the Saturday before Candlemas, burning the prior's manors, vills, churches, granges and corn, capturing and leading away his tenants, killing some, ransoming others, so that those remaining cannot maintain their land, oxen, cows, sheep, work-horses and farm implements being taken away, so that nothing remains on which to live, promote hospitality or sustain other charges. They crave the King, by his affection for St Cuthbert and the church of Durham, to ordain some aid and sustenance so they may live and maintain divine service there until God in his grace and royal aid brings improvement (AP 2160).

A nostre seignour le Roi e a son counseil moustrent ses Chapeleins le Priour e le Couent de Duresme qe comme il soient destrutz par la guerre descoce qe por grant temps ad dure, et par la suruenue des enemys descoce, qe souent les ount ars et destrutz, et por autres diuerses oppressions il ount suffert par resun de la guerre, e nomement par la drein venue des auantditz enemys descoce par acord et assent des ascuns enemys le dit nostre seignour le Roi Dengleterre en Engleterre, issi qe par la demoere des ditz enemys descoce del venderdi apres la seint Hillar' iusqes la samadie proschein deuant le Chaundelour les manoirs le dit Priour, ses viles, ses eglises, ses graunges e ses bleez arstrent e destruistrent, ses tenantz pristrent e esmeneient, ascuns tuerent, asquns mistrent por rauncoun, issi qe ceux qe sont demorez ne sont de poer a terre tenir, ses boefs, vasches, Berby, cheuaux de Harace e tut autre manere de moeble pristrent e emporterent et enchacerent, par quoi rien ne lour demora de quoi il pount viure, hospitaute tenir ou autres charges sustenir, dont il prient nostre seignour le Roi qe pur laffeccion qil ad deuers le gloriouse corps seint Cuthbert e leglise de Duresme e por les almes de ses auncestres, por oeure de charite e pur le bien de lui mesmes, qil voille ordeiner asqune eide e sustenance por eux dont il pount viure e la seruice dieu meintenir en mesme le lieu, tanqe deus par sa grace e le eide de lui y mette amendement.

Endorsed: Coram Rege—Herl[aston]

1322. On 'the Friday after St Hilary 1321' [15 January 1322] Thomas Randolf, earl of Moray and leader of a Scottish invasion party, issued from Corbridge a safe-conduct for emissaries from Thomas of Lancaster to last until 15 August following (*CCR 1318–1323*, p. 525; cf Barrow, p. 343). This incursion may be the one referred to by Robert de Graystanes, when the Scots burnt the priory granges 'full of grain' and by a feint towards Richmondshire were able to take in their beds the men and women who had rashly returned from places of refuge in Cleveland in the belief that the Scots had gone south. Strictly construed, however, the chronicler is writing of a raid in 1323 (*Scrip Tres*, 102).

134

The King's poor men of Auckland petition the King that whereas they have nothing on which to live through many devastations by the Scots, and to save their lives they took victuals sold at Newcastle upon Tyne amounting to £19 12s and have nothing from which to raise the money, they crave his highness to consider their great losses suffered and their readiness to suffer for his honour in the future. May he allow towards this debt a bill of £30 due to them from the time that sir Roger de Northburgh was Treasurer of his Wardrobe, and may they have letters to the collectors of his money at Durham to accept this bill in allowance of the debt (AP 13516).

A nostre seignur le Roi prient ses poures gentz de Aukeland de si come il nauoient rien dont viuere pur plusurs destructions qil ount eu par les Escoces mes pristrent pur lour vie sauuer de ses vitailles qe furunt venduz a Noef Chastel sur Tyne a la mountaunce de .xix. li' .xij. s. e il nount riens dount leuer ceux deners, Mes prient a sa haut seignur quil enueille auoir regard a lour grauntz damages quil suffrirent e autre foitz prest serrunt a suffrir pur son honur, qil les vueille allouer en cele dete vne bille de .xxx. li' dues a ceux del temps qe sire Roger de Northburgh' fust son tresorer de sa garderobe e quil enpuissont auoir ses lettres as coillours de ses deners a Duresme qil enueillent prendre cele bille en allouaunce de la dette auantdite.

Endorsed: Le Rey veut estre payr de la vente et payera ses dettes

quant il verra etc.   videtur consilio quod est faciendum
si placeat Regi set tamen coram Rege.

c. 1323. Roger Northburgh was Keeper of the Wardrobe between
February 1316 and May 1322 (*HBC*, p. 78). A directive requiring
strict payment for surplus victuals was issued to the Treasurer
of the Exchequer on 4 December 1323 (PRO, QR Mem Roll
97 m 30; cf. *North'd Pet*, pp. 148, 189, 194–7, 243).

135

The prior and convent of Hexham petition the King that they
are destroyed by the Scottish war and crave as aid towards their
maintenance the escheated land in Silksworth of Sir Thomas, late
earl of Lancaster, to hold of the King at the assised rent. They
held land of Thomas in the township in [free] alms (AP 15562).

A nostre [seignur le Roy prien]t ces pouers Chapeleyns Priour
et Couent de Hextildesham qi sount destrutz par la guer descoce
qil les voille granter d . . . . . com en eyde de lour sustenaunce,
pur lamour de deu et les almes ces Auncestres, la tere qe luy est
escheu en la ville de Silkesword' par la mort monsz Thomas iadis
Count de Lancastre a tenir de nostre seignur le Roy enrendaunt
a son escheker la Rente assise, en quele ville ces dits [Chap]eleyns
⟨tyndrent⟩ de dist Thomas partye des teres en almones.

Endorsed: Coram Rege

c. 1323. Silksworth had formed part of the estates of John
Marmaduke, lord of Horden, whose son Richard alienated part
of these lands to the earl of Lancaster in exchange for estates further
to the south (G. A. Holmes, *The Estates of the Higher Nobility
in XIV century England* (1957), p. 137; cf. Durham, Misc Charters
6261–72). In the event Silksworth went to Richard Emeldon,
mayor of Newcastle and King's agent in northern parts, who had
been appointed in May 1322 to seek out and keep the lands lately
of Thomas of Lancaster. On 5 June 1323 he was made an interim
grant of two-thirds of Silksworth, converted to a permanent grant
on 24 March 1324, with the dower reversion (*CPR 1321–24*,
pp. 161, 292, 398). Cf. nos 191, 192 below.

136

Gilbert de Toutheby petitions the King that for his great losses from the Scots on his lands in the bishopric of Durham he may be pardoned a debt of £67 10s owed for wardship of the land and the heir of Robert de Bauent, bought of the King's father (AP 3778).

A nostre seignur le Roi pri Gilbert de Toutheby que pur les grantz pertes qil ad eu par resoun de les Escoc[es] de totes ses terres qil ad en Leuesche de Duresme, qil luy plese de sa grace perdoner luy .lxvij. li' .x. s. queux il luy deit pur la garde de le terre et del heir Robert de Bauent, la quele il achata de nostre seignur le Roi son pere que dieux absoille.

Endorsed: Il semble al counseyl qe ceo est almoyne a faire sil plest al Roi.   Il plest au Roi et pur ceo eyt pardoun.

1327. Toutheby was a lawyer who served on the council of Bishop Bek (*Bek*, pp. 103, 206; *Boldon Buke*, p. xxxv) and later was a serjeant at law to Edward II (*Select Pleas . . . IV* (Selden Soc. 74; 1955), p. 120). On 18 October 1320 he fined in 350 marks payable in instalments of 58 marks 4s 5d for wardship of the lands lately of Robert de Bavent, tenant in chief, with marriage of the heir (*CFR* iii, 35–36). His pardon for £67 10s out of 300 marks for the wardship was granted on 26 September 1327 (*CPR 1327–30*, p. 171).

137

Roger de Esshe petitions the King and Council that when the King was at Stanhope in the bishopric of Durham his men came in force to Esh and seized, cut and carried his corn and his hay worth £40, and took and drove off from him and his men 32 great beasts and 88 muttons without making payment. He craves an enquiry in consideration of his great loss, as often before he was burnt and destroyed by the Scots (AP 2237).

A nostre seignur le Roi et a son conseil moustre Roger de Esshe qe come nostre dit seignur le Roi fut en leuesche de Duresme

a Stanhope la vyndrent les gentz le Roi a force a Esshe et les
bleez le dit Roger et ses preez a la value de qaraunt liures sierent,
faucherent et emporterent, et trent et deux gros bestes et quatre
vyntz et ouyt motouns de luy et de ses gentz pristerent et enchacerent sanz paiement faire: dount le dit Roger prie a nostre
dit seignur le Roi qe il voille de sa grace faire enquere la verite
et faire a luy ascun regarde de sa grant perde auantdit, desicome
il ad souent este en temps passe ars et destrut par les enemys
Descoce.

Endorsed: Soient certeines gentz assignez denquere la manere de
cest fait et lenqueste ent returne en Chauncellerie soit fait droit.

1327. Edward III was at Stanhope in pursuit of the Scots in July
1327 (R. Nicholson, *Edward III and the Scots*, (1965), pp. 29–30).
Roger de Eshe was a substantial landowner near Durham (*Reg
Pal Dun* i, 256–58). He served as a justice of assize on numerous
occasions for Bishop Bury (Deputy Keeper's Report XXXI,
(1870), 61, 103–5).
AP 2238 is a duplicate, endorsed 'coram rege'.

138

The prior and convent of Durham petition the bishop of Winchester, chancellor of England, that whereas they had victuals of
the late King, father of the present King, amounting to £300,
of which they have paid £200, the house of Durham is devastated
by the Scots, namely their lands in Northumberland, in the
bishopric, and in Scotland, and often has been burdened by the
coming of kings. They crave for the love of God and St. Cuthbert
a writ and aid from the King for release from the £100, as was
done for all other abbeys and priories in Northumberland. All
the bulk of their sustenance was in the county of Northumberland
(AP 2159).

A treshonurable piere en dieu Leuesqe de Wyncestre Chaunceler
Dengleterre prient le Priour et le Couent de Duresme qe come
ils aueient des vitailes du Roi qi mort est, piere nostre seignur
le Roi qore est, a la mountant de .CCC. li' des queux ils vnt

pae les .CC., et la maison de Duresme est destruyt par les enemis
Descoce comme de lour terres de Northumbr', et Lesueschee et
de Escoce, et est souent chargee pur venuz des Rois; qe vous,
sire, por dieu et pur lamour de seynt Cuthbert voillez faire le
bref et mettre vostre bone eide deuers nostre dit seignur le Roi
qe les dites .C. li' seient relessez sicome qeles est fait as tous autres
Abbayes et Priouries de Northumbr'. Et, sire, tote la force de
nostre sustenance fust en le dit Contee de Northumbr'.

Endorsed: Y semble au conseil sil plese au Roi, pur ceo qe les ditz
Priour et Couent ount suffert et pris grantz malz par les Enemis
et le Roi ad fait pardoun au tutz autres de pais, qe le Roi pardonir
a eaux les dites cent liures come est demande en la peticion.

1333. On 2 August 1333 the prior and convent of Durham were
pardoned their outstanding debt of £100 (*CPR 1330–34*, p. 461).

139

Their poor chaplains the prior and convent of Durham petition
the King and Council that whereas the great part of their
sustenance is in northern parts on the Scottish border, of which
the greater part is destroyed by the Scots, and one of their cells,
called Coldingham and Coldinghamshire, within the border is
worth 1000 marks a year, of which they and their predecessors
were always in peaceful seisin both in time of war as in time of
peace as of right of their church of St. Cuthbert and as parcel
of the kingdom of England: they were ousted from the cell by
Robert Stuward, guardian of Scotland, who claims he is King
of Scotland, and it is occupied by the earl of the Scottish March
to the disinheritance of the King and his crown and the destruction
of the house of the prior and convent of Durham. They request
the King and Council to ordain some remedy as now they hear
that at Scottish instigation the pope has provided a cardinal to
the cell (AP 5312).

A nostre seignour le Roi et son conseil moustrent ses pours
Chapeleyns le Prior et Couent de Duresme qe par la eu le grant
partie de leur sustenance si est es parties de North' sur lez Marche
Descoce, dont le greyndre partie est destruyt par enemys Descoce,

et vn lour selle appelle Coldyngham et Coldynghamshire, dedeinz les Marche susditz de la value de .Mille. marcz par an, de quele ils et lours predecessours de tout temps sibien en temps de guerre come en temps de Pees ount este seises peisiblement come de dreit de lour eglise de seint Cuthbert de Duresme et come parcelle del Roialme Dengleterre, de quele selle les ditz Priour et Couent sont oustez par Robert Stuward' gardeyn du Roialme Descoce qe se dit le Roi Descoce et ocupie par le Count de Marche Descoce en desheritesoun nostre seignour le Roi et sa corone et distruccion del Meson les ditz Priour et Couent de Duresme: Pur qei pleise a nostre tresexcellent seignour le Roi et son tresnoble conseil en oeure de charite et pur lamour le gloriousse confessour seinte Cuthbert de Duresme ent ordeigner remedie, et ore de nouelle, com les ditz Priour et couent ount entenduz, a le instance Descocez le seint Pier lappostelle ad puruieu vn Cardinale a mesme le selle, ad quele auxint les ditz Priour et couent Priount remedie.

Endorsed: Soient les sieurs qi serront apres Nowel a le grant iour de la Marche chargez de ent treter diligeaument pur le reparement auoir par due manere des ditz attemptatz.

1346–57. During the captivity of David II in England his nephew Robert Steward acted as guardian of Scotland. A memorandum of ?1358 written by the chamberlain of Berwick admitted that at the release of King David the barony of Coldingham in Scotland was 'by negligence' given to the Scots and the King's lieges mulcted in large sums for customs on wool etc by the 'priseur' (Bain iv, 5). As regards the implied claim that Coldingham contributed materially to the revenue of Durham priory, tithes and other receipts from the churches of Earlston, Ednam, Aldcambus and Edrom in 1328/9 amounted to £143 14s 8d, as was recorded on Durham, Bursars Account, but later ceased. The Coldingham priory receipts as printed suggest two hiatuses. There is a reference to shortage of tenants in 1345, and the assized rents, which were worth £81 13s 8½d in 1355/6, had fallen to £6 13s 6d in 1356/7 (*The Priory of Coldingham*, ed. J. Raine, (Surtees Soc 12; 1841), 32, xvii, xxx, xxxi).

Clerical

The clerical petitions are mainly to request the King to reverse presentments to livings made during vacancies of the see. One alleged the deliberate manipulation of a jury of enquiry (no. 144). The King's aid was invoked in the long-standing process by the Prior and Convent of Durham to obtain the appropriation of Hemingbrough (no. 145). Eventually in 1427 Prior Wessington secured permission to convert the rectory into a college, which at least enabled the Convent to reward its friends and clerical advisers with prebends (R. B. Dobson, *Durham Priory: 1400–1450* (1973), pp. 93, 156–62).

Ancient Petitions 3072, 3524, 3695, 5024, 5315, 5336, 7949, 9151, 11088, 12008, 12390, 12491, 12497, 12967.

140

John de Sneyton petitions the King that whereas Richard, lately bishop of Durham, in his lifetime gave him the church of Whitburn, then void by the resignation of sir William de Ayremynne, and he was in peaceful possession in the bishop's lifetime, Nicholas de Welleburn later gave the King to understand that the church was void following the bishop's death, and by reason of this untruth had presentation by the King and had John wrongfully ejected. John sued Nicholas in the Court Christian touching this, but Nicholas used forged public instruments and by allegation that this matter touched the King's right brought royal letters under the privy seal to the judges and others, whereby John was unduly delayed in his suit. He petitions the King for instructions to the judges and others to do justice to him in this matter, according to Holy Church; and the King should ask sir William de Ayremynne the truth of the matter, as he knows it well (AP 3695).

A nostre seignur le Roy moustre Johan de Sneynton' que com Richard iadys Euesque de Durrem ly auoit en sa vie done la eglise de Whitebern' que adonque fust voide par le resignement sire William de Ayremynne et le dit Johan feust en peisible possession

de cele eglise viuaunt le dit Euesque, Nichol de Welleburn' apres
fist entendaunt au dit nostre seignur le Roy que la eglise feust
voide apres la mort le dit Euesque, par quele suggestion noun
verraie il auoit presentement de nostre seignur le Roy a cele eglise
e par colur de cel presentement est le dit Johan ouste de cele eglise
a tort, e de ceo se est pleynt en la Court Cristien countre le dit
Nichol sicom appent a la conissaunce de saynte eglise en tiel cas,
en quele busoigne le dit Nichol ad faus Instrumentz publiz, e les
ad vse en Iugement e ia du meyns, par suggestion qil fait a nostre
seignur le Roi que cele busoigne touche son droit, porte lettres
de nostre seignur le Roy sur sa targe as Juges e autres du conseil
le dit Johan countre ly pur le dit Nichol de requeste et maundement: Issint que le dit Johan est delaie en le sute noun duement
par tieles lettres: par quoi il prie a nostre seignur le Roi qil voille
maunder as ditz Juges e autres qe lentente nostre seignur le Roy
nest pas qe par encheison de ses requestes ne maundementz eux
ne lessent de faire droit al dit Johan sur la dite busoigne, sicom
appent a seynte eglise. E de ceste chose pleise a nostre seignur
le Roy denquerre la verite de sire William de Ayremynne, car
il le siet bien.

Endorsed: Mandetur per breue de Magno sigillo Judicibus et aliis
ad quos pars ipsa petere voluerit, et quod voluntatis seu intencionis
Regis nunquam extitit nec existit quod ob aliquem ipsius rogatum
seu mandatum omittere debeant quicquam quod ad ipsos dino-
scitur pertinere in suis processibus per censuram ecclesiasticam
factis vel in hac parte faciendis.

1317. The presentation of Ayremynne to Whitburn had been
made by Edward II *sede vacante*, following the resignation on
14 April 1311 by William de Bordis, bishop-elect of Lectoure.
The pope substituted Berald de Farges, whose proctor, John de
Pollowe, disputed the attempt to present Ayremynne (*Reg Pal
Dun* i, 181–85). On 28 September 1312 a commission was issued
by Bishop Kellawe to remove Farges in favour of Ayremynne:
and Ayremynne was instituted on 13 June 1313, following an
agreement reached with Farges's proctor on 16 May and suit in
the King's court (*ibid.*, i, 199, 354–55, 357–59: ii, 933–34).
Ayremynne, who was a King's clerk, resigned Whitburn in 1316,
when Bishop Kellawe granted the living on 24 June 1316 to Master

John de Snayton junior, nephew of Master John de Snayton, the bishop's proctor at Rome (*ibid.*, ii, 811, 1403). With the death of Bishop Kellawe on 9 October 1316, however, Nicholas de Welburn obtained from Edward II a writ of presentation to Whitburn dated 23 October 1316 (*CPR 1313–17*, p. 556). On 18 May 1317 the King ordered the keeper of the spiritualities of the archbishopric of York to proceed with Snayton's appeal, but this order was reversed on 16 June 1317. Subsequently the King obtained a judgment in court against Kellawe's successor, Bishop Beaumont, and on 15 July 1323 a royal prohibition was issued against any disturbing Welburn in his possession of Whitburn (*CCR 1313–18*, pp. 409, 471, 483; *CPR 1321–24*, p. 325). The rectory was valued at £40 in 1292, although it fell to £26 13s 4d in the new assessment of 1318 (*Taxatio Papae Nicholai IV*, (1802), p. 314). Cf. no. 24 above.

141

Hugh de Mohaut, master of Kepier Hospital near Durham by collation of the bishop of Durham, petitions the King and Council that Simon de Eycot of the King's household wrongfully came to Kepier Hospital on Sunday, 31 October 1316, and claimed the King's collation to the hospital on supposition that it was void, whereas it was full and occupied by Hugh, and he ejected him by force and wasted and destroyed his goods. He craves restitution of possession (AP 3072).

A nostre seignur le Roi et a son conseil moustre son chapelyn dan Hugh' de Mohaut, Mestre del Hospital de Kypier pres de Durem de la collacion Leuesque de Durem et seisi fust tout son temps, qe Symond de Eycot de son menage atort vient le dymange en la eueille de touz seynz lan du regne nostre seignur le Roi qe dieu gard disme al dit Hospital de Kypier disant sei auoir collacion de nostre seignur le Roi del dit Hospital, en supposant le Hospital estre voide ou il est pleyn et councilie del dit dan Hugh', et lui emeta del Hospital susdit a force et les biens de la eyntz gaste et destrut atort, dount il pri a nostre seignur le Roi grace qil puisse estre restitut a sa possessioun desicome il fust sanz agarde et iugement oste.

Endorsed: Habeat breue de Cancellaria de venire faciendo Clericum Regis coram ipso Rege ad certum diem et ibi fiat partibus Justicia. Irrotulatur

1316 x 1320. Hugh de Mohaut was receiver-general to Bishop Kellawe from 1311 to 1314 and master of Kepier between 1311 and 1316 and again between 1320 and 1340 (*Reg Pal Dun* i, 128, 492; *Fasti*, p. 89). Simon de Eycote was granted custody of Kepier by Edward II on 17 October 1316 and ejected Mohaut a fortnight later; but on 22 November 1320 Mohaut was reinstated, the King's warrant being notified by Master Robert de Baldock (*CPR 1317–21*, p. 529).

142

His chaplains, the Prior and Convent of Durham, petition the King for the love of God and St. Cuthbert to confirm the deeds of his father and his ancestors and the bishops of Durham, for the health of his church of Durham and honour of the saint's body, which has been reverenced by him and his ancestors (AP 12008).

A nostre seignour le Roy prient ses Chapeleyns le Priour et le Couent de Duresme qe li voille de sa grace, pur lamour de dieu et de seint Cuthbert, confermer les faitz de soun Peer et de sez Auncestres et des Euesqes de Duresme, pur saluacioun de sa Eglise de Duresme et honour del Corps seint, qe molt ad este honure de lui et de sez Auncestres.

No endorsement

1319. The warrant for execution is dated 16 September 1319 from 'the siege of Berwick' (*Cal Chancery Warrants* i, 502).

143

Robert de Warthecoppe, parson of Washington, petitions the King and Council that whereas his church is charged with divers pensions and a portion totalling 22 marks [£14 13s 4d] appropriated to various religious houses in the bishopric of Durham, the church with these being assessed at £22 10s, and he is ready to pay the tenth granted to the King in respect of his share, less the portion and pensions, the collectors of the tenth in the bishopric have levied a tenth on the total assessment, so favouring the monasteries. Whereas he is not required to pay on the 22 marks, which are spiritual rent, the collectors have charged him beyond his share with a tenth on the portion and pensions, amounting to 2 marks 2s 8d [29s 4d] for each tenth granted to the King, as well as other papal impositions and the finding of expenses of the cardinals, without regard for the heavy annual charges on the church. He craves the King and Council for a writ to the collectors, that those deriving pensions and the portion be charged with the royal tenth according to their share and that allowance be made to him of what they levied additionally from him (AP 12967).

Au nostre seignur le Roi et son conseil prie son cler Robert de Warthecoppe, persone de la eglise de Wessyngton', qe come sa dite eglise soit charge de diuerses empensions et dune porcion qe amontent a .xxij. marcs apropers a diuers mesons de Religion en leueschee de Duresme, et mesme leglise ensemblement ouesqe celle empensions et portion sont taxez a. .xxij. li' et .x. s., et tout soit ceo qe la dite persone soit prest de paier la disme grantee au nostre seignur le Roi si auant come a sa por[cion] auient de la dite taxe, outre la somme des porcion et empensions susdites lui ont uieyns, les Coilliours des dismes en le dit Eueschee en fauour des dits Religiouses ont leue de dit Robert la disme de tote la taxe susdite issint qe la ou le dit Robert ne nest tenuz de paier qe .xxij. marcs des empensions et porcion susdites quele sont rentes espritiels si auant come la dite eglise, ⟨de⟩ ceo lui ont desditz Coillours charge de paier outre sa porcion de leglise, cest assauoir la disme pur mesme les porcion et empensions qe amontent a .ij. marcz .ij. s. viij. d. en chescune disme grantee al Rei et auxi des autres imposicions par le pape ou a trouer despenses des Cardinals, nemye eiant regard as greuouse charges de denairs dont leglise est annuelment charge. Pleise al dit nostre seignur et son bone counseil comander brief as ditz Coilliours qe les parnours des empensions et porcion susditz soient chargez chescun solonc sa porcion de paer dismes al Roi, qe de celles dismes allouance soit fait al dit Robert de ceo qils leue de lui outre la Rate de la taxe auantdit.

Endorsed: Eit bref as Tresorer et Barons de lescheqer qils facent venir deuant eux les ditz religiouses a certein iour a moustrer sils sacheit riens dire pur quei ils ne deuient estre chargez de la disme, chescun solonc les pensions et porcions qils pernent de la dite eglise et illoqes d... les resons dune partie et dautre outre soit fait droit et reson a la dite persone.

1353 x 1366. There is no indication of recipients of portions or pensions at Washington in the *Taxatio* of 1292. Robert of Warcop, keeper of the King's victuals in 1341 and a chancery clerk, exchanged the rectory of Spettisbury, co. Dorset, for Washington in 1353 (*CPR 1350–54*, p. 485; *Fasti*, p. 136). His tenure was challenged in 1363, when Thomas de Penreth, priest, was presented by Pope Urban V on the grounds that Warthecoppe was holding the benefice without dispensation for the fact that he was illegitimate. Subsequently Warthecoppe's position was regularised on 15 March 1364 (*Cal Pap Reg: Petitions* i, 419, 483).

<h1 style="text-align:center">144</h1>

Alan de Schutlyngdon, clerk, lately keeper of Sherburn Hospital in the bishopric of Durham, petitions the King and Council that whereas he held the same for long time by gift of the present Bishop of Durham, a writ of *quare impedit* was served on him at the King's suit on supposition that the hospital fell void in the time of Richard de Bury, late Bishop of Durham, following the death of Thomas de Hessewell, then master, and remained vacant until the temporalities came into the King's hand after the death of Bury. In fact in the time of Bury the hospital was given to Master Thomas de Neville immediately after Hessewell's death by Master John de Why[t]chirch, the bishop's vicar-general, having full power to donate all benefices and hospitals in his patronage (the bishop being abroad on the King's business at Antwerp), which was subsequently granted and confirmed by the bishop to Master Thomas. Master Thomas held the hospital for years under Bury and a further 16 years under the present bishop until his death, so that the hospital could not be void after the death of Bury, when the temporalities were in the King's hands, nor by any other cause might its presentation belong to the King. Now of late, as Schutlyngdon is willing to prove, a panel was summoned by a *nisi prius* before the King's judges at Newcastle,

consisting of men drawn from the furthest parts of Northumberland and of little worth, having neither sufficient land to be
knight nor sergeant, and some no land at all, not summoned by
the sheriff nor on a given day, but suddenly brought to the town
the day after the *nisi prius* at sunrise by Sir Alan de Heton and
other enemies of the said Alan de Schutlyngdon. On such testimony and disregarding consideration of the rights of Schutlyngdon the only verdict that they could give was that the hospital
was void, as they were informed by the enemies of Schutlyngdon,
and judgment was given against him, and he was ejected contrary
to right. He craves the King and Council for remedy and the
discovery of his right, and reconsideration as justice requires, notwithstanding the process and judgment above given. Because
none can have remedy by common process of law where the
King is a party without special leave, may it please the King to
summon before the same judges the sheriff, undersheriff and other
ministers present at the inquest, to be examined on oath about
the truth of these things, and may he have a verdict passed by
the knights and the better-informed of those parts, for other than
by King and Council the complainant may not have his right
adjudged (AP 3524).

A nostre seignur le Roi et a son consail moustre Alein de
Schutlyngdon' clerk, nadgaire gardein del hospital de Schirburn
deinz leueschee de Duresme, qe com il eust et tignt le dit hospital de lung' temps del doun leuesqe de Duresme qore est et ia vn
bref de quare impedit estoit porte sur lui a la suit nostre dit
seignur le Roi de mesme lospital, supposant le dit hospital estre
voide en le temps Richard de Bury nadgairs Euesqe de Duresme
apres la mort Thomas de Hessewell' adonqes meistre du dit
Hospital et ensi voide demurrir tanqe les temporaltes deuindrent
en les meins nostre dit seignur le Roi apres la mort le dit
Richard de Bury; la ou en le temps le dit Richard de Bury le
dit Hospital estoit done a meistre Thomas de Neuille immediat
apres la mort le dit Thomas de Hessewell' par mestre Johan de
Why[t]chirch, viker general le dit Euesqe Richard, eiant de lui
plein poair et general de donir toutz les benefices et hospitals de
son patronage (lui esteant en le message nostre seignur le Roi es
parties de delai a Andewerp), et puis par le dit Euesqe Richard
le dit Hospital grauntez et confermez au dit meistre Thomas, par

qeux doune et confermement le dit meistre Thomas tigne le dit
Hospital ans et iours en le temps le dit Richard de Bury et sesze
ans en le temps leuesqe qore est, toutefoitz continuant sa
possession tanqe sa mort, issint qe le dit Hospital en nulle maner
purroit estre voide apres la mort du dit Richard, esteantz les
temporaltes en les meins nostre dit seignur le Roi, ne par tielle
cause ne par autre cause, colour ou droit purroit acrestre a nostre
seignur le Roi auantdit de donir le dit Hospital; et ia tarde par
vertu dun Nisi prius pris deuant les Justices nostre seignur le Roi
a Neofchastiell' par gentz loingteins de pluis foreins lieus del
Countee de Northumbr' et de gentz de petit valu n[i]ent eiantz
terres suffisantz Chiualer ne seriant, de valu leinz et ascuns nulle
terre eiant', ne vnqes somons par viscont ne iour auoient mes
sudungnement mene a la ville lendemain [apres] la iour del Nisi
prius a houre de prime par sire Alein de Heton et autres
aduersairs du dit Alein de Shutlyngdon' et par lour deuys en-
panellez et mesme le panel ensemblement od le brief adonqes et
venuz deuant liuerez au dit viscont, come le dit Alein est et touz
iours serra prest de moustrer a nostre dit seignur le Roi et a son
consail auandit par toutz les voies qe a son dit seignur plerra et a
son sage consail ordeigner; et sur ceo pur verdit de tiels gentz
procurez et nient eiantz ne auoir voillantz conissaunce de con-
sideracion du droit de dit Alein coment qil lour moustra son droit
deuant les Justices nostre seignur le Roi par les euidences des-
suisdits, les qeux il est vnqore prest a moustrer, ne vnqes ne
sauoient verdit donire mes qe lospital fust voide come ils estoient
enfourmez par les aduersairs du dit Alain, iuggement est rendu
encontre lui et le dit Alein mis hors de son hospital auandit,
encontre dreite et bone conscience; qe plese a nostre tresexcellent
seignur le Roi et a son consail pur lamour de dieu et en oeure
de charite ordeiner qe le dit Alein poesse auoir remedie en celle
partie et descoueir son droit et de ceo fair discussion solonc ceo
qe bone conscience et dreit demandent, nientcontreestant les
proces et le iuggement en la fourme suisdit sur ceo renduz; dis-
sicome nulle ne poet auoir remedie par voie datteint la ou nostre
dit seignur le Roi est partie sanz especial conge de lui et en cas
qe plerroit a nostre dit seignur le Roi de sa grace, fair venir
deuant mesmes les Justices, viscont, et southviscont et autres
ministres nostre seignur le Roi qe furent presente au [jour] du dit
enqueste pres destre iurez examinez sur la verite de choses suis-

ditz, sit autre ent grantir, qe le dit Alein purra auoir latteint a passer par chiualers et meuth auuez de celles parties, car a autre qe a sa tresgracious seignurie et a son consail ne poet home compleint ne pursuit de son droit aiugez.

No endorsement

1362 x 1366. Alan of Shitlington was vicar-general and steward of Bishop Hatfield. His benefices included Middleton St. George, 1339–65, and Hemingburgh (E. Yorkshire), 1348–75 (*Fasti*, p. 118). In 1366 Pope Urban V deprived him of Sherburn hospital as he held no scholastic degree and collated Walter de Wandsworth, BA and scholar in theology (*Cal Pap Reg: Petitions* i, 536–37). In 1348 Alan had received a papal dispensation to study canon or civil law at some university (*ibid.*, 144).

AP 7949 is an alternative version, with the endorsement:
   Soit le Roi pleinement enfourme de ceste matire et sur ce dit sa volunte

145

The King's chaplains, the Prior and Convent of Durham, petition the King and Council that whereas the King gave them leave to appropriate the church of Hemingbrough in return for great spiritual charges on behalf of the King, his heirs and progenitors when the appropriation should be accomplished, and in return his chaplains released to the King the annual sum of £40 from the subsidy on wool at Berwick, granted by King Edward the King's grandfather and confirmed by the present King. And although the King often requested the Pope for this appropriation and the chaplains worked diligently at great expense and cost, they could not bring about the appropriation and were given a negative answer. Therefore they crave that the patent for £40 from the customs be renewed and re-affirmed as before, having regard to the fact that since the time of the release leave was given by the Pope for the appropriation of Simonburn church to Windsor chapel at the King's request, and also that the cell of Coldingham in Scotland is taken from them, from which they should have had great profit, so that on all sides they are grievously brought to nothing unless they can be relieved by the King (AP 5336).

A lour redote seignur nostre seignur le Roy et son grant
consaille prient ses Chapelleyns Priour et Couent de Duresme qe
come nostre dit seignur de sa grace especiale dona congie as
cez ditz Chapeleins daropriere a eux et lours successours la
eglise de Hemmyngburgh, supportanz grand' gargez (*sic*) espiritels
pur le dit congie pur nostre dit seignur le Roi, cez heirs et cez
progenitours pur la dite esglise qant ele serra aproprie duement,
en recompensacon de quel grant ses dit chapeleins relesseront a
nostre dit seignur .xl. li.' annuele del subsidie des leins a Berwyk
sur Twede grante a eux par le Roi Edward laiel et comferme par
nostre dit seignur le Roy qorest perpetuelment a durere. E
coment qe nostre dit seignur le Roy souent par ces lettres ad
supplie a nostre seint Piere le pape pur lapropriacoun de la
dite esglise et qe cez ditz chapeleins, as greuouse mises et
costages, eient mys lour diligence en celle partie ils ne poent
ascunment aue[nire] a la dite apropriacoun mes sont respondu
autrement qe iammes ne le aueront. Pur quei plese en oeure de
charite auoir regard a la bene feie et conscience et comander
qe la dite patent de la custome de .xl. li' soit renouelle et
afferme adurere en le primer course qils le auoient deuant la
dite relesse, eiant regard qe entre la dite relesse faite a dit
seignur ils donerent congie daproprier la esglise de Simondburn'
a la chapell de Windesore a la request nostre dit seignur le
Roy. Et auxint qe la celle de Coldyngham en la terre Descoce
leur est tollet de quel celle ils soleit reporter grant profit, issint
qe de toutez pars ils sont grantement anientz et si par vostre
graciouse seignurie eus poent estre releuez.

No endorsement

?1376–77. The assignment on the Berwick customs was made by
Edward I in September 1296 (*Rot Scot* i, 34). The process for
appropriation of Hemingbrough was started by 1319, when the
Prior and Convent of Durham petitioned the Pope on the
grounds of their losses at the hands of the Scots (*Scrip Tres*, pp.
cxxii–iii). Despite his licence to Bishop Bury on 25 June 1338
to appropriate Simonburn to the use of the Durham monks'
cell at Oxford as a thank-offering for victory at Halidon Hill,

Edward III in 1351 granted the advowson and other property to the college of St. George at Windsor. This Simonburn appropriation had taken effect by 1367 (*NCH* xv, 168 [a very muddled account, as Hemingbrough had belonged to Durham from the eleventh century]). The King had signified his approval of the appropriation of Hemingbrough by the Prior and Convent on 6 March 1356 (*CPR 1354–58*, pp. 357, 363–64, 443). This was confirmed by the Pope on 22 October 1363, after approval had been given by the Archbishop of York (*Cal Pap Reg: Petitions* i, 464). Among the reasons for papal hesitation should be noted an order of 21 December 1372 from Pope Gregory XI to his nuncio in England, Simon, cardinal of St. Sixtus, to inform Edward III in response to representations on behalf of Durham that the house already had four dependent abbeys and two cells, all with reduced inmates, thirteen parish churches etc, and only 56 monks resident at Durham, who 'spend more on food and clothing than befits the modesty of their religion'. Rather than grant an unconditional appropriation Gregory threatened to order an enquiry into how many more monks the house could add, the value of the church, and provision for a perpetual vicar, should Hemingbrough be appropriated (*Cal Pap Reg* iv, 117–18). A papal order was sent on 28 January 1376 to the Official of York to confirm Thomas de Walleworth, clerk, if fit, to the church of Hemingbrough, vacant by the death of Alan de Schotlyngton (*ibid.*, 222). On 22 March 1381 Richard II confirmed the various licences of Edward III relating to Hemingbrough (*CPR 1381–85*, p. 10).

AP 5315 is virtually identical except for the reference to the late King Edward the King's grandfather. This is endorsed:
  Soient veues les endentures de couenantz ent faitz et autres euidences, si nulles y soient parentre le ditz Roy et Priour et Couent, et sur ce nostre seignur le Roi par auys de son conseil y ferra reson chescune part.

146

Thomas del Chaumbre and his fellows, farmers from a cardinal of Bishopwearmouth church in the bishopric of Durham, petition the King and Council that whereas for a year past they farmed the church from a Raymond Pelegryn, the cardinal's proctor, for specific terms of which two remain, a petition was submitted in the present parliament that no liege of the King be servant, proctor or farmer of cardinals or other aliens for benefices in this kingdom on pain of life and limb and forfeiture of their goods, which if granted in general would result in great loss and damage to Thomas and his fellow-farmers in respect of their tithes this year, their wheat sown and handiwork in the glebe, and many others of the kingdom are in the same plight, and also all such farmers will be excommunicated and lose great sums in which they are pledged to the papal chamber if they fail to pay their farm, both for the time when they take no profits from the churches and when they enjoyed them with profits. May it please the King and Council to consider the damage, and order that exception be made of farmers of churches leased from aliens previous to this present parliament, or otherwise ordain that they can occupy the churches for one year, until they have fully levied their profits, since they must necessarily be charged to pay the farms of the current year (AP 5024).

A nostre tresdoute et tresgraciouse seignur le Roi et a son sage conseille Moustre Thomas del Chaumbre et autres ses compaignons fermers a vn Cardinall' de lesglise de Bysshop' Warmouth deinz leueschie de Duresme, et par vn an passe furent fermers de la esglise suisdit de le lesse vn Raymond' Pelegryn procuratour de dit Cardinall' pur certeins termes deuz queux vnqore duront, qe com vne peticion soit mys sus en cest present parlement qe nulle liege home nostre dit seignur le Roi ne serra seruant, procuratour ou fermour as Cardinalx ou autres aliens de lour benefices en cest Roialme sur peine de vie et de membre et forfaiture de lour biens, quele peticion sil fuisse generalment grante serreit tresgrande perde et damage a dit Thomas et a ses compaignons fermers de lesglise suisdite de lour dismes a prendre de cest an et de lour blez semez et meynoeur faitz en les terres le dit personage, et a plusours autres de Roialme esteant en mesme le plite, et auxint touz tieux fermers susditz serront escomengez et perdrent grantz somes en queux ils sont liez al Chaumbre le Pape si eux ne paierent lour ferme sibien de temps qe eux ne pernerent my les profitz des ditz esglises com de temps qe eux occupierent et pristerent profitz, qe plese a nostre dit seignur le

Roi et a son conseille pur dieu et en oeure de charite de Veier et regarder as damages et meschiefs susditz, dordeigner qe forsprys soit fait des fermours des esglises des ditz aliens lessez a ferme deuant cest present parlement ou autrement ordeigner qe les ditz fermers puissent occupier les ditz esglises pur cest an tanqe eux eient pleinement leuie lours profit de lour esglises susditz, puisqe eux couient de necessite pleinement estre chargez de paier les fermes de cest an auantdit.

No endorsement

?1378. Robert of Geneva, cardinal-priest of the Twelve Apostles, leased his rectory of Bishopwearmouth in 1375 to John del Chambre and three others for five years at a rent of £250. This would suggest that the petition was presented at the October parliament of 1378. The statute, however, prohibiting foreign clerics from holding or leasing benefices in England was enacted in January 1380 (3 Ric II, c. 3). The cardinal's estates were subsequently sequestered by the King to pay for the ransom of one of his clerks. In 1378 Robert was elected as the anti-pope Clement VII against Urban VI, the pope recognised by Richard II (*Fasti*, p. 49–50).

147

The King by advice of Chancery has granted this bill.

Laurence de Allerthorp, master of the Hospital of St. Edmund at Gateshead, petitions the King that whereas he held the hospital by the collation of John, bishop of Durham, the patron, where institution and induction belongs to the ordinary, the King sued a *quare impedit* against the bishop and master Adam Fenrother, lately master, upon which writ they are at issue before the judges of Common Pleas; and now a Richard de Leuesham, to whom the King gave the hospital while the issue was still untried, has wrongly informed the King that he was properly in peaceful possession of the hospital collation and had been forcibly ejected, whereas he never had possession by institution and induction, as the law demands. In virtue of this allegation the King by letters patent under the great seal at Nottingham on 5 August [1383] assigned Thomas de Claxton, cousin of Richard, and William

Emeldon or one of them to maintain Richard and his proctors
in possession, by colour of which commission they purpose to
eject Laurence from possession. He craves a *supersedeas* directed
to Thomas and William to cease from execution of the commission as contrary to law and reason, as the plea is still before the
King's court (AP 11088).

le Roy ad graunter ceste bille par lauyz de chaunceleri.

Mountagu

A nostre tresredote seignur le Roy moustre laurence de Aller-
thorp' Mestre de lospital seynt Esmon de Gatesheued qe come il
tient le dit Hospital del la collacion lonorable pier en dieu Johan
Euesqe de Duresme, patron del dit Hospital, a quel Hospital apent
institucioun et induccion del Ordinar', et nostre dit seignur le
Roy ad porte vn quare impedit del dit Hospital deuers le dit
Euesqe et Mestre Adam Fenrother nadgaires Mestre del dit
Hospital, sur quel brief nostre dit seignur le Roy et les ditz
Euesqe et Adam sount a issue de pais come pleinement poet
apparer par le plee ent pendant deuant les Justices del comune
Bank', et ore vn Richard de leuesham, a qi nostre dit seignur le
Roy ad done le dit Hospital pendant le dit issue vnqore nient
trie, ad nonduement enfourme nostre dit seignur le Roi qe le
dit Richard est duement adhept (*sic*) paissible possession du dit
Hospital par vertu de la collacion auantdit, et qe ascuns safforcent
de luy oster induement de sa dite possession, la ou le dit Richard
nauoit vnqes possession par institucion et induccion del dit
Hospital sicome le ley demand'; par vertu de quelle suggestion
nostre dit seignur le Roi par ses lettres patentz de son grant seal
a Notingham le quint iour Daugst (*sic*) lan de soun regne septisme
ad assignez Thomas de Claxton', quest cosyn le dit Richard, et
William Emeldon ou lun deux de maintenir le dit Richard et ses
procuratours en possession del dit Hospital, par colour de quelle
comission les ditz Thomas et William sount [en] purpes douster
le dit laurence de sa dite possession del Hospital auantdit; qe pleast
nostre dit seignur le Roy de granter vn supersedeas direct' as
ditz Thomas et William de surseer del execution del dit comission
issint encontre ley et resone grante, consideres qe le plee est
vnqore ent pendant en la Court de Roy.

No written endorsement but a cruciform trace of red wax

1383. A royal order was issued on 30 October to Thomas de Claxton and William Elmeden to supersede their maintenance of Levisham and his proctors in the hospital of St. Edmund at Gateshead following the above petition. The collation had been made by the King pending a plea between the King and Bishop Fordham (with Adam Fenrothour) concerning the patronage of the hospital. John Montague was steward of the King's household between 1381 and 1387 (*CCR 1381–8*, pp. 406–7: *HBC*, p. 75).

148

The King has granted *scire facias*, and afterwards let justice be done

Thomas Cotham, holder of the prebend of the late John Kyngeston in the church of St. Cuthbert, Darlington, petitions that whereas by colour of a royal collation on behalf of a Robert Dalton, clerk, who has no right to it, Thomas has been disturbed in possession and vexed and sued in the King's courts against right and justice; he craves the King's majesty to command his Chancellor to issue a *scire facias* to summon Robert into the Chancery to show his pretended title, and unless he can show that the King has a clear right to grant the prebend the Chancellor is to revoke the King's letters patent of enfeofment and allow Thomas to sue in whatever court, church or lay, that seems best to secure peaceful possession. (AP 9151).

le Roy ad grante scire facias et apres la dite commission qe droit soit fait

A le tresexcellent tresredoute et tresgraciouse seignure seyngur le Roy Supplie vostre humble lige Thomas Cothom', prebender de la Prebende quele Johan Kyngeston' nadgaires quant il vesquis auoit en leglise de seint Cuthbert de derlyngton', qe come par colour dune vostre collacion fait de la dite Prebende a vn Robert Dalton' Clerc qi null' droit ad a ycelle le dit Thomas soit enquiete et destourbez de la possession quelle il ad en mesme sa prebende, et soit auxint par celle cause nonduement vexez et desesz en vos Courtz, contre tout droit et iustice: Plese a vostre roial maijeste commander vostre Chanceller qil face venir par vostre brief de Scire facias le dit Robert en vostre Chancellerie pur moustrer le title quel il le pretende dauoir en la dite prebende, et sil ne sceit moustrer qe vous auiez cler droit de la doner mesme la Prebende, adonqes vostre dit Chanceller face casser et reuoquer voz lettres patentes au dit Robert enfaites, seoffrant et grantant au dit Thomas depursuir en qeconqe Court Christiene ou seculer qil verra estre affaire pur peisible possession auoir en sa Prebende susdite, sicome reson est, en oeuere de charite.

1389. Dalton is listed as a canon of Darlington between 1390 and 1403 (*Fasti*, p. 33). On 5 July 1390 Bishop Skirlawe or his vicar-general were ordered to arrest and bring before the King and Council all presuming to thrust out Robert de Dalton, chaplain, from his prebend in St. Cuthbert's, Darlington, where he had been collated by the Crown. It had been lately held by William de Lynton, clerk, and was vacant, but certain men had procured a great number of inhibitions to the detriment of the King's right (*CCR 1389–92*, p. 196). Dalton was 'ratified' in possession by Richard II on 15 October 1390 (*CPR 1388–92*, p. 307). The warrant for consideration of the petition is dated 1389 (PRO, Chancery Warrant 1/509/5663).

149

John Kyllome, clerk, petitions the King that whereas he had a provision of the late Pope Urban [VI] directed to the bishop of Durham for a benefice with cure of souls worth 25 marks and for a benefice without cure worth 18 marks, there was a portion in the parish church of Norton in the said diocese, being without cure and worth only 9 marks and of the patronage of the bishop by right of the church of St. Cuthbert of Durham. To this John de Fordame, lately bishop of Durham, collated Robert de Scampston and instituted and inducted him in corporal possession. This portion came void by the death of the said Robert long before 29 January 1390, and Kyllome on the strength of the provision took the portion and was put in corporal possession by the executors of his bulls, and this long before the 29th day, and continued until a William Ryall, clerk, suggested falsely to the

King's majesty that it was in the King's gift, and was given collation by royal letters patent, on the strength of which the bishop of Durham accepted, instituted, inducted and put him in corporal possession and ejected Killome, to the eternal setback of his estate. He craves an order to the Chancellor to summon William into Chancery to show the royal title to grant the portion and do right and reason, notwithstanding the admission, institution and induction (AP 12497).

A nostre tresgracious et tresexcellent seignur le Roy, Supplie humblement son poure orator Johan Kyllome Clerc' qe come le dit Johan auoit vn prouision de la Pape Vrban darein qe dieux assoile ... la collacion et auowre leueqe de Durcsme qe pur le temps serroit, cest assauoir de benefice cure de taxe de vynt et cynk marcs et benefice nient cure de taxe de dys et oyt marcs, la y ad vn porcion en leglise parochiele de Norton' deinz la diocese le dit Euesqe qest benifice nient cure et de taxe de noef marcs tantsoulement et qest du patronage du dit Euesqe come de droit de sa eglise seint Cutberd' de Duresme, et a quele porcion Johan de Fordame nadgaires Euesqe de Duresme fist collacioun a Robert de Scampston' et lui fist institucion et induccion en ycell' estre mys en corporele possession, la quele porcion voida par la mort le dit Robert long' temps deuant le vynt et noefisme ⟨iour⟩ de Januer lan de vostre regne treszisme, le quel Johan kyllome par force de sa dite prouision susdit accepta la dite porcioun et par executours de ses bulles en ycell' fuist mys en corporele possession et ce long temps deuant le dit vynt et neofisme ⟨iour⟩ et celle possession continua tanqe vn William Ryall' Clerc, fesant suggestioun nient veritable a vostre roiale mageste vous auoir droit a doner la dite porcion, et sur ce auoit collacioun du dit porcion de vostre Haut seignurie par voz lettres patentes, par force de quell' collacion le dit William est par le reuerent piere en dieu leuesqe du Duresme a dite porcion accepte et institut et induit et mys en corporele possession et vostre dit poure oratour Johan Killome du dite porcion ouste en perpetuel aririsement de son estat: Qe pleise a vostre hautesse et roiale mageste de commander vostre tresreuerent Chanceller de faire venir le dit William en vostre Chancellerie pur moustrer et declarer illoeqes vostre title a doner la dite porcion et outre qe vostre Chanceller face droit et reson a le dit poure suppliant en ceste cas, non obstantz les admission, institucion et induction susditz, pur dieu et en oeure de charitee.

No endorsement

1391. The warrant for consideration of the petition is dated 1391 (PRO, Chancery Warrant 1/529/7665). The significance of 29 January 1390 was that it was the date of limitation fixed in the re-enactment of the Statute of Provisors in 1391 (cf *Rot Parl* iii, 267). William Rial occurs as portioner of Norton in 1390, and John Kyllome as vicar of Billingham in 1396 (*Fasti*, pp. 73, 178).

150

John Herle, clerk, petitions the King that whereas he had a provision of the late Pope Urban [VI] for a prebend in the collegiate church of Our Lady in Chester le Street in the franchise of Durham between Tyne and Tees, where a prebend called 'of Lamesley' is of the patronage of the bishop of Durham and which John Fordam, lately bishop of Durham, gave to Robert Scampston, clerk, and instituted, inducted and put him in corporal possession, and this prebend was void long before 29 January 1930. Herle, in virtue of his provision, took the prebend and was put in corporal possession by the executors of the papal bull long before the said 29 January, and continued in peaceable possession until he was ejected by colour of the King's collation made to a Thomas de Westminster, clerk, by letters patent on his false suggestion that the prebend was void and of royal collation, to the petitioner's great damage. He craves a writ of *scire facias* out of Chancery to warn Thomas to appear before the King and Chancellor to show why the royal letters patent appointing him to the prebend be not repealed and annulled and the plaintiff restored (AP 12491).

A tresexcellent et tresredoute seignur le Roy Supplie humblement vostre poure liege Johan Herle Clerk qe come il auoit prouision del pape Vrbane darrein a vn prebende en lesglise colligiall' de nostre Dame en Cestre en le strete deinz le Fraunchise de duresme parentre les ewes appelle Tyne et Tese, en le quel Esglise est vn prebende appelle le prebende de lameslay le quel

est del patronage del Euesqe de duresme et la quel prebende
Johan Fordam iadys Euesqe de duresme dona a Robert Scampston'
Clerc' et luy instituer et inducter et en corporele possession dycelle
fist metter, la quel prebende par la mort de dit Robert fust voide
par long' temps deuant le vynt et noefisme iour de Januer' lan
de vostre reigne treszisme: et le dit Johan Herle par vertue de
sa prouision suisdit mesme le prebende accepta et par executours
de cez bulles fuist mys en corporele possessioun dycelle par long'
temps deuaunt le dit vynt et noefisme iour de Januar' et mesme
la possessioun continua pesablement et quitement tanqe il ent fuist
ouste par colour de vostre collacioun fait a vn Thomas de Westm-
[inster] Clerc' par voz lettres patent a sa mayns verra suggestion
deuant a vous a entendre qe le dit prebende fuist void
et de vostre collacion, ou ele ne fuist pas, a grant damage de dit
suppliant; qe pleise a vostre tresexcellent et tresreall' mageste
graunt' voz brief de scire facias hors de vostre Chauncellarie de
fayre garnir le dit Thomas destre deuant vous et vostre Chaun-
cellar' de moustrere pur quoy voz lettres patentz a luy faitez del
dit prebende ne serront my repellez et anullez et le dit suppliant
al dit prebende restitut, pur dieux et en oeure de charite.

No endorsement

1393/4. Robert Scampston exchanged the vicarage of Catwick,
Yorkshire, for the prebend of Norton in 1383. In 1387 he was
made a canon of York, and in 1388 was confirmed as canon of
Chester le Street, Norton and Lanchester (*Fasti*, p. 115). John
Herle was confirmed as prebend of Chester in 1398 (*ibid.*, p. 60).
The warrant for consideration of the petition is dated 1393/4
(PRO, Chancery Warrant 1/545/9212).

151

John Stafford, parson of St. Nicholas, Durham, petitions the
King to ratify his possession of that church (AP 12390).

Plaise a nostre souerein seignur le Roy granter a vostre tres-
humble oratour Johan Stafford, parsone de leglise de saint Nicholas en la Citee de Duresme, ratificacion de sa dite eglise pour dieu
et en oeure de charite.

No endorsement

1407. Stafford was presented by the King to the rectory of Sharn-ford, diocese of Lincoln. in August 1405. The ratification of St. Nicholas, Durham, was approved by Henry IV on 31 October 1407 (*CPR 1405–08*, pp. 54, 367).

Financial

The financial petitions are mainly concerned with persuading the King to respite debts owed to him or to honour assign-ments in the petitioner's favour. The only tax mentioned is the papal tenth of 1318 (no. 157).

Ancient Petitions 107, 417, 2123, 2150A–B, 2156, 2169, 2214, 4095, 5217, 7807, 8737.

152

The Prior and Convent of Durham thank the King for his benefits and labours to put the church of Durham in good state, and assure him that the Bishop has done his visitation, ensuring unity, charity, almsgiving and hospitality.

As he found that goods of the house had been dispersed, they crave the King to order the sheriffs of York and Northumber-land to restore them if found in their bailiwicks.

Whereas some said that the Bishop of Durham had appro-priated to himself goods of the house, they deny this and allege that he had greatly used his own for their relief.

They crave again that monks of the house suing in the King's court be commanded to return to their house and obedience, and they are ready to obey the King's will in whatever he com-mands (AP 8737).

Le Priour e le Couent de Dureme mercient a nostre seignur le Roi de touz biens faitz e especialment de grant peyne qil en ad mys a mettre leglise de Dureme en bon estat, e font assauer a luy qe le Euesqe de Dureme ad fet sa visitacion en si bone manere qil ad la dieu merci en la meson de Dureme vnyte, charite, amones e hospitalite.

E pur ceo qil troua en sa visitacion qe les biens de la meson sont aloignez grantment hors de soen poer, si prie le Priour et le Couent auantdit nostre s[eignur le] Roy qil ly pleyse maunder vn brief au visconte de Euerwyk et vn autre au visconte de Northumberland' qil facent les biens apurtenant as meson de Dureme en lurs baillies trouez alauantdite meson estre restorez.

E pur ceo qe ascune gent vnt dit qe le Euesqe de Dureme auoit aproprie a luy des biens de la meson, dient il fraunchement qe ceste chose ne contint nule verite, eyns en ad il mys grantment du soen e mettra enqe la meson soit releuee.

E prient vncore qe les Moynes de la meson qe se courent par la court le Roys soient comandez qil viegnent a lur meson e a lur obedience, e prest serront eaux e tut le Couent ala volonte le Roys, qant il les vodra comander.

No endorsement

?1301. This honeyed account of an episcopal visitation suggests that the writer was Henry de Luceby, the prior of Durham intruded by Bishop Bek after his tempestuous visitation of 20 May 1300, in the course of which he suspended from office most of the existing obedientiaries, including the prior, Richard de Hoton. Hoton and his proctors were busy during 1301 and 1302 presenting their case against Bishop Bek for exceeding his spiritual and temporal powers, which led to the confiscation of the franchise of Durham by Edward I on 7 July 1302 (*Bek*, pp. 131–58, 176–8, 181–3). Cf. no. 177 below.

153

Richard, prior of Durham, and the convent petition the King and Council that whereas the King granted them by charter an annuity of £40 to be received twice a year from the Exchequer at Berwick, viz at Martinmas and Whitsun, to be distributed to 6,000 poor people at the two feasts of St. Cuthbert, viz at the main feast [20 March] 3,000 and at the translation [4 September] 3,000, each receiving a penny, and for a pittance to the convent on the same feast days of 50s, and for maintenance of four candles about the saint's feretory, two of 20 lb. of wax, and for a chaplain to sing in the Galilee within the church every day, and for two comparable candles in the chantry: the prior and convent were seised of the £40 by sir Hugh de Cressingham by the King's letter in the 24th year of his reign [1296], and from then to the present have fulfilled the almsgiving as the charter wanted, but they have had no allowance since the year of the gift. They crave from the King the arrears and an order to the Treasurer of Scotland for future regular payment to maintain the almsgiving in accordance with the charter (AP 417).

A nostre seignur le Rey e a son Counsail Moustre Richard Priour de Dureme e le Couent qe par la ou nostre seignur le Rey fraunchement par sa Chartre graunta as ditz Priour e le Couent de la vaunt dite Mesoun de Dureme .xl. lj. dargent, a receiuer de an en an al Escheker de Berwyk' a deus termes del an, ceo est a sauoir a la feste de seint Martin en yver la vne Moite, e a la Pentecost' prochein suant lautre Moite sicum contenutz est en sa Chartre, pur distribucione fere a .vj. Milles poueres en les deus festes de seint Cutbert par an: Cest a sauoyr en la principale feste a treis Milles e al translacione a autres treis Milles, e a cheskun de poueres .i. d. E estre ceo pur pitaunce au Couent de la vauntdite Mesoun, en cheskun des iours de seint Cutbert auauntditz .l. s. E pur soustenir .iiij. sierges entour le fiertre del vauntdit Cors seint, dount chescun des deus serra de .xx. li. de cire, e les autres deux de auenaunte Mesure, sicum la Chartre voet: E pur trouer vn Chaplein chauntaunt cheskun iour del an en lauauntdite Eglise de Dureme en vn lu qil apelent la Galyleie: E a soustenir ileoskes oueoskes cele Chaunterie deux sierges auenaunces. Des qeux auauntditz .xl. li. le Priour e le Couent de la vauntdite Mesoun de Dureme furent seisi par la lyuere sir Hugh' de Cressingham e par la lettre le Rey, lan de son Regne .xxiiij. e puis ceu temps ieskes enca le Priour e le Couent auauntditz ount Meintenuz lauauntdit aumoigne entierement de an en an solome ceo qe la Chartre voet, e nul alowaunce nount en-puis lan qe le doun sei fist ieskes ⟨aea⟩, dount il prient a nostre seignur le Rey les arrerrages e qe il voille si pleysir luy seit comaunder a son tresorer de Eschoce qe la paie seit fete de an en an en tens auenir, issi qe lauauntdit aumoyngne peusse estre Meintenuz, solome le purport de la Chartre.

Endorsed: Duresme Coram Rege
Mandetur Camerario Scocie quod soluat de exitibus Scocie eis
et illis de Beuerlaco similiter arreragia et decetero annuatim secundum Tenorem Cartarum.

?1305. The original warrant to Cressingham to pay the pension
of £40 was sent on 16 September 1296 (*Rot Scot* i, 34). Payment
for arrears for four years was authorised by Edward II on 4
August 1309 (*ibid.*, 67). Cf. no. 145 above.

154

The Prior and Convent of Durham petition the King that
whereas the present King by his charter granted £40 to be taken
from his Exchequer at Berwick until other provision be made
of land or benefice worth £40 for alms as in his charter, these
were often detained to their loss and labour. To accomplish this
alms, costing £40, they crave land or benefice in a suitable place
near the Border where they can have ready access (AP 2123).

A nostre seignur le Roi mustrent le priour e le Couent de
Doream qe la ou nostre seignur le Roi qi ore est par sa chartre
graunta .xl. li' a prendre par an de sa escheker de Berewick' tant
cum il les aueit purueu aillors tere ou benefice de seint Eglise a
la vaillaunce de .xl. li' pur certain asmoun fair, cum contenu est
en sa chartre, les quels .xl. li' les sunt souent detenutz par quei
il sunt mult perdant et traueilletz, einceo qil poent les deners
auoir e si funt il lasmoun qe enioint les est qe amountz a les
.xl. li'; dunt il prient nostre seignur le Roi qil les voille graunter
alcun certein chose en tere ou en benefice de seint eglise en lieu
couenable pres de la Marche ou il les puissent prestement auoir.

Endorsed: Mandetur per breue de Cancellaria Custodi et Camerario Scocie quod inquirant vbi Rex melius possit prouidere
eisdem de petitis et tantum Canonicis Ecclesie de Beuerlaco
⟨et super hoc certificent Regem *in a different hand*⟩. Irrotulatur

c. 1305. See no. 153 above.

155

Robert de Barton petitions the King and Council that whereas he was appointed receiver by royal commission of the issues of the temporalities of the bishopric of Durham, vacant after the death of Antony de Bek, at the same rate of expenses as the former receivers of Bishop Antony, and the King graciously and hurriedly delivered the temporalities to Richard de Kellawe, elected in succession to the same Antony, and ordered Sir Henry de Percy, now dead, then keeper of the bishopric, and himself to deliver the same, provided that they levied all the appurtenant issues: they then were over £1000 in arrears, and to collect these issues he stayed a half year beyond the date of restoration. Nevertheless the Treasurer and Barons of the Exchequer would not allow him his expenses after the day of delivery of the temporalities to the bishop-elect. He craves allowance for his expenses for the time while he stayed about levying the issues, because they can find by good testimony or reasonable evidence that he stayed on business. They should consider that he was many times burnt and devastated by the enemy, so that nothing remains to him but bare land (AP 7807).

A nostre seignur le Roi et a son counseill' moustre Robert de Barton' qe come il fust assigne resceuur par commissioun nostre seignur le Roi des issues de la Temporaulte del Eueschee de Duresme vacaunte par la mort Antoyn de Bek, de prendre a tant pur ses despens pur la demoere qil froit en cel office come pristerount les resceuurs le dit Antoyn en soen temps. Et ia soit y ceo qe en fauour de Richard de Kellawe, eslit de cele eueschee apres la morte le dit Antoyn, pur diuers resouns le Roi liuera graciousement et hastiuement la dite Temporaulte al dit eslit' et maunda a sire Henri de Percy qui mort est, adonqe gardein de mesme leueschee, et a lauantdit Robert qeuls (sic) liuerassent al dit eslit la Temporaulte auantdite, issint totes voies qe les issues append-auntz al Roi de la dite voidance fuissent pleinement leuez a soen oeps, a quel temps il furent arere plus de .M. li' des dites issues, entoure le leuer de quels issues le dit Robert demurra vn demi an outre le iour de la liuere de la dite Temporaulte, nepurkant le Tresorer et les barouns del esckeker ne volent allouer al dit Robert ses despens forsqe al iour de la deliueraunce de la dite

Temporaulte al dit eslit': Par quei le dit Robert prie qe ses despens ly soient allouez taunt de temps come il demurra entoure le leuer des dites issues, sicom euls purrount trouer par bone tesmoignaunce ou par autre resonable demoustrance qil demurre taunt de temps besoignablement: Eauntz regarde sil lour plest qil ad estee taunte foitz arz et destruz par les enemis, qe a poy rene ly demure forsqe la terre nue.

Endorsed: Soit mande bref as Tresorer et Barons del Escheqer qe se enforment par enqueste ou en autre manere combien il demorra par necessite entour les issues del Euesche leuer ⟨apres la liuere fait al Euesqe de la Temporaulte⟩ et pur tant de temps li facent due allouance.

1316. Barton was summoned to account at the Exchequer in February 1313 for the issues of the bishopric during the vacancy, as also for the manor of Wark on Tyne (PRO, QR Mem Roll 85 m 71d). The following Michaelmas his accounts were still outstanding, when his clerk, Robert Parninke, appeared for him and presented a view of account (ib, 86 mm 101, 141d). He was still unable to clear his accounts at Michaelmas 1314, because the local bailiffs had not accounted with him (ib 87 mm 115, 135). The final balance was drawn up at Easter 1316, when he was found to have collected £1424 10s 3d, of which over £90 was still outstanding at the Exchequer (ib 88 m 197). Henry de Percy died in October 1315.

156

The Prior and Convent of Durham petition the King and Council that whereas Eustace de Vescy, former lord of Swinhoe in Northumberland, granted by charter to God, our Lady and St. Cuthbert and the monks of Farne Island 5 quarters of wheat each year for ever from his manor of Swinhoe, and William de Vescy, son and heir of the said Eustace, and John de Vescy, son and heir of William, confirmed it, as is shown by charters transcripts of which are attached, the Prior and Convent of Durham and their predecessors were seised thereof since the making of the charters until the death of Sir Henry de Percy. After his death the manor of Swinhoe was seized into the King's hand through the nonage of the heir, and the wheat withheld (AP 107).

A nostre seignur le Roi et a son conseil Prient le Prior de Durrem et le Couent qe come Eustace de Vescy iadis seignur de Swynhow en le Contee de Northumbr' granta a dieu et a nostre dame et a seynt Cuthbert et a les Moynes del yle de Farneland cynk quarters de furment chescun an pur tous iours par sa chartre a prendre de son Maner de Swynhow, et Williame de Vescy fitz et heyr le dit Eustace et Johan de Vescy fitz et heyr le dit Williame ceo confermerent sicome il pert par chartres des queux les transescritz sont atachez a ceste peticion, et des queux cyn quarters le Prior de Durrem et le Couent et lur predecessores ount este seisi pus la confeccion des dites chartres tanqe a la Mort sir Henri de Percy, qe du maner de Swynhow morust seysi, apres qi mort par le nounage le heyr le dit sir Henri le Maner de Swynhow fust seysi en la meyne nostre seignur le Roi et le dit furment southtret, dount il priont remedie.

Endorsed: Quia carte de quibus mencio fit in peticione coram consilio vise fuerunt, mandetur Escaetori Regis vltra Trentam quod per sacramentum etc. inquirat vtrum Prior seisitus fuerit de frumento illo vsque ad mortem Henrici de Percy ⟨sicut per peticionem asserit se fuisse⟩ necne; et si sic, tunc per cuius donum et per cuius manus illud recepit et vbi et ad quos terminos ⟨et a quo tempore⟩ et qualiter et quo modo et de aliis articulis premissa contingentibus etc, vt dominus Rex, inde per inquisitionem illam debite certioratus, vlterius faciat quod de iure viderit faciendum.

Irrotulatur   Coram Cancellario et Thesaurario

1316. Following an inquest taken by Robert de Cliderhou, escheator north of Trent, an order was sent on 25 September 1316 to John de Felton, constable of Alnwick Castle, to deliver yearly at Martinmas the five quarters of wheat to the prior, convent and brethren of Farne from the manors of Tughall and Swinhoe (*CCR 1313–18*, p. 366). The petition is summarized on the parliament roll (*Rot Parl* i, 340).

AP 108 is the transcript of the charters, minus witnesses and dates. (The original charters are printed in J. Raine, *North Durham* [1852], App. pp. 122–3.)

157

The clergy of the bishopric of Durham petition the King that whereas the country was often destroyed by the coming of the Scots and much impoverished by this, wherefore the King on another occasion made a new assessment of benefices when various aids were granted to the King, and the aids were levied according to the new assessment. Now the Pope has granted the King a tenth from the clergy of England for his aid. May it please the King out of charity to consider their poverty and damages over a long time and order the levy of the tenth in accordance with the last assessment made by his order, for they cannot bear it otherwise because their estate is not yet relieved, and several benefices are assessed at great value, from which none can take anything on account of the great destruction done there (AP 4095).

A nostre seignur le Roi prie le Clerge del Euesche de Durem qe come cel pays souente fiez eit este destrut par la venue des enemis Descoce e de ceo feit mout enpouery, par que altre foiz en diuers aeides que lui furent grantez de lour Benefices le dit nostre seignur le Roi fit taxer de nouel par son Bref meismes ceux Benefices e solonc le Tax ensi fet de nouel i fit leuer les eides, e ore eit le Pape grante al dit nostre seignur le Roi la dime du Clerge Dengleterre en aeide de lui, qil pleise al dit nostre seignur le Roi par charite auer regard a lour pouerte e meschiefs qil ount e lungement vnt eu, e comander a leuer de eux ceste dime solonc le dit drener Tax qe fut fait par son comaundement, qar dautre ne poont il vncore estre chargez, pur ceo que lour estat nest de riens vncore releue, et plusors benefices sont taxez a grant value des quex homme ne peut rien prendre pur la grant destruction qe ad este fete sur eux.

Endorsed: Le Roy ad graunte a ceste foiz qe la disme soit done solom la nouele taxacion, sauue son dreit autrefoiz.
Deleted: Vocentur Thesaurarius et Barones de Scaccario et fiat per eorum consilium

1319. Permission was granted on 25 May 1319 to the collectors to accept the tenth according to the new valuation (*CCR 1318–23*, p. 69). Cf. no. 101 above.

158

The Prior of Durham petitions the King and Council that whereas Sir William de Fellyng, formerly constable of Roxburgh Castle, bought from the predecessor of the present Prior for stocking the same castle while it was in the hands of the King's father the tithes of ... ham for £13 6s 8d, which is still due as appears by a bill of the Chamberlain of Scotland of that time: he craves allowance of the sum against debts owed the King for victuals bought of the King and his father in their great distress.

Also the Prior of Durham petitions the King and Council that whereas Edward, the King's grandfather, granted the Prior, predecessor of the present, an annual rent of £40 from his exchequer at Berwick, payable at Whitsun and Martinmas equally, to provide certain alms for him and his heirs as more fully appears in the King's charter, of which a transcript is attached, this rent is now £220 in arrears from the time the town was in the hands of the King's father, as appears by a bill of the then Chamberlain of Scotland, and during this time the Prior and Convent distributed the said alms: he craves allowance of part of this sum against debts for victuals bought from the King's father, and for the remainder payment or suitable assignment, and that the King may ordain some allowance for maintaining the alms or else discharge him from the obligation.

Also the Prior of Durham petitions the King and Council that whereas by destruction of war occurring in Northumberland it was ordained in parliament that no writ of *cessavit* should run for arrears arising in time of war, the Prior was bound to pay the Prior of Kirkham an annuity of 4 marks for certain tithes in the parish of Edlingham in that county, and great arrears have accumulated in time of war through which the Prior could have no profit from this tithe, and the Prior of Kirkham has sued against the Prior of Durham a writ of annuity before the judges of Common Pleas: he craves the King for a writ to the judges to discharge him from arrears incurred in time of war whereby no tithes remained, the annuity representing these tithes, as fully appears in the writing which the Prior of Kirkham has concerning the annuity (AP 2150A).

A nostre seignur le Roi et a son conseil prie le Priour de

Duresme qe come sire William de Fellying, iadis Cones[table vostre] Chastel de Rokesburgh', pur ganesture de mesme le Chastell' taunt come le dit Chastell' fust en la mei[ne le Roi] .E. pere nostre seignur le Roi qore est, achata du Priour de Duresme predecessour le priour qore est les dismes de ... ham pur tresze liures .vj. s. .viij. d. les queux sount vnqor dues au dite, come pert par vn bille del Chaumberleyn [Deschoce] qe au ceux temps fust de ceo en fait, par quoy le dit Priour prie a nostre seignur le Roi qe les ditz Tresze liures .vj. s. .viij. d. puissount estre alouwes en dettes qil doit doit [sic] a nostre seignur le Roi pur vitailles qil achata de dit nostre seignur le Roi et de son pere en son graunt meschefs.

Estre ceo le ditte Priour de Duresme prie a nostre [seignur le] Roi et a son counseil qe come le Roi .E. ael nostre seignur le [Roi.E.] qore est graunta au Priour de Duresme, predecessour le Priour qore est, vne Annuelle rent de qarant liures a re[ceiuer de an] en an de sa Escheker de Berwik sur Twede a la fest de Pentecost' et de seint Martyn en yuer par [egales] porciouns pur fair certein aumoigne pur lui e ces heires, sicom plus pleinement apert par la chartre le ditte Roi .E. [lauauntdit] le transescrit de quele est cusu a cest peticion, de quele rent arer est au dit Priour deux cenz [et vynt liures du] temps qe la ditte ville fust en la meine le Roi .E. pere nostre seignur le Roi qore est, come apert par un bille du Chaumberleyn deschoce qe au ceux temps fust, et en quele temps le Priour e le Couent feiscent le ditt aumoigne et ... fount graunt partie, par quey le dit Priour prie a nostre seignur le Roi qe lui plese a lower partie de les ditz deux cens et vynt liures en dettes qil doit a nostre seignur le Roi pur vitailles qil achata de son piere et pur ..... et du remenaunt qil puisse auoir paiment ou couenable assignement, et qil pleise a nostre seignur le Roi ordeine aschun porcioun dount cest aumoigne poer estre meintenus, ou dunke lui descharger de i cele.

Estre ceo le dit Priour de Duresme prie a nostre seignur le Roi et a son counseil qe come par meschef' e destruction de Guer qauoit este en Counte de Northumberland, ordene fust en parlement qe nulle bref de Cessauit dust Curz ne lieu tener des areragez en coruz ne de cesser feat en temps de Guer, e le ditte Priour soit tenuz au Priour de [Kirk]ham en vne annuete de quatre Marce par an pur certein disme denz la paroch' de Edlyngham en le ditte Counte, de quele annuete graunt arrerages sount en coruz en temps de guer pur ceo qe le ditte Priour illoqes vnke disme ne nulle profist de sa

Eglise poat auoir, les queux arrerages le ditte Priour de Kirkham demande vers le ditte Priour de Duresme par bref dannuite deuant les Justices de Baunk', par quoy le dit Priour de Duresme prie a nostre seignur le Roi qe lui plest comaunder bref a Justices du baunk' qil ne soit charge des arerages en curuz en temps de guer en queux il nulles dismes iloqes restent, pur queles Dismes ladite annuite fust graunte come pleinement apert par lescritte qe le ditte Priour de Kirkham ad de la ditte annuite.

Endorsed: Quant au primer point et auxi quant au second' en droit des billes, qil ad come il dist: ⟨*soit mande as Tresorer, Barons et Chaumberleins del escheqir qe vewes les billes, sil troessent qe la dette soit vncore due, qil lur facent auer allouance en dettes qil deit au Roi, Resceiuantz etc⟩

Quant au second' point, en droit de recompensacion qil demande pur la Chanterie: ⟨*se auise ou il purra auoir ascun benefice de seinte eglise a la value de .xl. li' et certifie le Roi.⟩

Quant au tierz point − nichil

[*Written in different ink]

post 1328. As the petition refers to the King as grandson of Edward I the petitioner should be identified with Prior William de Couton [1321–41] whose priorate began in the reign of Edward II. William de Fellingg received on 18 January 1313 assignments on tallages from York and Newcastle amounting to £124 4s 2d towards a total sum of £324 4s 2d owed in arrears of wages for himself, 36 squires, 15 hobelars, 3 sergeants, 20 crossbowmen and 51 archers in garrison at Roxburgh and as compensation for horses lost in action. He was succeeded as Constable of Roxburgh by Ivo de Aldeburgh in May 1313 (*CPR 1307–13*, p. 589; *CCR 1307–13*, pp. 506, 513). The tithes were presumably sold to him by Prior William de Tanfield [1308–13]. On 3 November 1328 an order was issued to the King's judges to cease hearing pleas relating to Northumberland and brought by the writ *cessavit*, as had been agreed in parliament at Salisbury [October 1328]. This was on account of war-damage at the hands of the Scots, and the moratorium was to last until the Christmas following (*CCR 1327–39*, p. 341).

AP 2150B is the enclosure mentioned, being a slightly mutilated copy of

Edward I's donation of £40 for candles and a dole in honour of St. Cuthbert, dated 16 September 1296 at Yarmouth.

159

The men of the franchise of Durham and Norham petition the King and Council for a writ to the Treasurer and Barons of the Exchequer touching the pardon by the King to the men of Northumberland of debts incurred with the King for victuals and other things like the other people of the county, as the franchises are inside the county (AP 2169).

A nostre seignur le Roi et a son consail prient les gentz de la franchise de Duresme et de Norham qils pount auoir bref as Tresorer et Barons del escheker sur le pardon feat par nostre dit seignur le Roi a les gentz du Conte de Northumbreland des dettes qils ... a nostre seignur le Roi por les vitaile et par autre enchesons auxi com autres gentz de mesme le Counte ount, de puis qe les dites franchises sount deinz mesme le Conte.

Endorsed: Coram Rege et magno consilio
Eient bref auxi come les autres genz du dit Countee du dit pardoun pur coi qe Leuesche et la dite franchise sont deinz le corps du dit Countee et parcele de mesme le Countee *cancelled*
    Pur ce qe ceste grace est faite a les gentz de Northumb' le conseil ne ose mie estendre la grace faite as genz de Northumbr' a les genz del euesche sanz auiser le Roi.

1332–4. After an initial pardon of money due at the Exchequer from the men of Northumberland, dated 3 October 1331, a further pardon in view of losses in the late wars was issued on 27 October 1332 for debts from victuals bought from the King at Newcastle, Carlisle and Skinburness (*CPR 1330–34*, pp. 169, 361). On 1 March 1334 the men of Durham were pardoned all debts for victuals arising before 12 February 1327, as earlier conceded to the men of Northumberland (*CPR 1330–34*, p. 528).

160

The King's poor chaplains the Prior and Convent of Durham petition the King and Council that whereas they bought victuals

from the King's father and also from the present King for their
sustenance to the sum of £400 of which sir Robert de Nottingham
by the King's order levied from them £100, and now the King of
his grace has pardoned the men of Northumberland within
which the priory is situated: although the Prior sued a writ to the
Treasurer and Barons of the King's exchequer to discharge them
from this debt for victuals they would not discharge them because
the priory is within the franchise of Durham. The Prior craves the
King to consider their great losses through the war, and now their
house of Coldingham has been destroyed and the monks there are
all come to Durham. May he command issue of a writ of discharge,
because all the franchise of Durham is within the county of
Northumberland (AP 2156).

A nostre seignur le Roi et a son conseil moustrent ces pouers
chapeleins le Priour et le Couent de Duresme que come ils
achateront des vitailles le Roi .E. pere nostre seignur le Roi et
auxint de nostre seignur le Roi qore [est] pur lour sustenance ala
montanz de quatre Centz liures, de quele soume sire Robert de
Notingham par mandement nostre seignur le Roi leua deux
taunqe a Cent liures, et ore nostre seignur le Roi de sa bone grace
ad pardone ales gentz ⟨del Conte⟩ de Northumberland' deinz quel
Counte sa Priory et ces terres sont, et mesqe le dit Priour ad sui
brief as Tresorer et barons de lescheker nostre seignur le Roi de
lui descharger de ceo que due est par lui des ditz vitailles, les ditz
Tresorer et barons ne lui volont descharger pur ceo qe sa priory est
deinz la franchise de Duresme; par que le dit priour prie a nostre
seignur le Roi que lui pleisse auoir regarde ales granz perdz qil
ad eu par la guere et ad de iour en autre, et ore est destruit de sa
meson de Coldingham et les moynes illoqes soleint estre toux sount
venuz a Duresme, et comander brief si lui plest de lui descharger qar
tote la franchise de Duresme est deinz le Counte de Norhumber-
land.

Endorsed: Coram Rege et magno consilio
   Pur ce qe ceste grace est faite a les genz de Northumbr', le
Conseil ne ose mie estendre la grace faite as genz de Northumbr' a
les genz del euesche sanz auiser le Roi.

1332–33. On 2 August 1333 a pardon was issued for £100 still due
from £300 owed for victuals, it being granted in view of losses

from Scottish forays (*CRP 1330–34*, p. 461). Cf. no. 159 above. The assertion that Durham was part of Northumberland was advanced with more enthusiasm by the commons of Durham than the Bishop, who emphasised the separate character of his franchise. See nos 159, 169; cf. no. 203.

161

Nicholas de Ellerker petitions the King and Council that whereas the father of the present King was beholden to Nicholas and his brother John, now deceased and whose executor he is, in 200 marks being an advance which the King acknowledged by letters under privy seal, and Nicholas sued in the previous parliament by petition and was given a writ to the Treasurer, Barons and Chamberlains of the Exchequer to make payment or assignment, by virtue of this writ he was given an assignment on the Prior of Durham as collector of money for victuals sold by the King's father: and Nicholas having received a tally and writ to the Prior, delivered up his obligatory letter to the Exchequer. Now he can have no payment from the Prior because of another assigment made to sir Robert de Wodehous and also to William de Denum, and the Prior claims that he can meet nothing beyond these two. Nicholas craves an assignment elsewhere, as without aid in this debt he is undone for ever (AP 2214).

A nostre seignur le Roi et a son conseil moustre Nichol de Ellerker qe come nostre seignur le Roi, piere nostre seignur le Roi qore est, feust tenuz au dit Nichol et a Johan son frere qi mort est, qi executour il est, en .CC. mars, les queux il apresterent au dit Roi et des queux le dit Roi lour fist ses lettres obligatories de son priue seal, et sur ceo le dit Nichol suyst par peticion en drein parlement, ou feust agarde qil eust bref as Tresorer, Barons et Chaumberleins de Lescheker de faire a lui paiement ou assignement, et par vertue de quel bref il feust assigne au priour de Doresme, Coillour des deneres pur vitails venduz par le dit Roi le piere, et sur ceo taile leue et bref mande au dit Priour, et le dit Nichol livera sus la dite lettre obligatorie en Lescheker; et ore le dit Nichol ne poet auoir nul paiement du dit Priour par reson de vn autre assignement que est fait a sire Robert de Wodehous et auxint par vn assignement fait a William de Denum, et outre les queux deux assignementz le dit

Priour ne poet leuer nul dener auxi come il dist, par quoi le dit
Nichol prie pur dieu et pur lalme le dit Roi le piere qil poet estre
aillours assigne, qar sil ne soit eide de cest dette il est touz iours mis a
meschef'.

Endorsed: Soit mande par bref de Chauncellerie as Tresorer, Barons
et Chaumberleins del escheqer qe vewe la taille qil ad, sil troessent
qe autres sont assignez au dit Priour, issint qe le dit Nichol ne poet
la estre serui, qe adonqes il soit aillours assigne ou il purra
prestement estre serui, Receiuantz sa taille.   Irrotulatur

post 1332. Nicholas de Ellerker was a wool merchant, shipping
from Newcastle in 1326 and 1334 (PRO, Customs Accts 105/5, 6).
On 30 December 1333 he received a licence in mortmain to grant 6
marks of rent to St. Mary's Hospital, Westgate, Newcastle, for a
chantry. He and his brother John are also associated with a chantry
dedicated to St. Catherine in St. Nicholas's, Newcastle (*CPR
1330–34*, p. 488; Brand, *History of Newcastle* [1789], i, 252–53).
Robert de Wodehouse was Keeper of the Wardrobe to both
Edward II and Edward III, 1323–28, and Treasurer 1329–30
(*HBC*, pp. 78, 101). William de Denum was a sergeant at law and a
Baron of the Exchequer, 1331–32 (E. Foss, *The Judges of England*
(1870), p. 220).

162

Thomas, bishop of Durham, petitions the King and Council
that whereas the Bishop loaned the King his late grandfather 4000
marks for great and pressing business during the time the Bishop of
Exeter and Richard Lescrope were Treasurers, for which the
Bishop of Durham had a dozen tallies from the said Treasurers, for
payment of which he long sued but could obtain nothing,
whereon Alice Perers, who was staying with his grandfather as one
of his household, came to the Bishop of Durham at his manor of
Charing in Middlesex in October 49 Edward III [1376]: when he
begged Alice to help him obtain payment of the said 4000 marks,
and this she promised him, whereupon the Bishop handed over all
the tallies. Because she owed the King's grandfather great sums of
money she sued in the royal Receipt and delivered there two of the
said tallies standing in the Bishop's name, without warrant or

authority from him, neither in person nor by attorney, for which delivery of tallies she was allowed 1000 marks of her own debt to the King in money received from the Treasury, to the deceit of the King's court and the great hardship of the Bishop and delay in the repayment of the rest of the debt. He craves the King to summon Sir William de Windesore and the said Alice now his wife before the King and Council and provide a remedy (AP 5217).

A nostre tresredote seignour le Roi et a son tresnoble conseil moustre Thomas Euesqe de Duresme qe com le dit Euesqe apresta a nostre seignur le Roi vostre aiel qe dieu assoille pur grosses et chargaunces busoignes du diz aiel qatre Milles Marcs en temps qe leuesqe Dexcestre et mousieur Richard lescrop' estoient tresorers au dit aiel, de quele summe le dit Euesqe de Duresme auoit dusze tailles de les ditz Tresorers, pur le paiement des queles il pursuyt longement mes il ne poet riens auoir, sur qoi Alice Perers qe fust demoraunt deuers le dit aiel com de sa meyne vigne au dit Euesqe de Duresme a soun Manoir a Charrynge en le Counte de Middelsex le Mois Doctobr' lan du reigne dudit aiel .xlixme ou il pria la dit Alice de lui eider qil serroit paie de les auantditz qatre Milles marcz et ele lui promist a ceo faire, sur qoi le dit Euesqe deliuera touz les ditz tailles a la dite Alice et par la ou ele estoit dettes a nostre dit seignur le Roi laiel de grande somme de deniers ele pursuyt en la receite du dit aiel et liuera illoeqes deux de ditz tailles computantz la summe de qatre .M. Marcz en noun de dit Euesqe sanz garrant ou auctorite de lui, la ou il nestoit en propre persoun ne par actourne, pur quel liuere des tailles ele auoit alowance de Mille marcz de soun dette propre quel ele deuoit au dit aiel ou en deniers receuz de sa tresorie, en deceite de la court nostre seignur le Roi et a grant damage du dit Euesqe et delaye del remenant de soun paiement. Plese a vostre treshaute seignourie de faire venir mousieur William de Windesore chiualer et la dite Alice ore sa femme deuant vous et defaire remedie au dit Euesqe de Duresme de la matiere auantdite.

No endorsement

1377 x 1381. Bishop Hatfield [1345–81] had worked his way through the King's household administration, serving as receiver of the chamber [1338–44] and keeper of the privy seal [1344], and then became Bishop of Durham (*HBC*, p. 91). The Treasurers referred to were Thomas Brantingham, Treasurer from 1369 to 1371 and Bishop of Exeter from 1370 to 1394, who was succeeded by Richard, Lord Scrope of Bolton, on 27 March 1371. Scrope was replaced on 26 September 1375 (*ibid*. p. 101). The malign influence of Alice Perrers was a grievance of the Good Parliament of 1376.

Legal

A number of petitions were directed to the King either by the Bishop of Durham or his 'subjects' to remedy deficiencies in the repertoire of writs available from the Durham chancery for suitors (nos 170–73). With these must be associated contradictory claims that eyres in Durham were both essential for swift justice, and to be avoided literally at all cost (nos 169, 175). Three concern feudal rights, where the King had assumed custody of all the lands of the late earl of Warwick, Guy de Beauchamp, during the minority of his heir (nos 164–66). Goods seized by Hartlepool 'pirates' were firmly held by the local townspeople, despite the representations of the rightful owners (no. 167).

Ancient Petitions 588, 1935, 2165, 3509, 3693, 6408, 7191, 7333, 7972, 9633B, 10278, 10872, 13709, 15515.

163

John son of John de Maidenestan petitions the King that whereas he sued a writ of *mort dancestor* before sir William de Ormesby and sir Henry de Guldeford, lately the King's judges in the bishopric of Durham, concerning his father, and pleadings were later resumed before sir William de Bereford and sir Roger de Heygham, the King's judges in the same bishopric, against Antony, Bishop of Durham, touching two parts of the manor of Thorpe Thewles and against Aveline, widow of Robert de Thorp, for the third part, whom the Bishop had warranted in court and for the whole alleged that John was a bastard: and it was ordered that the Archbishop of Canterbury certify the King of John's condition, and the Archbishop certified that he was born in wedlock. Therefore sir Roger Brabanzon sent the record and process to sir

Henry de Guldeford and his fellow royal judges in the bishopric of Durham by chancery warrant to examine the record and do right, and in the commission it was expressed that the sheriff of Northumberland should execute the judges' orders. Later the king forbade by word of mouth the sheriff of Northumberland to enter the bishopric of Durham to execute any manner of office, wherefore the judges had no power to proceed in the case without another executive commission to the sheriff of Durham. John craves that a writ be sent to the chancellor of Durham to authorise a commission to the King's judges in the bishopric to examine the record and process and do right as first ordered, in order that John be not disinherited, as the sisters of the late John have been induced by the Bishop and his council to sue a writ of *mort dancestor* against the Bishop for the same holdings. He craves that as it has been certified that he was lawful son of the said John an order be sent to the judges in the bishopric not to delay his right through the malicious suit of his aunts, and that the judges inquire into the conspiracy and collusion (AP 13709).

A nostre seignour le Roi mustre Johan le fiz Johan de Maidenestan qe la ou il porta sun bref de mortdauncestre deuant sire William de Ormesby e sire Henr' de Guldeford', nad gueres Justice nostre seignour le Roi en la vesche de Durem, de la mort Johan son pere e apres feust la parole resumouns deuant sire William de Bereford' et sire Roger de Heygham Justice nostre seignour le Roi en mesme leueschee vers Antoun Eueske de Durem de les deus parties del Maner de Thorpthewles e vers Auelyn, qe fust la femme Robert de Thorp, de la tierce partie de mesme le Maner, a la quele Auelyn ledit Eueske garauntist en Court e respundist de lentier e dist qe le dit Johan fust bastard, et sur ceo fust maunde al Erceueske de Cauntirbirs qil certifia le Roi del estat le dit Johan et le dit Erceueske certefiast quil fust muliere e nient bastard, dunt sire Roger Brabanzon maunda le record' et le processe a sire Henr' de Guldeford' et a ses compaignons, Justices nostre seignour le Roi en le veschee de Dueram, par commission hors de la Chauncelerie qil examinassent le record et feissent dreit a les parties, en la quele commission fust contenuz qe le viscont' de Northumbr' fust entendaunt a les ditz Justices a office de viscont' faire en le processe auantdite; e apres ceo nostre seignour le Roi defendist de buche qe le viscont de Northumbr' ne entrast'

leueschee de Doream a nule manere de office faire, par quoi les ditz
Justices ne auent poer de aler auant en le dit processe saunz autre
commission qe le viscont' de Doream fust entendaunt a office de
vescont' faire en le dit processe: dunt le dit Johan prie a nostre
seignour le Roy qil voille graunter bref' a son Chaunceler de
Doream qil face comission a les Justices nostre seignour le Roy en
la dite Eueschee qil examinent les ditz recorde et processe et qil
facent droit a les parties solonc le recorde et le processe a eux primes
maundees, e qe le viscont de Doream a ceo soit entendant', solom la
volente nostre seignour le Roy qe le dit Johan ne soit desherite, qe
le dit Eueske e son consail vnt mene les soers le dit Johan de qi mort
le bref est porte, qe vnt porte bref de mort dauncestre vers le dit
Eueske de meme les tenemenz de la mort le dit Johan lour frere,
pere cesti Johan, deuant les Justices en le veschee de Durem; dunt il
prie a nostre seignour le Roy, desicom la Court est a certe qil est
fiz le dit Johan e muliere, quil voille maunder a ses Justices en la dite
Eueschee qe par la sute des Auntes le dit Johan Maliciusement e en
sa desheritaunce compasse, qil ne soit delaie de son droit e qe
les dites Justices enquergent de la conspiracie e la collusioun
auantdites.

Endorsed: Mandetur Justiciariis quod ipsi procedant in Loquela
iuxta formam prime commissionis sue eis inde directe.

1306. This petition, which was heard in parliament in 1307 (*Rot
Parl* i, 198), highlights the practical aspect of Durham autonomy,
namely that the sheriff of Durham, who acted only on the bidding
of the Bishop (or the royal *locum tenens*), was the sole recognized
executive officer for the 'county' (*Placita de Quo Warranto* (1818),
p. 604; *Rot Parl* i, 117–19).

164

Ralph son of William petitions the King and Council that
Antony, Bishop of Durham, gave him a messuage and two
carucates of land in Langton, being an escheat of Barnard Castle,
which messuage was seized into the King's hand, and he craves to
have it safe (AP 9633B).

A nostre seyngnur le Rey e soun Conseyle Moustre Rauf le fiz

William qe la ou Antoyn Eweske de Duremme Luy dona vn Mes'
et deus carues de tere o Les aportenaunz en La vyle de Langeton, qe
fut vne Eschete del chastel Bernand, le quel Mes est seysy en la
mayne nostre Seyngur le Rey: Dount le dit Rauf' prye la grace
nostre seyngur le Roy qe il pusse le auauntdit Mes o Les
apurtenaunces tenir sauer si luy plest.

Endorsed: Ostendat cartam Episcopi Dunelmensis.

1306–7. Barnard Castle, forfeited as part of the English estates of
John de Balliol, was taken into royal custody in December 1306
(*Bek*, pp. 204–5).

165

Thomas Surtees petitions the King and Council that whereas
Robert de Middilton, now dead, held the manor of Westwick as of
the fee of Barnard Castle, which is in the King's hand by reason of
the minority of the son and heir of the earl of Warwick, and the
same Robert held other lands in Middleton on Tees of Thomas by
knight service, which are of older enfeofment than Westwick, Sir
Henry fitz Hugh, the King's keeper of the castle, has taken Robert,
son and heir of the said Robert, who is a minor, claiming
wardship, to the disinheritance of Thomas. He craves an enquiry as
to priority of enfeofment, and that right be done according to
Magna Carta, that the King have no greater advantage than the
earl if he were alive (AP 7972).

A nostre seigneur le Roi et a son consail moustre Thomas
Surtays qe par la ou Robert de Middilton', qe mort est, tint le
Maneir de West Wyk' du fie du chastiel Bernard, quest en la Mayn
nostre seigneur le Roi par raison du nonage le filz et heir le Conte
de Warwyk': Et mesme celui Robert tint autres terres en la vile de
Middilton' souz tees de lauantdit Thomas par seruice de Cheualier,
Les queux terres sont de aisne feffement qe nest le dit Manoir de
Westwyk': Si a monsieur Henry le filz Hue, gardein dudit chastiel
depar nostre seigneur le Roi, fait prendre Robert filz et heir le dit
Robert qe est dedaunz age, enclamant auoir la guarde du dit corps
le dit enfaunt pur la cause dessusdite en desheriteson du dit Thomas:
Par quoi il prie a nostre seigneur le Roi qe il li plaise faire enquerre

de la priorite du feffement des dites terres et commander qe droit li
en soit fait, de sicomme il est contenuz en la grant chartre des
fraunchises, qe le Roi en tiel cas nul autre auantage naura qe
nauroit le Conte sil fuest en vie.

Endorsed: Mandetur Henrico filio Hugonis Constabulario etc,
quod inquirat per sacramentum etc de balliua sua in presencia
partis per ipsum premuniende, si interesse voluerit etc, super
contentis in peticione et vlterius vtrum Robertus de Middelton'
tenuerit alibi de Rege necne et de aliis articulis etc, et inquisicio
returnetur in Cancellaria. Et si inueniatur per inquisicionem illam
quod suggestio sit vera et quod dominus Rex non habet aliam
causam ad custodiam heredis ipsius Roberti nisi racione custodie
heredis Comitis etc, tunc mandetur prefato Henrico quod amoueat
manum etc.   Irrotulatur

1318 x 1329. Guy de Beauchamp, earl of Warwick, died on 12
August 1315, and Henry fitz Hugh was appointed constable of
Barnard Castle in December 1315 (*CFR* ii, 267). Thomas, son and
heir of Nicholas Surtees, had livery in October 1318 of his father's
lands of Dinsdale, Coatham and Studhoe, held of the earl of
Warwick for the fee of one knight. He also held Over Middleton,
alias Middleton One Row (*ibid.*, 376; *VCH: Durham* iii, 218, 294).
The Warwick lands were restored to the Beauchamp heir on 20
February 1329 (*HBC*, p. 453). Robert Surtees was unable to trace a
Middleton 'of Barnard Castle' earlier than the time of Richard II
(Surtees iv, pt. 1, p. 70).

166

Emma, widow of Alan de Tesdale, petitions the King and
Council that whereas Sir John de Bailol, former lord of Barnard
Castle in the bishopric of Durham, gave by charter to Alan and his
heirs a rent of £10 from Longnewton, appendant to the said castle,
of which Alan was seised as of fee, the castle and honour now are
in the King's hand by reason of the minority of the son and heir
of the earl of Warwick, against whom she cannot have writ of
dower (AP 7191).

A nostre seignur le Roi e a son conseil moustre Emme qe fust la

femme Alayn de Tesdale qe come monsz Johan de Bailol iadis
seignur du Chastel Bernard en Leuesche de Duresme dona par sa
chartre au dit Alayn e a ses heirs dis liuere de rente en la ville de
Lange Neuton' qest apendant au dit Chastel, de la quele rente le dit
Alayn fust seisi en son demeyn come de fee par le doun auantdit, le
quel Chastel oue le honour est ore en la mayn nostre dit seignur le
Roi par le nounage le fuiz e heir le Counte de Warrewyk' vers qui
ele ne poet auoir son bref de dowair, dount ele prie remedi.

Endorsed: Mandetur Custodi Castri de Castro Bernardi quod
informet se pleniori modo quo poterit super contentis in peticione
et vtrum Alanus vir suus obierit seisitus de redditu illo in dominico
suo vt de feodo per quod vxor sua debeat inde dotari, an Comes
Warr' obierit inde seisitus, per cuius mortem redditus ille captus
fuit in manum Regis et de omnibus articulis etc, et informacio
illa mittatur in Cancellariam, vt Rex vlterius faciat quod de iure
fore viderit faciendum, et certificet totam veritatem facti.

Irrotulatur

1326 x 1329. Alan de Tesdale, who was still alive in 1326, had been
a retainer of the Balliols and a leader of the Durham commons
against Bishop Bek in 1302 (*Bek*, p. 215 n5). He later served Hugh
Despenser the younger and Edward II (*CCR 1323–27*, p. 532;
CFR iii, 397). See no 165 above.

167

Matthew son of William son of Robert de Wolferton petitions
the King and Council that whereas he and his fellows had lately
charged a ship of Zeeland at Lynn with wool and other goods
worth £500 to cross to Zierikzee in Zeeland to trade, John Arthur
of Hartlepool and divers others of the same town boarded the ship
at Cromer in Norfolk and drove off all the people therein except
for one man and took the ship with all the goods to Hartlepool and
still hold them: and Matthew and his fellows have often come to
John and the other people of the town who received the said goods
and craved their restitution, but could have no recovery nor right
on account of the franchise of the bishopric of Durham (AP 7333).

A nostre seignur le Roi et a son conseil mustre Mayheu le Fiuz
William fiuz Robert de Wolferton' qe come il et ses compaignons

eussent nadgeres charge vne neef de Selande a Lenne de leynes et autres biens a la value de .D. li' a passer a seryce en Selande pur marchaunder de les ditz biens, la vynt Johan Arthur de Hertelpol et plusours autres de meismes la ville de Hertelpol et la dite Nef a Croumere en Norff' assaillerent et totes les gentz qe leynz furent sauue vn soul homme enchacerent et la dite nef oue touz les biens auantditz tanqe a Hertelpol menerunt et illuqes encore les detienent, dont les ditz Mayheu et ses compaignons sont souent puis venuz au dit Johan et les autres gentz de la dite ville qe vnt les ditz biens en la manere recettes et prie restitucion de lour biens auantditz, et il nule manere de restitucion ne de droit vers eux ne poent auoir ⟨pur la franchise del Euesche de Dureme⟩: par quoi il prie pur lamur de dieu grace qe remedie et lei lour soit fait.

No endorsement

1326. On 24 April 1326 pardons of outlawry were granted to Nicholas de Bruntoft and 47 others, including John Arthurgh, for a trespass (unspecified) in Norfolk on condition that they surrendered to the Marshalsea prison and stood trial on a plea brought by William de Neuton and John de Refham (*CPR 1324–27*, p. 263). On 10 June 1334 John Arthur of Hartlepool was appointed tronager in Hartlepool (*CPR 1330–34*, p. 539).

168

Elizabeth de Umframville, countess of Angus, petitions the King and Council that whereas formerly the King by letters patent granted her £50 a year from the issues of Longnewton and Newsham on Tees in the honour of Barnard Castle for her maintenance, and she had sued by writ and otherwise the castle's constables for the money, she was unable to have any money for four years, to the detriment of her condition. She craves the King and Council to have pity as she has had no profit from lands in England or Scotland for—years and indeed lived [in poverty], and order that she be paid her arrears, and she will repay any surplus to the grant (AP 10872).

A nostre seignur le Roi et son conseil moustre Elizabeth' de Umframuille Countesse de Anegos qe com nadgairs nostre dit

seignur le Roi ly [granta] par sa lettre patente .l. li' par an a
resceiure des issues des villes de Langeneuton' et Neusem sur These,
qe sount al [honour] du Chastel Bernard', a sa volentz en eide de sa
sustenance et ia soit ceo qe la dite Elizabeth' ad sui par brefs et autre
manere as Conestables du dit Chastel por le dit argent auoir selonc
le grant auantdit, ia dumeins ele ne poet nul dener auoir ces quatre
aunz en grant arerissement de son estate, par quei ele prie a nostre
seignur le Roi e son conseil pur dieu qil voillent auoir pite . . . qe ele
ne resceut nul profit de ses terres en Engleterre ne en escoce ces . . .
auns, mes contriours ad vesqui a . . . , et comander qele soit paie de
ceo qe arere lui est et ele rendra a nostre seignur le Roi la profit . . .
[q]e le ad du grant auandit.

⟨Bauuill' *different hand*⟩

Endorsed: Coram Rege Por ceo qe les . . . es grauntes par les Roi . . .
pare sewe deuers nostre seignur le Roi qe ore est.

1327. The endorsement suggests the recent accession of Edward III.
Elizabeth de Umfraville was daughter of Alexander Comyn, earl
of Buchan. Her husband Gilbert had died in 1307. In response to an
earlier petition of 1323, craving that the £50 be assigned on the
customs of Newcastle and Hartlepool, the constable of Barnard
Castle was ordered on 26 July 1323 to allow the dowager countess
to take £50 from the tenants of Longnewton and Newsham (*CCR
1323–27*, p. 10). In 1329 an enquiry was held at Bywell which
testified that Elizabeth held in Northumberland the manors of
Birtley, Harlow and Otterburn for life, much of the land being
waste on account of the Scots (Bain iii, 176–77). Her inquest *post
mortem* was held on 17 February 1333 (*Cal Inq pm* vii, 156). Cf.
North'd Pet., p. 189.

169

The men of the franchise of Durham petition the King and
Council that whereas the King summoned an eyre in Durham
while the temporalities were in his hand following the death of
Louis, lately Bishop of Durham, by writ of chancery directed to
the keeper of the franchise and summons of five weeks, and
summoned the men of the counties of Norham and of Sadberge to
be at Durham on the day of eyre, whereas no eyre was summoned

in Northumberland, within which the franchise is situated, which seems contrary to the law of the land and to the franchise, for summons of eyre should be for six weeks and should be made by the sheriff, and the men of Norham and Sadberge should not have to leave their counties for an eyre: and neither the King, nor the Bishop *sede plena* ever started an eyre before Northumberland, and to prevent such mischief and disinheritance of the church the men made ransom of 1000 marks to the King, as the advisors about the King disregarded the mischiefs that the men had suffered through the war, amounting to more than £20,000. For the affection shown by his ancestors to the franchise and to prevent the church's destruction may the King grant aid similar to that given to the men of Northumberland within which the franchise lies, and give letters of respite under his great seal as to other men for all manner of debts for victuals and grant to the present Bishop that no eyre be held unless first summoned in Northumberland as previously done by the King's ancestors and the Bishop's predecessors (AP 588).

A nostre seignur le Roi et a son consail Moustrent les gentz de la franchise de Duresme qe come nostre seignur le Roi, les temporalte de la dite euesche pur la mort lowys nadgairs euesqe de Duresme en la mein nostre dit seignur le Roi esteauns, fist somoundre son eyr a Duresme par bref de sa Chancellerie [direct a] gardein de la dite franchise et de la somouns de Cink' simeins et fist somoundre par mesme le bref les gentz del counte de Norham et [del counte de Sadbergh de]stre a Duresme a iour del eyr assis, par la ou nul eyr fu sumounis en le counte de Northumbr' dedenz quel counte [la franchise est, la quele chose] a ceo qe semble a les dites gentz fu feat encountre la ley de la tere et encountre la franchise auauntdit, qar la s[omouns del eyr par ley deit] comprendre le temps de sis simeins, et la somouns par ley deit estre feat par viscount; estre ceo les gentz des countes de [Norham et] de Sadbergh ne soleint en nul temps a nul eyr issir les ditz countes. Estre ceo le Roi ne leuesqe le see pleine unkes en nul temps auaunt illokes eir ... si leur ad eprimes ne fu comence en le counte de Northumbr', pur queles mechef et disheritanz de la eglise eschuer les ditz gentz fesount Raunceoun de Mile Marz a nostre seignur le Roi, qar le counsail qe fu pres du Roi adonk' a les resounz auantdit ne a les ... meschiefs qe les dites gentz auoient soefert par la guere

nauoient regard. Par quei les dites gentz prieunt a nostre seignur le
Roi qe luy pleise auoir [regard a les] resounz auauntdites, et as
meschefs qils ount soefertz par la guere et a les grantz
raunceouns qils ount paier les gentz descoce [qe amountent] a
pluis qe vint Mile liures, et ala franchise de quel ses progenitours ount este mult tendre, et qe luy pleise pur les . . . . nt
pur eschuer la disheritanz de la eglise grantes plus . . . qe pur nul
autre resoun grantere qils puissent estre aydes par le . . . de
Northumbr' deinz quel counte la dite franchise est, de totes
Manere des dettes et des vitailes et de . . . et de ceo ses lettres desouz
son grant seal granter solunc ceo qil ad feat as autres gentz [e qe lui]
pleise granter par ses lettres a leuesqe qore est qe mes eyr ne soit
illoke tenuz si el ny soit primes [comence en le counte] de
Northumbr', ne auterement qe les progenitours nostre dit seignur
le Roi et les predecessours leuesqe lount vse de totes iours.

Endorsed: Coram Rege et magno consilio
    Eient respit tanqe a la feste de seint Michel prochein auenir qe le
Roi endemettres purra faire ce qil par son bon conseil verra qe soit
a faire.

1333–34. Following a petition of the Bishop of Durham to the
King and Council in parliament an order was sent on 1 March 1334
to the Treasurer and Barons of the Exchequer to respite until
Michaelmas payment of a fine of 1000 marks by the men of
Durham, as an eyre ought not to be summoned in the bishopric
unless first summoned in Northumberland. The fine had been
agreed for supersession of an eyre summoned for 22 November
1333 during the vacancy after the death of Bishop Beaumont on 25
September 1333, and the 1000 marks were paid into the Exchequer
by Bishop Bury on 2 June 1335 (*CCR 1333–37*, p. 305; *CPR
1330–34*, p. 475; *1334–38*, p. 118). Later the men of the franchise of
Durham again petitioned in parliament concerning this summons
of an eyre at Durham before William de Herle and his fellow royal
justices during the vacancy after the death of Bishop Beaumont.
They claimed that when they drew the King's attention to the
matter at Clarendon he had disallowed the precedents because 'les
sages de son Conseill' were absent: and to settle the matter they had
agreed to pay 1000 marks as fine. On account of the fact that the
summons was contrary to law, and their great charges because of

the war, they requested a discharge of the final 100 marks now due, 900 marks having been already paid. In the answer it was noted that an eyre had been summoned in Durham after the death of Bishop Bek although none was summoned in Northumberland. The memoranda rolls of the Exchequer were to be searched and consideration deferred to the next parliament (*Rot Parl* ii, 99–100).

170

Richard de Sayton petitions the King and Council that whereas the King granted a writ to the Bishop of Durham to do him right in respect of tenements given in fee tail to his father and mother of which Conan de Aske deforced him, the Bishop granted Richard a writ of *formedon* before his judges, but the holder came to the King's chancery and suggested that such pleas should not be pleaded except before itinerant judges in the same franchise, as the writ was ordained by Statute of Westminster II, made since the last eyre held in those parts. By reason of this the Bishop's judges ceased to proceed with the plea, to the disinheritance of Richard and against the law. He craves that the King and Council consider that for tenements given in fee one had remedy at common law by writs of right and of *mort dancestor*, which writs have been pleadable in the franchise for all time and which have been lopped by statute. May a writ be sent to the Bishop to proceed with the plea, as otherwise he will be disinherited by a statute made to inherit and not disinherit (AP 3509).

A nostre seignur le Roi et a son conseil moustre Richard de Sayton' qe come nostre seignur le Roi lui granta brief al Euesqe de Duresme qil lui deust fere droit et remedie des tenementz donez a son pier et sa Miere en fee taille, les queux tenementz Conan de Ask' lui deforcea, et le dit Euesqe granta au dit Richard vne brief de forme de doun des tenementz auanditz deuant ces Justices, par vertu de quel brief auandit come il fust tenuz par reson par la est le dit tenaunt venuz en la chauncelrie nostre seignur le Roi et ad fait sa sugestion qe tieles pleez ne doient estre pledez mes deuant les Justices erranz en mesme la franchise, par la ou le dit brief est ordeine par estatutz de Westminster seconde, le quel estatut fut fait puis le drein Eir tenuz en celes parties: par reson de quel brief les Justice le dit Euesqe ont sursiz daler auant en le dit plee en

desheritance le dit Richard' et en countre la lei de la terre: par quei
le dit Richard prie a nostre seignur le Roi et a son conseil qe lour
pleise auoir regarde a ceo qe des tenementz donez en fee taille
homme auoit remedie a la commone lei par bref (*sic*) de droit et par
brief de Mordauncestre, les queux briefs ount este pledables denz la
dit franchise de tote temps et les queux briefs ... collettes par
estatut; qe lur pleise comander par son brief au dit Euesqe daler
auant en le dit plee, qar outrement est desherite par lestatut qe fust
fait pur les gentz enheriter et noun pas disheriter.

Endorsed: Coram Rege et magno consilio
La peticion de la commune est respondu en ce cas, qe ont prie qe
le Roi voille de sa grace granter al Euesqe qil peusse pleder tieux
brefs, issint supposent il qe tieux brefs ne poessent estre pledez en
leuesche aore.

?1334. The question of whether new writs could be introduced
into Durham outside of eyre became of increasing urgency with
the collapse of the eyre system elsewhere in England. The name of
Conan occurs frequently in the family of Aske of Aske and Marrick
in Richmondshire. The deforcer here may have been the husband
of Eleanor Widdrington, who gained through this marriage claims
to Silksworth (PRO, Durham 13/223 m 8; *VCH: North Yorkshire* i,
60; *NCH* xii, 320). He also had interests in Hardwick by the Sea
(Hesleden) and Sheraton (Surtees i, 51, 54–55). In 1321 a Conan de
Aske and Emma his wife leased the tithes of Sheraton from the
convent of Durham (Durham, Misc Charter 4017). The writ of
formedon was used at the Bishop's assizes before William Basset and
his fellows on 3 January 1345 (PRO, Durham 13/221 m 2).

171
Agnes, widow of Alan of Sleekburn, petitions the King and
Council that whereas she and her husband were jointly enfeoffed
of land in Cornforth in the franchise of the bishopric of Durham
and her husband alienated it in fee, she is disinherited because the
Bishop ought not to issue the writs of *cui in vita*, entry, or *formedon*.
She craves that the Bishop be ordered to do right so that she can
recover the land, because the King's writ does not run in the
franchise (AP 3693).

A nostre seignur le Roy et a son conseil pri Auneys que feust la femme Alain de Slikburn que come son baron et lui feurrent iount feffez en vne terre en la ville de Corneford' en la franchise del Eueschie de Duresme et son baron en pleine vie aliena mesme la terre em fee, en quele franchise Leuesque ne doit granter bref de cui in vita, bref de entre, ne bref de forme de doun, par quei la dite Auneys est desherite: que lui plise de sa grace commander au dit Euesque qil face auer droit a la dite Auneys par que ele puisse receuerir la dite terre, de puis le bref le Roy ne Court pas en la dit Franchise.

Endorsed: soit maunde a leuesque brefe qil luy face dreit solom les vsages de celes parties

?1334. See nos 170 above, 172 and 173 below.

172

John of Crossgate, chaplain, petitions the King's Council that whereas in the franchise of the bishopric of Durham from time immemorial until now no original writ of free tenement may issue from the Bishop's chancery nor be pleaded before his judges except the writ of right, the writ of dower, and assizes of *mort dancestor* and of *novel disseisin*: the Bishop and his predecessors have been powerless to issue all other original writs, saving the power of the King in time of vacancy and in eyre. Nevertheless William son of John Hunter sued John by a Bishop's writ of [*mort d]ael* for two parts of a messuage, a mill and a carucate of land in Aldingrange in the said franchise before the Bishop's judges, contrary to the royal dignity and customary usage (AP 10278).

Au counseille nostre seignur le Roi moustre Joun de Crossegate Chapeleyn qe come deinz la fraunchise de Leuesche de Duresme du temps dount il ny aed memore taunqe en cea nul bref' leuesqe ne ses predecessours original de fraunc tenement ne soleit istre (*sic*) de la Chauncelrie leuesqe ne ses predecessours, ne deinz la dite fraunchise deuaunt les Justices Leuesqe ne ses predecesseurs estre plede, fors seulement bref de droit, bref de dower et assises de mort dauncestre et de nouele disseisine, et de totes autres brefs originales leuesqe et ses predecessours tut temps ount este saunz power et de

ceaux power salue a nostre seignur le Roi en temps de vacacion et
en Eyre, La aed William le fitz Johan Hunter tret en plee le dit Joun
par bref Leuesqe de ael de les deux parties dun Mies, vn Molyn et
vne Carue de terre oue les apurtenaunces en Aldyngrigge deinz la
fraunchise auauntdite deuaunt les Justices Leuesqe de Dureme
qore est, encountre la Coroune et la dignete nostre seignur le Roi et
les vsages auaunt nomez, dount il pri remedie et le supersedeas a
Leuesqe et a ses Justices.

Endorsed: Soit sur ceste peticion fait brief tiel come ad este fait auant
ses heures en semblable cas.

post 1334. This petition compared with nos 170–171 above neatly
underlines the dilemma facing the Bishop's courts. If justice was
done in the new fashion it was a cause for counter-appeal to the
King's court. Aldingrange belonged to Finchale Priory, having
been the original endowment of Henry Puiset for his proposed
Augustinian house of *Bacstaneford* (Surtees iv, pt. 2, p. 105).

173

Marmaduke Basset petitions the King and Council that whereas
Walter de Wessington gave the manor of Offerton in the
franchise of Durham to Marmaduke Basset his grandfather and his
heirs by the body of Isabel, daughter of the said Walter, and
Marmaduke the elder died so seised: after his death William Basset
entered as son and heir and alienated the estate and Marmaduke the
younger often sued the Bishop of Durham for a writ of *formedon*
[the lack of which will lead] to his disinheritance (AP 15515).

[A nostre seignur le Roi] et a son bon conseil prie Marmeduke
Basset qe come Wauter de Wessyngton' dona le Manoir de
Offerton' oue les appurtenaunces [qe sont deinz la fran] chise de
Duresme a Marmeduke Basset, son ael qi eir il est, et les heirs qil
engendra du corps Isabel la fiele le dit Wauter ... Marmeduke
deuya de ceo seisi, apres son mort entra William Basset come fitz et
heir, le quel William aliena le [dit Manoir et] ... [fa]ire diuerses
descordes par la forme de doun auantdit au dit Marmeduke, qi ore
se pleint come a fuiz et heir ... [le dit] Marmeduke est couent ... le
Euesqe de Duresme et lui ad prie qil lui grant ad vne bref' de forme

du doun, la ... desheritaunce le dit Marmeduke dont il prie remedie.

Endorsed: Soit mande al euesqe par bref de la chauncellerie comparnaunt la suggestion contenue en cele peticion, qil fait droit a Marmeduke.

c. 1330 x 1340. Walter de Wessington was a leading Durham knight (cf *Bek* pp. 92, 106, 135). His son-in-law Marmaduke was dead before 1310, when William Basset sold Offerton to John de Denum, a local man of law. The ill-feeling between Marmaduke Basset junior and the Denum family culminated in a fight at Penshaw in the autumn of 1328 when Margaret, lady of Offerton, met Basset, who promptly assaulted one of her retinue with an axe. She cried: 'Peace, peace, peace! Any evil done shall be made good to you'. He retorted: 'there can be no peace as long as that perverse man Thomas of Seaton is near you and in your company'. A further clash saw Seaton with a halberd in his back and Basset disarmed by a sword blow. Lady Margaret intervened to save Basset, who was lying on the ground with his enemies hacking at his legs, wounding him in seven places. The battle ended with Seaton shot through the windpipe and above the left breast, and the hue and cry raised after Basset's two henchmen, Thomas of *Miridon* and John of Burton Agnes (C. M. Fraser & K. Emsley, 'Law and Society in Northumberland and Durham, 1290 to 1350', *AA*[4] XLVII, 1969, pp. 62–3). For the inability of the Durham chancery to issue the writ *formedon*, see nos 170 and 171 above; cf. no. 175 below.

174

Ralph de Neville petitions the King and Council that whereas Thomas son of Robert de Rokeby, William Scop' of Cotherstone and John de Lythum, staying in Yorkshire, came to the park of Ralph at Raby in the franchise of Durham and broke into it and hunted and took wild beasts there, for which he sued them in the bishop's court before his judges at Durham there deputed, and they were outlawed in consequence, he can have no recovery because they have neither lands nor tenements within the bishopric (AP 6408).

A nostre seignur le Roi et a son counseil moustre Rauf de Neuille qe com Thomas le fitz Robert de Rokeby, Willeam Scop' de Cotheliston et Johan de Lythum demoraunz en le Counte de Euerwyk' vyndrount taunt' au park le dit Rauf a Raby deyns la fraunchise de Duresme et le dit park abruserunt et ses bestes sauuages leyns trouez chaserunt et pristrent, de quele trespas il les enpleda en la court le dit Euesqe deuaunt ses Justices a Duresme qe a ceo la furent deputez, et taunt sui qils sont utlaiges illoeqs a sa sute, ⟨et autre recouerir ne poet il auoir illeoqs par reison qe les ditz meffesours nont terres ne tenementz deinz le dit Eueschee, sour quoi il prie remedie *different hand.*⟩.

Endorsed: Soit mande al Euesqe de Duresme par bref du grant seal qil mande le record' et proces tochantz ceste bosoigne en Chancellerie ⟨et quant le record'⟩ vendra en Chancellerie, soit bref mande de prendre les corps de ceux qe sont vtlagez par le dit record' as viscontes des Countez ou ils sont demorantz.

1337. Ralph de Neville was Lord of Raby from 1331 to 1367 (Surtees iv, pt. 1, p.158). The park was at Langley by Durham. The original suit was to have been heard before Roger de Esshe and his fellow judges at Durham on Wednesday, 5 June 1336, when the park-breakers defaulted. After three further defaults the sheriff of Durham was ordered to have them in court for 3 February 1337, when in view of their continued contumacy the court adjudged them outlawed. On Thursday, 5 June 1337 Neville laid an information before the King that the park-breakers were at large in Yorkshire and obtained a royal writ for their arrest, addressed to the sheriff of Yorkshire: and the record of the Durham proceedings was entered on the *Coram Rege* Roll for Easter, with a hearing fixed for 1 July 1337 (*Reg Pal Dun* iv, 215–21).

175

The men of the franchise of Durham and Norhamshire petition the King and Council that whereas the Bishop of Durham should have in his franchises of Durham and Norhamshire royal jurisdiction and writs, and is bound to do justice to all therein wishing to plead, and any kind of writ ought to be available in his eyre, as with all his predecessors, and in former times eyres in these parts were held so often that none needed nor wished to plead out of eyre writs of entry or escheat or other common writs of land, because of the delay out of eyre and the speedy remedy in eyre: but eyres have not been held for a long time, wherefore many are disinherited and many are about to be unless a remedy be ordained. When men of the said franchises come to the Bishop's chancery and request writs of entry and other writs ordained by statute since the last eyre held in those franchises the Bishop will not grant these writs because they have not been pleaded there out of eyre, wherefore they crave the King and Council that as he is held to do right to all in his kingdom, within as well as outside franchises, to order the Bishop to do right to the people in his franchise through whatsoever writ they need, lest justice is lacking there more than elsewhere (AP 2165).

A nostre seignur le Roi e a son conseil moustront les gentz de la franchise de Duresme e de Norhamshire qe come Leuesqe de Duresme qe pur le temps sera ad e auer doit denz ces franchises de Duresme e de Norham franchise reale e ces briefs icoront, e droit par ces briefs est tenu a [fair a] toux yceux de mesme la franchise qe pleindre se vodrent, e en son Eire doit pleder chescun manere de brief, e toux ces predecessours tote temps ent fait; e en aunciene temps les Eires vers ceux parties soleint estre tenuz si souerment qe hors de Eire en cele franchise nule homme mester auoit ne ne voleit pleder par briefs dentre ne deschet nautre briefs communes des terres et tenementz dedeinz la dite franchise pur les grand delaie qil auoient hors deire e pur le hastiue remedie qils auoient en Eire; mes les Eires vers ceux parties ne sont pas este tenuz de grant temps, dont plusours gentz sont desherites pur toux iours e plusours en point destre desherites *forsqe* remedie en soit ordeine; e par la ou les gentz de les dites franchises venont a la Chauncelerie ledit Euesqe e priont briefs dentre e dascun autre briefs qe sont ordeinz par estatut' puis le dreyn Eire tenuz en celes franchise, le dit Euesqe ne les veot pas granter les ditz briefs pur ceo qe les briefs nont pas este pledez en la dit franchise hors de Eire, par quoi les ditz gentz prient a nostre seignur le Roi e a son conseil puis qil est tenuz a fair droit a toux iceux deinz son realme auxi bien deinz franchise come de hors e son brief ne ... pas ... qil diegne en comandement au dit Euesqe de faire droit deinz sa franchise al people par qequner brief qe lour besoigne auoient ... se, issint qe droit ne faile pas illoeqes e pluys qalours deinz le roialme.

Endorsed: Coram Rege et magno consilio
    Ceste requeste touche change de ley et ne purreit estre fait si
noun a la requeste Leuesqe de Doresme e la comunalte del Euesche
e par assent du Roi e des prelatz, Countes e Barons e autres grantz
de la terre e ce en parlement si riens deust estre fait; par que riens ne
poet estre fait a ore.

post 1345. The popularity of eyres contrasts with no 169 above,
suggesting that their other implications had been forgotten. The
last recorded eyre held in Durham was in 1279 (PRO, Assize Roll
225). For examples of cases hampered by the limited repertoire of
recognised writs in Durham, see nos 170–173 above.

176

    William de Claxton, knight, petitions the King and Council that
whereas he had sued for long time by writ of *formedon* against a
John de Drileton in the court of the Bishop of Durham and been
delayed about four years or more by divers false delays and
imaginary hindrances, and now the process being brought to an
issue to try the right of William by inquest, John, by false
suggestion that he was about to journey with the Duke of
Clarence, has sued for a royal protection to delay William in the
recovery of his right, to his great hurt: and John is staying in
England and not in the Duke's company, nor ever has served in
peace or war him or any other lord before this protection was
granted, nor is in service, as William understands. He craves that
the King and Council revoke the protection and order that such
protections be not granted hereafter to the delay and disinheritance
of him and his cause (AP 1935).

    A nostre seignur le Roi et a son conseil moustre William de
Claxton' Cheualer qe come il ad sui par grant temps vn brief de
fourme doun vers vn Johan de Drileton' en la Court leuesqe de
Duresme, en quel brief il ad este deslaie enuiron quatre ans ou pluis
par diuerses fauces deslaies et coniectementz ymaginez par le dit
Johan, et ore par processe contenue le plee est mys a issue a trier le
droit le dit William par enqueste, la ad le dit Johan, par fauce
suggestion allegeant qil estoit en alant oue le Duc de Clarence en sa
veiage, sui vn protection nostre seignur le Roi par cause de deslaier
le dit William de son droit recouerir a grant damage et desheritison

de lui, et si est le dit Johan remys et demurant deinz le Roialme Dengleterre et ne mie en la compaignie le dit Duc' ne vnqes estoit seruant de pees ne de guere a lui ne a nulle autre seignurage deuant celle protection a lui grante ne vnqores est, a ceo qe le dit William entende: Par qoi le dit William prie as ditz son seignur le Roi et a son conseil qe lour pleise repeller la dite protection et ordeiner par bone auisement ore en ceste conseil qe tieux protections ne soient grantez desore en auant en deslaie et desheritison de lui et en sa suite.

Endorsed: sue brief' de deceite pur ses damages recouerir sil voille, et sil voille defaire la protection le Roi sue en la Chancellerie de certifier le Roi sil soit demurant en Engleterre et ne mie a aler outre meer, quelle certificacion eue soet la protection repeller.

1364 x 1368. The journey of the Duke of Clarence to Ireland was arranged in 1364 (*CPR 1364–67*, pp. 10ff), and in 1368 the Duke died. Sir William de Claxton succeeded to Claxton in 1349 (Surtees iii, 142).

Prerogative

One of the burning issues during the first half of the fourteenth century was whether the Bishops of Durham could secure royal recognition of their right to lands forfeited within their franchise for treason (nos 180, 183–184, 189–190, 193–194, 196–198, 201–206). It had been conceded by Henry III in May 1267 (*CPR 1266–72*, p. 63), and tacitly accepted by Edward I in 1296 (*Reg Pal Dun* iii, 28–32). After the act of 1534 which reserved such forfeitures to the Crown, Bishop Tunstall was still able in 1539 and 1544 to dispose of lands forfeited by Sir John Bulmer. Queen Elizabeth finally put an end to the pretention by an act of attainder against the earl of Westmorland, passed in 1570, which specifically claimed the Durham forfeitures (Lapsley, 47–49).

Whereas the claims for prerogative forfeiture came from the Bishop, his 'subjects' complained of the disability whereby the sheriffs of Yorkshire and Northumberland were unable to execute royal writs within the regalian liberty (nos 177–178, 198). Prerogative wardship was at issue in no 182; rights of coinage in no 186: profits of the wool-staple at Hartlepool in no 195: profits from distraint of knighthood in no 201: profits from prevention of the illegal export of bullion in no202: and exemption from taxation in no 203.

Ancient Petitions E456, E770, 120A–E, 345, 393–94, 2121, 2147, 2151–52, 2155, 2157A–D, 2158, 2166, 2168, 3660–61, 3845, 4025, 4096, 4208, 4963, 5256, 5381, 5384, 8626–27, 8950, 9095, 15784A, 15785A–B.

177

Richard, prior of Durham, petitions the King that whereas there were divers debates between Antony, Bishop of Durham, and himself and the convent and then they agreed on a form of peace in the King's presence, who guaranteed it, to the effect that all grievances done before the accord by the bishop to the prior should be redressed and the condition of the prior and his supporters be safeguarded: the bishop, however, did not redress any of the grievances, whose diversity is recorded in a roll presented to the King, but daily multiplied the causes of grievance, which also are recorded on the roll: and by the King's command a writ was brought before his chief justices which has been before them already half a year, but by false returns from the sheriff of Northumberland the suit is delayed, wherefore the prior craves the King's grace to consider the grievances done as well after the accord as before it, especially as committed contrary to his ordinance and in the King's despite, such as [electing] Henry de Luceby as prior, so that right be done before the King in parliament. Unless the King intervenes to help he cannot succeed in his suit because the Bishop will not return writs to the King's court and the sheriff of Northumberland will not, or dare not, answer nor return them, as is shown by earlier endorsements. He craves the King's peace and protection for him and his men in order that these outrages done to him and his be brought to an end by the King (AP 8950).

A nostre seignor le Roy Moustre Richard Priour de dureame e sen pleynt qe par la ou plusors desbat firent entre Antoyn Eueske de dureme dun part e lauantdist Priour e soen Couent dautre, e puys de ceo pleinement par acord dun part e dautre se asseinarent en forme de pees en la presence nostre seignor le Rey qe de la pees se

entremist la soweinertye dount issint par nostre seignor le Re fust
entre eaus assentuz e par eaus acorde qe totes les greuances deuant
lauauntdist ordonement alauantdist priour fetes par launantdist
Eueske serroient repelees e qe lestat le priour e des soens en totes
choses fust sauue e entiere e nient enblemy par reson de nul desbat
auantdist, sur ceo lauantdist Eueske nuls des greuances auantdistes,
qe plusors sont e deuerses sicom piert en vne roule qe de ceo fait est
prest a nostre seignor le Rey a sa voluntez a moustrer, ne aad
repelee mes de Jour en Jour autres greuances aad multipliez, les
queus aussint sont en Roule prest a nostre seignor le Rey a
moustrer, e sour ceo par le commandement nostre seignor le Rey
breef' est porteez deuant ses cheefs Justices soen leu tenantz, le queu
breef' aad este pendaunt deuant eaus ia demy an, mes par fauses
retours du vescomt de Northombrelond lauantdist seute est delaeez:
par quoy lauantdist Priour prye a nostre seignor le Roy de sa grace
si ly plest qe il voile les auantdistes greuances faites veer, aussi bien
aprees lordainment come deuant ⟨nomement cumme il sunt ausi
feces encontre sa ordenance e en despit de nostre seignur le Rey,
comme [lelection de Henry de Lu]ceby priour *inserted without
indication of position*⟩ e qe dreiture ly soit faite deuant le Roy
meismes si ly plest en soen parlement: Care si nostre seignor le Rey
ne mette la mayn de ly eider il ne poet lauantdist seute escheuir, pur
ceo qe endroit de breef' qe venent al Eueske les queus il dust en la
court le Roys retourner il ne les voet pur le mandement le Rey
retourner, e endroit des breefs qe venent au vescomte de
Northumbrelond', lauantdist vescomte ne se deigne nen ose en
forme de lay a nul breef' respondre ne lealment les[?] les retorner, si
com bien piert par les responses qe il aad donez. E prye a nostre
seignor le Rey de sa pees e de sa protection pur ly e pur ses gentz
tant qe cestes outrages faites a ly e a soens par nostre seignor le Rey
soient terminetz.

Endorsed: fiat protectio Ricardo etc, non nominando se priorem,
duratura per biennium. Et quo ad Transgressionem, habeat diem
coram Rege.

March 1301. This petition marks a turning-point in the clash
between Prior Hoton and Bishop Bek of Durham which had
begun with an attempt by the bishop to visit the convent of
Durham on 20 May 1300, followed by appeals, the deposition of
the prior, an arbitration by Edward I at Evenwood on 20 June

1300, the siege of the monks in Durham cathedral lasting a month, the intrusion of a new prior, and the escape of Prior Hoton from confinement to appeal for protection to the Pope and the King. Eventually the King enforced compliance on the bishop by confiscation of his temporal jurisdiction over Durham. This jurisdiction was suspended between July 1302 and July 1303, and again between December 1305 and September 1308. The dilemma of the sheriff of Northumberland was that his jurisdiction did not normally extend over Durham. See *Bek*, pp. 92–3, 123–52, 176–214, and nos 152 and 163 above.

178

The Prior of Durham petitions the King concerning damages awarded before sir William de Ormesby and sir Henry de Gildeford while the franchise of Durham was in the King's hand, the Bishop's officers being unwilling to levy them or make execution.

The same petitions that the beasts and goods of the convent of Durham have been removed by brother Henry de Lusceby, intruded prior, and held in Norham Castle by its keepers, and the Prior sued to replevy them before the sheriff, and was told that the King's bailiff could not enter without special royal warrant, and he craves remedy in order to have delivery according to the law (AP 9095).

A nostre seignur le Roi mustre le Priour de Dureme qe des damages qe la furent agardez et iugeez deuant sire William de Ormesby et sire Henry de Gildeford tant come la franchise de Duresme fu en la meyn le Roi, les ministres leueqe ne volent leuer ne nule execucion faire, dount le dit Priour prie remedie.

Idem mustre meisme le Priour qe ses bestes et autre biens de la meison de Dureme esloignez par Daun Henry de Lusceby qe se fist priour par intrusion, sont detenuz en Chastel de Norham par les gardeyns de meisme le lieu, et ha le Priour suy au .. visconte par gage et plegge solum la Ley, et est respoundu qe le baillif le Roi ne poet entrer saunz especial garant du Roi, dount le dit Priour prie remede qe la deliuerance de ses biens li soit faite solum la Ley.

No endorsement

1303–4. Henry de Luceby was intruded as Prior of Durham by

Bishop Bek in August 1300. Royal assizes were held before William de Ormesby and Henry de Gildeford in Durham in 1302/3 (PRO, JI/226). On 26 February 1304 'two petitions of the Prior of Durham' were referred to the King's justices and others of his council (*Cal Chancery Warrants* i, 204).

179

The commons of the bishopric of Durham between Tyne and Tees petition the King and Council that whereas they complained at the last parliament at Rose [i.e. Carlisle] of grievances done to them by officers of the Bishop of Durham, concerning which the Bishop was arraigned to redress them, and when he was unwilling to do this the King at the request of the commons sent him an order to redress them so that the need for action might not arise, and the Bishop did nothing in way of redress following the writ and since this order has done more grievous things than before. They request the King that in default of the Bishop their grievances and disinheritances in the franchise be redressed by order of the King's Council (AP E770).

A nostre seignur le Rey e a son conseil Moustre la Communaute del Euesche de Durem entre Tyne e Teise qi par la ou eus se pleynterent a [le] ... darreyn parlement a la Rose des greuaunces e de deserit aunces a eus fetes par les Ministres le Eueske de Durem, des queus le Eueske [souent] fuist arisone qe il les redresscast e il poynt ne le vout fere, parunt en defaute de ly Nostre seignur le Rey graunta a la requeste de meime la communaute [vn br]ef al Eueske E ly Maunda qe il feist redresser les greuaunces e les deseritaunces a eus fetes: Issynt qe il ne huyst mester de metter [la main, e le] dist Eueske pur ceo bref' a ly liuere ren ne fist, ne des articles des greuaunces a eus feces e a ly liuerez pleynement respoundis[t] qe .. . re fereit: Eynz, puys ceo Maundement a eus pluis a greuaunce ad fet qe deuaunt: Dount eus prient a nostre seignur le Rey qe en defaute del dist Eueske les greuaunces e deseritaunces a eus fetes en la fraunchyse auauntdiste si ly pleyse voyl redresser par le ordeyne-ment de ly e de son Conseyl.

Endorsed: Rex non potest respondere Communitati de re non certa, set si aliquis de re certa con[queri] voluerit, Rex faciet Justiciam.

1307. Parliament was held at Carlisle in January 1307. Administration of the franchise had been resumed by royal officers in December 1305 (*Bek*, pp. 197–8, 205–7).

180

Richard, bishop of Durham, petitions the King and Council that whereas his royal franchise of the church of Durham was such that from time immemorial between Tyne and Tees, in Norhamshire and Bedlingtonshire no royal officer, escheator nor other might enter to seize land or perform other office, sir Robert de Cliderhow, escheator north of Trent, entered the franchise, allegedly with a chancery writ, and seized the manor of Hart and Hartness with the appurtenances into the King's hand, to the prejudice of the franchise. And further a John le Irreis entered the franchise with an alleged commission from the King's Chancery and seized into the King's hand Barnard Castle and the manor of Gainford with their appurtenances within the said franchise, which are still in the King's hand. The Bishop craves the King, for the devotion he has to God and St. Cuthbert, that he will maintain the franchise in its ancient condition and lift his hand from the lands so seized and recall the writs issued from Chancery to the prejudice of the said franchise (AP 120A).

The petition is printed in *Reg Pal Dun* iv, 183–85: cf. 129–39.

1316. The seizures represented the aftermath of the forfeitures of Barnard Castle and Hartlepool by John de Balliol and Robert de Brus respectively. The former had been claimed in 1296 by Bishop Bek, but the latter forfeiture occurred in 1306 while the palatinate was in royal hands. Edward I had regranted Hartlepool to Robert de Clifford on 26 May 1306 and Barnard Castle to Guy de Beauchamp, earl of Warwick, on 2 February 1307 (*Bek*, pp. 203, 208). With Beauchamp's death in August 1315 Bishop Richard de Kellawe tried to reassert claims to wardship of Barnard Castle during the minority of the heir by presenting this petition at the Lincoln parliament of 1316 (*Reg Pal Dun* iii, 1–2). Copies of the writs to Clitherhow and Le Irreis with their returns (summarized in Kellawe's register, *ibid.*, 2–3) are attached as AP 120 B–E.

181

The Bishop of Durham petitions the King that whereas divers
oppressions have been done to him contrary to the franchise of the
church of St. Cuthbert of Durham, concerning which he delivered
petitions at Lincoln in the last parliament [January 1316] and was
adjourned for an answer at Westminster on the quindene of Easter,
he craves an order to Council to hear the petitions and that right be
done (AP E456).

A nostre seignur le Roi prie Leuesqe de Duresme qe come
diuerses oppressiouns e greuaunces soient faites a lui en countre
lestat e la fraunchise de sa esglise de seint Cudbert de Duresme,
dount il liura peticions en le dearreyn (sic) parlement tenu a
Nichole, e feust dilluqes aiourne destre respoundu a Westmoustier'
a la quindezeyn de Pasche, qil voil comaunder a soun conseil qe les
dites peticions soient oyes e qe dreit lui soit fait.

No endorsement

1316 See no. 180 above.

182

Robert de Welle petitions the King and Council that whereas
the King of his free lordship granted him all the lands and
appurtenances, fees and advowsons held in dower by his wife
Maud, among which they were seised of the service of Richard fitz
Marmaduke for the manor of Stranton in Hartness by assignment
of dower in the court of the Bishop of Durham of a third of the
manor of Hart: the present Bishop has come down on the manor,
claiming its custody by reason of his prerogative, to the King's
prejudice, to whom the reversion of the third belongs after
Robert's death. The King has sent a writ of Chancery to the
Bishop on three occasions to do right to Robert or show cause, and
on the fourth summoned him to appear before the King and
Council on the octave of St Hilary last [20 January] to answer, but
he would not answer nor come on the day assigned. Robert craves
an attachment on the Bishop or a summons to the Bishop and himself before Council, where the King's right may be tried (AP 3845).

A nostre seignur le Roi et a son conseil moustre son lige Robert de Welle qe come nostre dit seignur le Roi de sa fraunche seignurie et grace eust donez au dit Robert toutes les terres od les appurtenances, fiez et auowesons queux Mahaud sa femme tynt en dowaire, entre queux fiez les auantditz Robert et Mahaud furent seisi du seruise Richard le fuiz Marmeduke du Manoir de Stranton en Hertenesse par assignement de dowaire fait en la Court .. leuesqe de Doresme de la tierce partie du Manoir de Hert, Leuesqe de Doresme qe ore est se est abatuz en dit Manoir, enclamant auer la garde par reson de sa prerogatiue en preiudice nostre seignur le Roi a qi la reuersion de la dite tierce partie apent apres la mort le dit Robert. Et tout soit ce qe nostre seignur le Roi eit mande par bref de Chauncellerie au dit Euesqe qil faist a lauantdit Robert dreiture et reson et autrefoiz et la tierce foiz, ou qil signifiast la cause, et la quarte foiz, ou qil feust pardeuant le Roi et son conseil ⟨as vtaues de seint Hiller' derrein passer ou qe le Roi adonqes feust⟩ a respoundre sur la busoigne auantdite, as queux mandementz il nad volu respoundre ne venir ⟨au iour qe li fu assignez⟩, prie le dit Robert qe pleise nostre seignur le Roi comander atachement sur le dit Euesqe ou qe les ditz Euesqe et Robert soient appellez pardeuant son conseil et qe illoeqes le droit le Roi puisse estre triez et recom'

Endorsed: Habeat breue de attachiamento versus Episcopum quod sit coram Rege secundum processum priorum breuium.

c. 1318. Robert de Welle had married the widow of Robert de Clifford, lord of Appleby and Hartlepool, without royal licence, but was pardoned on 3 October 1316 (*CCR 1313–18*, p. 367). Bishop Kellawe died the following week, on 9 October, and Bishop Beaumont received the temporalities of Durham on 4 May 1317 (*HBC*, p. 220). Richard Marmaduke was murdered in 1318 (Surtees i, 26). Cf. no. 64 above.

183

The executors of Richard, lately bishop of Durham, petition the King and Council that whereas formerly in parliament at York they craved the King by petition to do right concerning wardship of the manors of Barnard Castle, Gainford, Whorlton

[and] Longnewton with their appurtenances in the bishopric of Durham, which John de Baillol and his ancestors held of the predecessors of Bishop Richard by knight service and which manors came into the seisin of the earl of Warwick lately dead, after whose death Bishop Richard seized the manors in the name of wardship through the minority of the earl's son and heir. These were taken from him by the King, for which reason he sued by petition in parliament at Lincoln to have remedy. This was sent from parliament to Chancery, where the Bishop sued until his death. The executors crave that right be done, so that they can pay the debts of the dead, who died suing his right. They crave an answer and that right be done them (AP 2168).

A nostre seignur le Roi e a son consail prient les executors Richard nadguers Euesqe de Duresme qe cum autrefoize en le parlement de Euerwik il prierent a nostre seingnur le Roy par peticioun illoqe liure qil le feist dreit de la garde des maners de chastel Bernard, Gaynesford, Quernington, Langneuton' oue les appurtenaunces en Leueschee de Duresme les queus Johan de Baillol e ses auncestres teindrount des predecessors le dit Euesqe Richard par seruice de chivaler, e les queus Maners apres deuyndrent en la seysine le Count de Warrewyk' qi drein Morust, apres qi mort Le dit Eueske Richard fist seysir les dites Maners en noun de garde par le nounage le fiz e le heir le dit Count, des queus nostre seignur le Roy li hosta, par quei il suist par peticioun en le parlement de Nicholle de Remedie auer, La quele fuit enuoie de parlement tauntke en chauncelerie ou le dit Euesqe suwist tauntke il morust, dount les dites executors prierent qe dreit lour fust fait si qil poaynt les dettes le dit Mort aquiter, qe morust ensuaunt son dreit. Dount il prient qil seient responduz a la dite peticioun e qe dreit les soit fait.

Endorsed: Quia Comes tenuit tenementa illa de domino Rege et non de Episcopo et dominus Rex est in possessione custodie predicte, consideratum est quod accio non co[ncedatur] executoribus.   Irrotulatur

c. 1319. See nos 180–181 above. There were parliaments held at York in May 1319 and January 1320 (*HBC*, p. 516).

184

Louis, Bishop of Durham, petitions the King and Council that whereas Walter de Selby held the manor of Felling in the bishopric of Durham, where the Bishop has royal franchise and royal prerogative and so should have within the bishopric both forfeiture of war and other escheats as had his predecessors, as appears by the King's confirmation, Walter was of the fealty of Robert de Brus in Scotland, where he stayed as an enemy, for which reason the Bishop seized the manor of Felling as the right of him and his church, and held it until the King gave it to Ralph de Epplyngdon and he was ejected by the sheriff of Northumberland (AP 2158).

A nostre seignur le Roi et a son counseil mustre Lowys Eueske de Duresme qe come Wauter de Selby tient le Maner de Fellyng oue les apurtenaunces dedenz leuesche de Duresme, ou le dit Eueske ad le Regal et fraunchise et prerogatiue reales par quei il doit auer dedenz le dit Euesche auxi bien forfetoure de guerre come dautres eschetes et ses predecessours ount eu, sicom il pert par fet le Roi le quel nostre seignur le Roi qore est ad conferme, et le dit Wauter sest mys a la foi Robert de Brus en escoce et la demoert come enemy, par quei le dit Eueske seisit le dit Maner de Fellyng' en sa Maine com son dreit et le droit de sa Eglise de seint Cutbert de Duresme par la forfetoure le dit Wauter, et en sa Maine le tient taunqe nostre seignur le Roi le dona par sa chartre a Rauf de Epplynden' et par son visconte de Northumbr' le dit Eueske osta: dount il pri qe remedi et droit lui soit fait.

Endorsed: Soient veues les chartres et ap[pell'] les parties et le Roy certefiez qen est trouez.
Irrotulatur   Coram Rege—Herl[aston]

1319 x 1323. The manor of Felling, confiscated by Bishop Beamont for Selby's participation in the rebellion of Gilbert de Middleton and the concurrent Scottish infiltration, was later granted by the Bishop to Amery de Trewe in 1331 and then to Sir Thomas Surtees of North Gosforth and Dinsdale (Durham, Misc Charter 5858; *CPR 1330–34*, p. 240). Edward II, however, treated Selby's lands as a royal forfeiture, and by a grant of 24 May 1319 gave Felling to Ralph de Epplingden, who subsequently was involved with Thomas of Lancaster and the earl of Hereford and forfeited the estate in turn (*CPR 1317–21*, p. 335; *FPD* 8–10 notes.) See no. 185 below.

185

Ralph de Epplingdeun petitions the King that whereas he holds the manor of Felling which used to be of Walter de Selby, who is an adherent of the Scots, by grant of the King by reason of Walter's forfeiture, which manor is held of the prior of Durham by certain service, and the prior distrained on Ralph for arrears of services for the time that the manor was in the King's hand for the forfeiture as well as for the time of Walter: may it please the King to ordain suitable remedy for this distress (AP 393).

A nostre seignur le Roi prie Rauf' de Epplingdeun', qe come il tient le Manoir de Felling' qe fust a Wauter de Selby, qi est ahertz a vos enemis de Scoce, de doun le dit ⟨nostre seignur le Roi⟩ par reison de la forfaiture le dit Wauter et le dit Monoir (*sic*) soit tenuz du Priour de Duresme par certeins seruices, et le dit Priour destreint le dit Rauf' pur ascunes seruices qe arere lui sont, a ceo qil dit, auxi bien du temps qe le dit Manoir estoit en la mayn le dit nostre seignur le Roi pur la dite forfaiture come du temps le dit Wauter, qil pleise a nostre seignur le Roi ⟨ordiner⟩ qe conuenable remedi soit fait au dit Rauf' de la dite destresce.

Endorsed: videtur consilio quod tenens non debet onerari de tempore Regis. Et ideo prosequatur Prior versus dominum Regem pro tempore suo si sibi viderit expedire. Et super hoc habeat tenens breue quod pro tempore Regis non distringatur.

Irrotulatur

1319–23. See no. 184 above. The Prior and Convent of Durham petitioned in parliament in 1325 for recovery of the issues from Felling, forfeited successively by Selby and Epplingdon, in view of their losses, and a writ of enquiry was to be sent to the sheriff of Northumberland (*Rot Parl* i, 431). According to this enquiry, held at Felling in the presence of the sheriff on 17 May 1326 the manor was held of the Prior of Durham by knight service and a rent of 2 marks, with fortnightly suit of court. It was then worth 40s a year nett, but 'before the burning of the bishopric' had been worth 8 marks, excluding the services (*FPD* 8–9 notes).

186

The King's chaplain, the Bishop of Durham, petitions the King that whereas the latter had granted him dies to mint money at Durham, and beyond the six pieces he granted him as a special favour three upper punches, these are now retained by the keepers of the Mint at the Tower without royal authority. He craves delivery of the three upper punches until the King himself orders otherwise (AP 4096).

A nostre seignur le Roi prie le soen chapelyn Le Euesqe de Durem qe com autre foiz il ly graunta ses coignes pur Monee faire a Durem, e outre .vj. peces qe ly furunt Liuerez pur la dite Monee faire ly graunta il treis peces de sa grace especial que sunt apellez trusseux a la volunte le dist nostre seignur le Roi, si com piert par son bref, les queus ly sont ore detenuz par les Gardeyns de la Monee a La Tour saunz comaundement nostre dist seignur, qe si ly plest voile comaunder qe les treis trusseus auaunditz lui seient liuerez arere, tauntqe par nostre seignur le Roi mesmes seit autre chose comaunde.

Endorsed: Le Roi lad grante tanqe de la Pasqe qe vendra en vn an prochein suiant.

1320. The authority for delivery of the punches is dated 20 November 1320 (*CCR 1318–23*, p. 281). Deliveries of dies to Bishop Beaumont from the royal Mint are recorded on the Memoranda Rolls for 1316/7, 1317/8 and 1320/1.

Following the initial warrant from Edward II, dated 1 June 1317, the exchequer officials examined the memoranda rolls and found precedents for previous deliveries of coin dies in June 1253 and November 1279, the latter being on the occasion of a new coinage. Augustine le Waleys, keeper of the King's exchange, was ordered in 1317 to engrave three new sets of dies, which were delivered by John de Merkingfeld, keeper of the dies in the King's exchange, to William de Ayreminne on behalf of the Bishop-elect in the form of three standards and three trussels. When Beaumont complained that a proper set consisted of two trussels to each standard, Edward II issued a further writ on 30 July 1317 authorizing three more 'duplicate' trussels, which were finally delivered on 31 October. The following year, on 22 May 1318, the bishop's brother, Henry de Beaumont, appeared at the Exchequer to complain that by recalling and reissuing dies the work of the Durham mint was being disrupted. Finally on Monday, 6 October 1320, William de Haustede, keeper of the King's mints at London and Canterbury, checked the Durham dies after they had been brought for renewal to the Exchequer by John of Durham, servant of Rainer the Lombard, keeper of the Durham exchange. A warrant was sent to Haustede on 1 December following to supply the additional three trussels, as petitioned by the bishop, to have for the term of a year after Easter, without prejudice to the King's rights, providing that the three trussels previously issued be returned to the exchange and that he have no more than two trussels for each standard (PRO, QR Mem Rolls 90 mm 46d, 119: 91 mm 12d, 114d, 160: 94 mm 24, 159).

187

The King's chaplain, the Abbot of St Mary, York, petitions that whereas one of his monks granted to Sir William Ridel, keeper of his castle of Barnard Castle, tithes for the sum of £50, provided he found sufficient security for payment, Sir William took the tithes by force for the upkeep of the castle. The abbot is loathe to become involved with royal officers and craves a remedy. Although the wrong was done in the franchise of Durham, yet because it concerns a royal officer he craves a royal remedy (AP 4025).

A nostre seignur le Roi prie le soen chapelein si li plest Labbe de nostre dame de Euerwyk' qe com vn de ses Moignes oet grante a sire William Ridel, gardein de son ⟨chastel⟩ Chastel Bernard', ascunes disme por .l. li' issint qil trouast suffisant seurte de la paye, le dit sire William ceo ne voleit et prist les dites dismes a force et armes por la sustenaunce du dit Chastel. Et por ceo sire qe le dit Abbe harreit moult dentagler vos Ministres, prie le dit Abbe a nostre seignur le Roi si li plest, qil li voille de ceo faire remedie. Et tot seit qe le dit trespas fust fait dentz la fraunchise de Duresme, iadumeyns por ceo qil touche le Ministre nostre seignur le Roi, il prie de li remedie si li plest.

Endorsed: Mandetur Willelmo Ridel quod si ita sit, tunc satisfaciat Abbati de debito, Ita quod dominus Rex inde iterato non audiat querelam, adiungendo quod dominus Rex alias mandauit quod decime non caperentur per huiusmodi sustentacionem.

1319–23. Sir William Ridel of Tillmouth, having been captured by the Scots in 1301, was sheriff of Northumberland from May to October 1315 and again from August 1317 to October 1319, when he was appointed keeper of Barnard Castle, an office he held until 6 July 1323. (*CFR* iii, 219; C. H. H. Blair, 'Sheriffs of Northumberland', AA⁴ XX (1942), pp. 41–2). According to the clerical taxation of 1291 the parish of Gainford which included the chapelry of Barnard Castle was appropriated to St. Mary's, York. In 1291 the church was assessed at £100 and the vicarage at £10, although by 1318 in the 'new taxation' the values had fallen to £40 and £1 respectively (*Taxatio Papae Nicholai iv*, p. 315).

188

Louis, bishop of Durham, petitions the King and Council that whereas Sir John de Eure died at Auckland in the bishopric of Durham where the Bishop is ordinary and to whom as ordinary belongs the right to sequestrate all goods found in his diocese of those who die therein until their wills are proved, Richard de Emeldon, commissioned by the King to seize land and goods of the King's enemies in those parts, came and seized the goods of Sir John found there. Sir John had died through persons unknown, without being attainted. He craves that the King out of regard for the franchise of Holy Church order Emeldon to lift his hand and restore the said goods so that he can order them as an ordinary should (AP 5256).

A nostre seignur le Roy et a son consail moustre Loys Euesqe de Duresme qe la ou sire Johan de Eure morut a Aukland en Leuesche de Duresme, ou le dit Euesqe est ordenor du lu, et a luy apent com a Ordinaire de sequestrer touz les biens et chateux trouez dedenz sa diocese de gentz qe moerent iloeke taunt qe lur testament soit proue, la vint Richard de Emeldon a qui nostre seignur le Roy auoit faet commission de seisir terres et tenementz, biens et chateux des enemis et rebels nostre seignur le Roy celes parties et a seisir les biens le dit sire Johan iloeqes trouez, le quel sire Johan fu mort iloeke par gentz desconutz saunz estre iloeke atteint: par quai il prie a nostre seignur le Roy qil vueille auoir regard al estat et la fraunchise de seinte Eglise et maunde al dit Richard qil oste sa main et luy rende les biens auauntditz, si qil porra des ditz biens faer ceo qe a Ordinaire apent.

Traces of red seal on face of petition

Endorsed: First endorsement obliterated
Por ceo qe Johan de Eure morust denz la franchise leuesqe de Dureme, seit maunde a Lesuesqe qil enquerge coment Johan de Eure morust, et sil fust tue, denquere par qi et coment et en quele manere, et certifie le Roi en Chauncellerie et seit fait droit.

Irrotulatur

1322. The circumstances of Eure's death were obscure, he having been involved with Thomas de Lancaster and present at the battle of Boroughbridge in which the rebellious earl was captured and subsequently executed. Emeldon had been appointed on 18 May 1322 as keeper of the lands of Thomas of Lancaster and his adherents in Northumberland, with power to evaluate these estates, to enquire what lands should be forfeited and whether there were any counterclaims, which lands were worth retaining for the King's benefit, and what would be more profitable to lease, and how much timber could be cut without detriment to the estate (*CPR 1321–24*, p. 161). The petitions of Eure's executors (AP 274), of the Bishop of Durham as ordinary (AP 275), and of the widow Agnes (AP 276) appear on the rolls of parliament (*Rot Parl* i, 403–4).

On 28 December 1326 John de Eure, son and heir, petitioned for livery of his father's lands, he then being 22 years of age; it was not, however, until 1360 and after payment of £400 that the Eure lands in Stokesley and Ingleby Greenhow in Yorkshire, and Kirkley with Berwick Hill, Throphill, Newton Underwood,

Mitford, Benridge, Lynemouth and Callerton Darreyns [Darras Hall] in Northumberland were returned (W. P. Hedley, *Northumberland Families* (Soc. of Antiquaries of Newcastle upon Tyne, 1968), i, 184). A pardon for those responsible for the deaths of John de Eure and Richard Uttyng of Topcliffe, chaplain, was issued by Edward II on 22 May 1322 (*ibid.*). Cf *Cal Inq Misc* ii, 121.

189

Louis, bishop of Durham, petitions the King and Council that whereas formerly he presented his petitions in parliament, craving his rights to the manors of Barnard Castle and Hart and other forfeitures of war in the bishopric of Durham and the advowson of Simonburn church and 50 librates of land in Tynedale, as included in these petitions, which remain unanswered: he craves an answer that right be done and not further delayed (AP 345).

? 1324. This petition is on the parliamentary roll (*Rot Parl* i, 418).

190

Louis, bishop of Durham, petitions the King and Council that whereas in this parliament [Candlemas, 1327] forfeiture of war was awarded him as a right of his church, and formerly it was awarded to his predecessor and writs were sent to the keepers of forfeited lands in his royal franchise to lift their hands from Barnard Castle, the manor of Gainford and other lands of the earl of Warwick, and Hart and Hartness of Sir Roger de Clifford, earlier forfeited through the forfeiture of Sir John de Bailliol and Robert de Brus within the franchise, the King having used his prerogative within the franchise, which does and should belong to the Bishop within the franchise as it belongs to the King outside. The Bishop craves orders to the keepers of the said lands to lift their hands and allow the Bishop to enjoy his franchise, where the King's writ should not run as of right nor the King enter to seize lands (AP 5384).

A nostre seignur le Roi et a soun counseil mustre Lowis Euesqe de Durem' qe come en icoe parlement forfeiture de guere luy seit aiuge come du droit de sa Eglise et autrefoiz fuste aiuge a soun predecessour, par quei briefs sount comaundes as gardeyns des terres forfaites de deinz sa franchise real qil oustait la meyn de par celes Chastel Bernard', le Manoir de Gaynesford et autres terres qe feurent a Count de Warewyk', Hert et Herternesse qe feurent a sire Roger de Clifford', autrefoitz feurent forfaites par la forfaitures sire Johan de Bailliolo et Roberd de Bruys sount deinz mesme la fraunchise, nostre seignur le Roy par resoun de la dit forfaiture vsaunt sa prerogatiue de deyntz la dite fraunchise, la quele prerogatiue est et estre doit al Euesqe de deinz la dite fraunchise come est au Roi de hors, ad seisy les dites terres en sa meyn qe point ne sount tenuz de luy, par quei le dit Euesqe prie audit nostre seignur le Roi qil voil comaunder bref as gardeyns de terres auantdites qil oustont la meyn de celes terres come des autres et suffrir le dit Euesqe auoir et ioyer sa fraunchise, ou le bref le Roi ne doit curer de droit ne nostre seignur le Roi illoques terre seiser.

Endorsed: Porce qe agarde est par le Roi qore est et son conseil en plein parlement qe leuesqe eit sa franchise reale come autrefer (*sic*) fust grante en temps le Roi Henri besael nostre dit seignur le Roi, est acorde qe le Roi ouste la mein de quant qil ad en sa mein par reson de iurisdiccion real, et aussint ses ministres ministrantz en office real.   Irrotulatur

1327. On 24 February 1327 the constable of Barnard Castle and the bailiff of Hart and Hartness were each ordered not to intermeddle with anything touching the regalian jurisdiction of the Bishop in Durham, it having been considered by the King and Council in parliament that the Bishop should have such royal liberties as were granted in the time of Henry III (*CCR 1327–30*, pp. 48–49). The full proceedings in parliament relating to Bishop Beaumont's suit are printed in *Rotuli Parliamentorum Anglie Hactenus Inediti*, (Royal Hist. Soc. Camden 3rd Ser LI, 1935, pp. 110–16).

191

Richard de Emeldon petitions the King and Council that whereas Edward, father of the present King, granted him by charter the manor of Silksworth, providing that if the King or his heirs wished for any reason to take back the manor when the whole manor came into Richard's hands after the death of Ida, widow of

John fitz Marmaduke, Richard or his heirs would have assignment and livery of 30 librates of land in a suitable place, as is shown by the charter whose transcript is attached. Now it has been ordained in parliament that all lands seized as forfeit through the dispute of the earl of Lancaster should be restored to those who should have them, and this manor was so seized. He craves that he be not ejected contrary to the form of the said charter, or that 30 librates of land be provided according to the tenor of the charter (AP 15784A).

A nostre seignur le Roi et son counsaille moustre Richard' de Emeldon' qe la ou sire Edward' piere nostre seignur le Roi qore est qui dieux garde dona et graunta par sa chartre au dit Richard' le Manoir de Sillesworth' ou les appurtenaunz, issint qe si le dit sire Edward ou ses ⟨heires⟩ volaient par asqunes causes reprendre le dit manoir en lour meyn del houre qe le manoir entier serra venu en la mayn le dit Richard ou de ses heires, lui ferroient assigner et liuerere trente Liure de terre en lieu couenable, sicom piert par la Chartre dount transescript est cosu a ceste peticoun, et come le manoir entier seit deuenu en la mayn le dit Richard' apres la mort Ide qe fust la femme John le fitz Marmaduke et iea soit ordine en parlement qe totes les terres qe furront seisis en la mayn le roi com forfetes pur la querele le Counte de Lancastre soient restitutz a ceux qe les deuoient, et ceo manoir si fust seisi en la mayn le Roi com tiele forfeture a ceo qil entent: prie le dit Richard' qil ne soit oste dudit manoir encountre la forme de la chartre auantdite ouqe trente Liure de terre lui soient liueres et assignes en lieu couenable solom la tenore de la Chartre auantdite.

Endorsed: Coram Rege et magno consilio
   Il nest pas del entencion du counseil qe les terres sire Robert li seient renduz come a cesti qe fut de la querele et le counseil ne li tient my de la querele.

c. 1327–29. The original grant to Emeldon is dated 24 March 1324 (*CPR 1321–24*, p. 398). The transcript is now AP 15784B. The estate had passed to Sir Robert de Holland, but nothing was returned to that family until 1329 (*CPR 1327–30*, p. 467). See no. 192 below.

192

Richard de Emeldon petitions the King and Council that whereas Edward, father of the King, granted by his charter, confirmed by the present King, to Richard the manor of Silksworth in the bishopric of Durham towards his long service and losses received through the Scottish wars, to have to him and his heirs for all time, so that neither he nor his heirs should be evicted before he was provided with 30 librates of land, as contained in these charters, now Sir Robert de Holand has put in question the manor, which is in the bishopric of Durham, by reason of a fine levied in the court of the Bishop between Sir Thomas lately earl of Lancaster and the said Robert wherein the earl recognised the manor as belonging to Robert by gift, in return for which Robert leased the manor to the earl for life. By this the manor should return after the earl's death to Robert and his heirs. Through this contention Richard has had no profit from the manor as he should. He craves an order to enable him and his heirs to have peaceful tenure (AP 15785A).

A nostre seignur le Roi et a son consail prie Richard de Emeldon qe come sire Edward' piere nostre seignur le Roi granta par sa Chartre la quele nostre seignur dit le Roi ad ia conferme par sa chartre au dit Richard le Manoir de Silkesworth oue les apurtenances en le Euesche de Duresme en partie de allouance de son longe seruice et pertz il ad resceu par la guerre Descoce et a auoir et a tenir au dit Richard' et as ses heirs a touz iours issint qe le dit Richard ne ses heirs ne deuient estre ostetz du dit Manoir auant qe puruer luy feust Trente liures de terre en couenable liu, sicom est contenu en les dites chartres, et ia Sire Robert de Holand' mette debat' en le dit Manoir, qe est en le Euesche de Duresme, par resun dune fin qe se leua en la Court le Euesqe de Duresme, dedenz qe Franchise real le dit Manoir est, entre sire Thomas iaditz Counte de Lancastre et le dit sire Robert, par quele fin le dit Counte conusoit le dit Manoir estre le droit le dit Robert come ceo qil auoit de son doun, et pur cele reconusance le dit Robert granta et rendit le dit Manoir au dit Counte a tenir a terme de sa vie si qe apres le desees le auantdit Counte le dit Manoir returnereit ale auantdit sire Robert et as ses heirs, issint qe le dit Richard' pur ceo debat ne fait mye son profist en le Manoir come deueroit faire: Par quei voilletz si il vous plest ordeyner pur lestat le dit Richard qil et ses heirs poent tenir mesme le Manoir paisiblement.

Endorsed: Por ceo qe tesmoigne est par la peticion qe Richard est seisi du Manoir [du] doun du Roi piere nostre seignur le Roi, et par agard du parlement est acorde qe li dit Richard, ne nul autre qe est seisi des tenementz qe feurent a dit Robert, ne serront mie oforz saunz responce a la commune lei, et adonqes si Richard soit de ceo emplede, il purra estre eide par la chartre le Roi et le Roi se auisera issint qil ne serra mie perdant.   Irrotulatur

c. 1329. On 20 November 1329 Edward III granted to Robert, son and heir of Robert de Holand and a minor, lands and rents valued at £26 in consideration of claims to Silksworth, granted as forfeited land to Richard de Emeldon (*CPR 1327–30*, pp. 39, 467, 469). The heirs of Richard de Emeldon were still successfully defending their right to Silksworth in the court of the Bishop of Durham in 1390, this time against the heirs of Richard Marmaduke, who had made the initial transfer of Silksworth to the earl of Lancaster (PRO, Durham 13/223 mm 8–9). AP 15785B is a copy of the confirmation by Edward III of his father's grant to Emeldon. Cf. nos. 135, 191 above.

193

Louis, Bishop of Durham, petitions the King and Council that whereas he seized the lands of Walter de Selby in his franchise of Durham as the right of himself and his church through the forfeiture of Walter as an adherent to the Scots: by reason of an agreement made between Robert de Umfraville, earl of Angus, Ralph de Greystoke and John de Eure on the one part and Walter on the other at the surrender of Mitford Castle, occupied by Walter by force of war, which agreement in Walter's belief bound Robert, Ralph and John to secure for Walter the peace of King Edward, father of the present King, despite his adherence to the Scots, a royal writ came to the Bishop to deliver to Walter all lands seized within the franchise by reason of his forfeiture. This writ, in the opinion of the Bishop, was issued contrary to the law, since the agreement made among the said Robert, Ralph, John and Walter, who were strangers to the Bishop, should not bind him by law nor deprive him of the right of himself and his church. These lands were seized by right of his church long before Walter occupied the castle on whose surrender the agreement was based as Walter believed. The Bishop craves that no such writ be used to his prejudice, and a transcript is attached (AP 2121).

A nostre seignur le Roi et a son consail mustre Loys, Eueske de Doresme, qe cum il auoit seisi les teres et tenemenz qe furent a Wauter de Selby deinz sa franchise de Doresme cum son droit et le droit de sa eglise par la forfeture le dit Wauter pur ceo qe le dit Wauter aerda a les ennemis descoz, par la par resoun de vn couenant feat entre Robert dunframuile counte Danegos, Rauf de Greystoke et Johan de Eure de vne parte et le dit Wauter dautre parte sur le rendre du chastel de Mitford et qe le dit Wauter ocupa par forz de guere, le quel couenant a ceo qe le dit Wauter ad supose fut qe les ditz Robert, Rauf, et Johan dussent feare le dit Wauter auoir la peas le Roi E[dward] le pier nostre dit seignur le Roi et totes ses teres et tenemenz qe furunt pris en la meine le dit Roi E[dward] le pier pur taunt qil aerda a les ennemis descotz: par la est bref venutz au dit eueske qil liure au dit Wauter totes ses teres et tenemenz les quez il auoit seisiz en sa meine deinz sa franchise auandit par la forfeture le dit Wauter: le quel bref, cum est avis au dit Eueske, est issu en contre ley entaunt qe le couenant feat entre les ditz Robert, Rauf et Johan et Wauter qe furunt estranges audit eueske ne ly doit par ley lier ne ly [t]oller son dreit ne le dreit de sa eglise des ditz teres et tenementz, les ques le dit eueske auoit seisi cum le droit de sa eglise long temps einz ceo qe le dit Wauter ocupa le dit chastel sur le rendre de quel le dit couenant se tailla cum le dit Wauter ad supose: par quoi le dit Eueske pri a nostre seignur le Roi qe mes tiel bref mse (sic) en preiudise de ly encontre ley et resoun, le transescrit de quel est cosu a cest.

Endorsed: se ei par voie de respons sil eit droit quant il vendra deuant le Roi ou ailloc' par proces.

The transcript is now missing

1329–31. The agreement had been reached in the autumn of 1321, after Selby had held Mitford Castle for two years on behalf of the Scots. Despite the guarantee that he would be treated leniently,

Selby was imprisoned in the Tower of London and was not
released until March 1327, when he received from Edward III a
general pardon and restoration of such lands as were still in the
King's hands. His case was examined in parliament in October
1328, and on 13 March 1329 orders were issued to the sheriff of
Northumberland and the Bishop of Durham to release his
forfeited lands. The case was re-opened in 1331 in parliament, but
the Bishop ignored royal directives and his judges preferred to
accept the validity of his charter granting Felling to Amery de
Treu (*NCH* ix, 59–61 and notes). Cf. nos 184, 185 above.

194

Louis, bishop of Durham, petitions the King and Council that
whereas in the first parliament of the present King at Westminster
it was considered on his petition that he should have forfeiture of
war and royal rights of franchise between Tyne and Tees and
elsewhere held by his predecessors as the right of the church of St.
Cuthbert of Durham from time immemorial, and he has a
chancellor and writs, so that the King by his officers should neither
seize land nor hold enquiries of land, suit or contract by reason of
royal jurisdiction unless through default of the Bishop, and it was
considered in the same parliament as previously considered by the
King and Council that the Bishop should have his royal franchise as
formerly granted in the time of King Henry, and that the King
should lift his hand, as should his officers, and on such endorsement
a writ was ordered and sent under seal to Roger de Mortemer,
keeper of Barnard Castle and the other lands of Guy de
Beauchamp formerly earl of Warwick in the bishopric of
Durham, or his deputy, the transcript of which is attached, but the
keeper so far has done nothing. He craves a similar writ to the
present keeper to lift his hand, as previously decided (AP 5381).

A nostre seignur le Roy et a son conseil mostre Loys Euesqe de
Duresme qe come en le primer parlement nostre seignur le Roy
qore est tenu a Westm' par sa peticion illoeqes mostree agarde
feust qil eust forfaiture de guerre et franchise et droiz reals de deinz
les Ewes de Tyne et de Teyse et aillours ou il a franchise reale de
deinz sa Eueschee et ses predecessours lount eu come le droit de
leglise de seint Cuthbert de Duresme de temps dunt memoyre ne

court, et y a son Chaunceler et son bref y court, si qe nostre seignur le Roy par ses Ministres ne de deinz sa dite franchise ne doit terre seisir ne conissance illoeqes auoir de terre ne de tenement, de querele ne de contract, par reyson de iurisdiccion reale si ceo ne soit defaute du dit Euesqe, et en mesme le parlement feust agarde qe pur ceo qe agarde feust illoeqes par le Roy qore est et son conseil qe le dit Euesqe eust sa franchise reale come autrefoitz feust grante au temps le Roy Herry (sic) besael nostre seignur le Roy qore est, feust adonqes acorde qe le Roy ostast la mayn de quant qil aueit par reyson de iurisdiccion reale et aussinqes ses Ministres ministranz en office reale, et sur cest endossement feust ordeine bref et mande south' cire a Roger de Mortemer, gardein de Chastel Bernardi et des autres terres et tenementz qe feurent a Guy de Beauchaump' iadis Counte de Warewyk' en leueschee de Duresme ou a son lieu tenant, le transescript de queu bref est attache a ceste peticioun, pur queu bref le gardeyn qe adunqes feust ne fist rien. Par quey il prie au tiel bref au gardein qore est qil oste la mayn, sicome deuant feust agarde.

Endorsed: Pur ceo qe autrefoitz feust accorde en parlement a Westm' lan primer qe leuesqe eust iurisdiccion reale deinz sa franchise auantdite et qe le Roi ostast sa meyn de quanqe il auoit en sa Mayn par reson de iurisdiccion real et auxi ses Ministres Ministrantz en office real et sur ce auoir bref a visconte et autres Ministres le Roi adonqes, eit ore autiel bref as Ministres le Roi qe ore sont.

c. 1332. The endorsement explains the reason for the masterly inactivity. As the King's officers ought not to act within Durham, there was no royal sheriff to ensure that the King's writs were obeyed. On 14 September 1332 an exemplification was made at the request of Bishop Beaumont of the writs of 24 February 1327 to the constable of Barnard Castle and to the bailiff of Hart and Hartness to cease exercising the King's authority within their bailiwicks, and a similar writ to William de Denum, farmer of certain escheats in Bedlingtonshire (*CPR 1330–34*, p. 360). Cf. no. 190 above.

195

The Bishop of Durham petitions the King and Council that whereas the King in his parliament at Westminster on the morrow of the Nativity of the Blessed Virgin [9 September] last past ordained for the profit of the realm that staples should be established in certain places and decreed pains, forfeits and ransoms on those disobeying, and whereas the Bishop should have first cognizance of all kinds of contract, covenant and trespass done within his royal franchise, with forfeitures and amerciaments, the King has reserved cognizance of such forfeitures to his judges and has sent the statute to the Bishop to proclaim and keep in his royal franchise to its detriment. The Bishop craves that the King and Council waive these points of the statute, so that he can have before his judges cognizance of trespasses against the statute as the King has elsewhere, as he and his predecessors have had in similar cases heretofore (AP 2155).

A nostre seignur le Roi et a son conseil moustre Leuesqe de Duresme qe come nostre dit seignur le Roi a son parlement tenuz a Westm' alendemeyn de la Natiuite nostre dame drein passe pur profist du roialme ordeina les estaples destre en son roialme en certeinz lieux et sur ceo ordeina certeinz peinz, forfaits et raunsons vers ceux qe. . . . rent encontre lordinance auandit, et par la out le dit Euesqe ad et auoir doit la primer conisaunz de chescun maner de contrate, couenant, Trespas fait deinz sa franchise reale et forfaiturs et amercimenz, la ad nostre seignur le Roi reserue deuers lui deuant ces Justices la conisance de tiels forfaiturs, et de ceo ad mande le dit Estatut a le dit Euesqe de crier et fermement garder deinz sa franchise reale, la quele chose est enblemisement de sa franchise: par qoi le dit Euesqe prie a nostre seignur le Roi et a son conseil qe lui plest celes pointz del Estatutz desbarer, issint qil peusse auoir deuant ces Justices la conisanz de trespas de ceux qe vindront encontre lestatut auandit auxi come le Roi doit auoir dehors, si come lui et ces predecessours ont eu de tote temps dedeinz la dit franchise reale en teux ceux cases semblables.

Endorsed: Coram Rege et magno consilio
Le Roi se auisera des choses contenues en ceste peticion.

1332–33. The home staples for wool were established by an act of parliament in September 1332, to take effect from Easter 1333, and were abolished by another act in March 1334 (Lloyd, p. 121).

196

Richard, Bishop of Durham, petitions the King and Council that whereas by reason of his royal franchise he and his predecessors had by right of the church of Durham at all times between Tyne and Tees, Norhamshire and Bedlingtonshire right of forfeiture of war, and formerly in the time of King Henry, great-grandfather of the present King, a Peter de Montfort forfeited by war the manor of Greatham within the royal franchise, and King Henry understanding that forfeiture of war was his by right within the franchise as elsewhere in the realm seized possession and gave it to a Thomas de Clare: and one Robert [Stichill], then Bishop of Durham, his predecessor, sued and showed his right and the King wholly revoked his collation made to Thomas, as is shown by the charter of King Henry, and later Sir Robert de Bruys forfeited by war the manor of Hart within the franchise and Antony, then Bishop, seized the manor as by right of his church, and was seised thereof until King Edward, grandfather of the present King, by royal power and without [legal] judgment ejected him and gave it by charter to Sir Robert de Clifford to hold of him and his heirs, saving the right of the church of Durham, the Bishop and his successors. The manor is now in the hand of Robert, son and heir of Robert de Clifford, and whereas at a parliament held at Westminster during the time of the present King it was awarded that Louis, then Bishop, should have forfeiture of war and that the King should release whatever he had for that reason within the franchise, nevertheless those holding such land by royal charter were not to be ejected without defence, Robert son of Robert now is of full age and the Bishop craves that the King have regard for the right of him and his church over the said manor from which his predecessor was ejected by royal power, so that he can preserve his right, and that he will revoke the collation made to Sir Robert de Clifford, just as King Henry revoked his collation of Greatham to Thomas de Clare (AP 2166).

Endorsed: Pur ce qil suppose par sa peticion qe monsieur Robert de

Clifford' est tenant du Manoir, sue deuers lui par bref a la comune lei.

This petition from Richard de Bury, bishop of Durham [1333–45], is printed in *Reg Pal Dun* iv, 182–83.

?1334. Robert de Clifford, who was born on 5 November 1306, had the estates of his deceased brother granted to him in February 1327 while still under age (*CFR* iv, 5; *Cal Inq pm* vii, 30). See also nos 189–90 above.

197

The King's bachelor Walter de Selby petitions the King that whereas he sued divers writs previously before the present Bishop and before Louis, late bishop of Durham, to deliver to him his lands in the franchise of Durham according to the terms contained in the writ of which a transcript is attached, the Bishop has done nothing yet because Thomas Surtays holds the same by grant of Louis, lately bishop of Durham his predecessor. Walter draws attention to the fact that he is in the King's services in Scotland and craves an order to the Bishop to take the lands and deliver them to him (AP 394).

A nostre seignur le Roy prie son bachelor lige Waltier de Selby, qe come il ad porte diuerse brefs auant ces heures al euesqe de Duresme et a Leuwys nadgaires Euesqe de Duresme son prede- cessour a deliuerer a lui ses terres deinz sa fraunchise de Duresme solonc' le purport des bref' dont le transescrit est cosu a ceste peticioune, pur queux bref' le dit Euesqe riens nad fait vncore pur ceo qe Thomas Surteys tient mesme les terres du doun Lowyz iadys Euesqe de Duresme predecessour le Euesqe qore est: qe lui pleise dauoir regard aceo qe le dit Waltier est en le seruice nostre dit seignur le Roy en Escoce, et mander au dit Euesqe qil face prendre les dites terres en sa main, et qe il les deliure au dit Wautier issint qe il ne soit plus delae contre reson.

Endorsed: soit vnqore bref mande al Euesqe qil face liuerer les terres selonc lautre mandement ou qil certifie la cause pur qoi il ne le doit faire et outre soit fait proces.

1333–36. On 27 January 1332 Edward III ratified the confirmation by the prior and convent of Durham, dated 10 January 1332, of a grant by Bishop Beaumont of 27 December 1331 of the manor of Felling to his kinsman Ameury de Trew together with Trew's subsequent grant of the manor to Thomas Surteyse (*CPR 1330–34*, p. 240). Surteyse had been appointed steward of the Durham priory lands in 1325 (Durham, Misc Charter 4281). See nos 184–5, 193 above, and no. 198 below.

198

The King's bachelor Walter [Selby] petitions the King and Council that whereas certain agreements were made by indenture between Robert de Umfranvyll, lately earl of Angus, Ralph de Craistoke, then lord of Greystoke, and Sir John de Eure on the one hand and Walter on the other for the surrender of Mitford Castle, namely that the earl, baron and John would cause Walter to have the King's peace and all his lands without loss, although taken into the King's hand as an adherent of the King's enemies. The King having granted this agreement should be held on all points, writs were sent to the sheriff of Northumberland to deliver to Walter all the lands in his bailiwick and to Louis, lately bishop of Durham, to do the same, as Walter was never attainted of felony through which he should forfeit. The sheriff by virtue of this order delivered him all his lands in the county but the Bishop would do nothing and made grants of all his lands in the franchise as escheats, so that the agreements were not observed therein. In view of his great labour in the King's service he craves restoration of his lands in the franchise in accordance with the agreements (AP 3660).

A nostre seignur le Roy et son conseil pri le son leige bacheler Waltier que come certeins couenances se firent par endenture entre Robert de vmfranuyll nadgairs Counte de Anegos, Rauf de Craistok' adunqe baron de Craistok' et Monsieur Johan de Eure dune part et le dit Waltier dautre part sur le rendit du Chastel de Mitford, cest assauer que le dit Counte, baron, et Johan feroient auer au dit Waltier la pees sire Edward' nadgairs Roy Dengleterre pier le dit nostre seignur le Roy et touz ses terres et tenementz santz deseriteson, queux furont pris en la main le dit pier par reson que fust dit qil estoit ahers a le enemys le dit pier, les quels couenances le dit nostre seignur le Roy ad grante auant ces heures qils soient tenues en touz pointz, et sur ceo ad mande par diuers brefs au viscont de Northumbreland' qil feist deliuerer au dit Waltier touz ses terres et tenementz deins sa baillie, et a Loys nadgairs Euesque de Duresme qil feist deliuerer touz les terres et tenementz le dit Waltier a mesme cele Waltier que furent deinz sa franchise de Durresme, pur ce que meisme celi Waltier vncque ne fust atteint de felonie pur qoi il deueroit forfaire: le quel viscont par vertu du dit mandement deliuera au dit Waltier touz ses terres et tenementz deinz le dit Countee, mes le dit Euesque rien ne voleit faire pur les ditz mandementz et ad done par sa chartre touz les terres et tenementz le dit Waltier deinz la dite franchise auxi come sa eschete, par qoi les couenances auandites ne sont mie tenues deinz la dite franchise: que leur pleise auer regarde al grant trauaille que le dit Waltier ad eu en la seruice nostre dit seignur le Roy et grante al meisme celi Waltier puisse auer ces terres et tenementz deins la dite franchise solonc' les couenances auandites, issint qil ne soit mie deserite.

Endorsed: Sue deuers Leuesque qil lui face droit, et sil ne face adonque sue en Chauncellerie de auoir bref a le Euesque qil lui face droit, et outre sue proces auxi come auant ces houres ad estee vsee.

1336. The petition was accompanied by a transcript of the writ of Edward III to Richard, bishop of Durham, dated 11 July 1336 (AP 3661). This summarises Selby's petition to King and Council in parliament at Salisbury [in October 1328] about the non-observance of the agreement which offset against the surrender of Mitford Castle the restoration of lands forfeited by Selby on account of his adherence to the Scots. In addition Selby had been held in prison. The terms of the agreement had been examined and orders issued to the sheriff of Northumberland and the Bishop of Durham to deliver to Selby those of his lands confiscated. Since Bishop Beaumont failed to obey, a second order required compliance unless the present Bishop [Bury] could show good cause. The text is printed in *NCH* ix, 61n. The original order to Bishop Bury does not appear to have been entered on the Close Roll, although a writ of 10 July 1336 to the bishop for payment of his expenses amounting to £100 can be found there (*CCR 1333–37*,

p. 596). See no. 193 above.

199

Richard, bishop of Durham, petitions the King and Council that whereas Hugh Pusat', formerly bishop of Durham, bought from King Richard the wapentake of Sadberge with the fees appurtenant to hold to him and his successors as freely as the bishop held his other lands within the franchise of Durham, as more fully appears by the charter and confirmation by King John, the transcripts of which are attached, and within which wapentake John de Bailliol held five knights' fees and a quarter fee, and John owed for castle-guard at Newcastle upon Tyne 5 marks and 40 pence a year. Later Balliol did homage for his services to one Robert, bishop of Durham, by order of King Henry, great-grandfather of the present King. By reason of an enrolment in Chancery on the Fine Roll of 18 Henry[1233/4]a transcript of which is attached, a summons for the 5 marks 40 pence had issued against the Bishop and his predecessors, and the Bishop craves that the King and Council consider the charters of the King's ancestors, acquitting him of all such services. May he have a writ to the Treasurer and Barons for acquittance (AP 2157A).

Transcript of charters of Richard I [7 December 1198] and John [1199/1200] granting and confirming the wapentake of Sadberge to the Bishops of Durham (AP 2157B)

Transcript of charter of Richard I, being the initial grant of Sadberge [18 September 1189] (AP 2157C).

This petition of Bishop Bury is printed in *Reg Pal Dun* iv, 180–82.

1337. On 18 March 1337 the Treasurer and Barons of the Exchequer were ordered to hear Bury's complaint about the reiterated demand for 5 marks 40 pence a year, and after inspection of the Exchequer rolls and memoranda, and if necessary consulting the justices of either bench, the demand if found valid was to be superseded until Christmas, so that the Bishop could pursue his discharge in the normal manner (*CCR 1333–37*, pp. 39–40; *Reg Pal Dun* iv, 211–12). The charters of Richard and John had earlier been enrolled at the instance of Bishop Beaumont in 1318 (*CChR* iii, 393–95). The attempts of the Bishops of Durham to consolidate their lordship between Tyne and Tees were constantly obstructed. The first John de Balliol had required repeated royal orders before he would do homage for Barnard Castle in the wapentake of Sadberge, and his successors were equally recalcitrant. On the other hand, despite the Exchequer's requirement that the annual due of 5 marks 40 pence be paid for castle-guard at Newcastle upon Tyne, the demands were consistently ignored, and by 1313/4 had grown to a notional debt of $367\frac{1}{2}$ marks at which point it was transferred to a roll of 'despaired debts' (PRO, Pipe Roll 159 m 44; *Bek*, p. 92 and note). The matter was still being argued in the Exchequer in 1343 (*CCR 1343–46*, p. 191).

200

Transcript of order made in council by Henry III on 10 April 1234 to John de Baillof' to do homage to the Bishop of Durham, on the understanding that the Bishop will undertake responsibility for castle-guard at Newcastle upon Tyne unless he can show why he should be quit. The sheriff of Northumberland is no longer to distrain on Bailliol for the castle-guard: dated 11 April 1234 (AP 2157D).

Rex in presencia Magnatum suorum apud Westmonasterium die Lune in Crastino dominice passionis domini anno etc .xviij. precepit Johanni de Baillof quod de feodo .v. Militum et quarte partis feodi .i. Militis qui pertinent ad custodiam Noui Castri super Tynam et qui tenent in Wapentaka de Sadbergh' homagium faciat venerabili patri R[icardo] Dunelmensi Episcopo et de seruicio eorumdem feodorum eidem Episcopo sit intendens et respondens. Ita quod idem Episcopus Regi respondebit de Warda que de eisdem feodis exigitur ad custodiam predicti Castri nisi Regi monstrare poterit ipsum de Warda predicta debere esse quietum per cartas Regis vel predecessorum suorum Regum Anglie. Et mandatum est vicecomiti Northumbr' quod ad predictam Wardam faciendum occasione predictorum feodorum ipsum Johannem non distringat. Teste Rege apud Westmonasterium .xj. die Aprilis, anno regni H[enriei] proaui Regis nunc decimo octauo.

      Irrotulatus in rotulo finium eodem anno
See no 199 above.

Richard, Bishop of Durham, petitions the King and Council that whereas within his franchises of Durham, Norhamshire and Bedlingtonshire he has royal franchise, royal jurisdiction and royal prerogative, issues, forfeits and all other forfeitures, and for this reason may distrain men of means to receive knighthood and have the forfeited revenues, a writ has issued from the Exchequer to the Bishop to distrain certain men in his franchise and answer for the revenues and have their bodies before the Barons of the Exchequer to hear judgement for failure to receive knighthood within a certain time according to the King's order, whereas in this matter the men of his franchise should answer only to him. He craves that the King and Council revoke the writ and cease the action (AP 2147).

This petition is printed in *Reg Pal Dun* iv, 265–66.

1337. Following its presentation in parliament the Treasurer and Barons of the Exchequer were ordered on 18 March 1337 to supersede until the following Christmas their demand for distraint of knighthood in Durham and to permit the Bishop to have cognisance thereof pending prosecution by Bishop Bury of his suit before the Treasurer and Barons (*CCR 1337–39*, p. 47; *Reg Pal Dun* iv, 211–12).

Richard, Bishop of Durham, petitions the King and Council that whereas he had within his franchise of Durham royal jurisdiction and prerogative and all kinds of forfeiture from time immemorial, so that the King's officers should not enter to exercise their office, and new statues were sent him to observe, and profits resulting belonged to the Bishop, now a new writ has been issued from Chancery contrary to law and reason, directed to the bailiffs of Hartlepool within the franchise to search the port to prevent silver, money or plate being taken out of the kingdom, as forbidden by statute, and such silver is to be seized for the King's use, whereas the Bishop should execute such arrests by his officers and have the profit. He craves that the King and Council order the

Chancellor to revoke the order and that he have a writ to the bailiffs forbidding their action, as the King's predecessors have done in respect of royal officers so acting, which writs were enrolled in the Chancery in the time of the present King (AP 2152).

This petition is printed in *Reg Pal Dun* iv, 264–65.

1337. The power of the Bishop of Durham in Hartlepool was circumscribed, and the pretentions of Bishop Bek to have customs officers utterly rejected. The customs collectors, however, accounted separately from those of Newcastle at the Exchequer, and on 25 March 1337 Edward III ordered Roger de Gosewyk and John Belle to cease enforcing their letters of scrutiny in the port of Hartlepool as Bishop Bury had shown that he had royal jurisdiction and profits there and the King had forbidden his officers to act within the liberty. The letters of scrutiny were thereby revoked (*CCR 1337–39*, p. 39; cf. *Reg Pal Dun* iv, 221–22; *Bek*, pp. 86–7, 191, 199).

203

The Bishop of Durham petitions the King and Council that whereas he and his predecessors until the time of the present King have held all their land within their franchises of Norhamshire, Bedlingtonshire and Holy Island in Northumberland and of Crayke in Yorkshire quit of all tax and tallage, ninths and fifteenths, as part of their royal franchise of Durham between Tyne and Tees, wherein as [county palatine] no writ runs except that of the Bishop, the sheriff of Northumberland by warrant from the Exchequer [entered] as royal officer and distrained on the Bishop's tenants within the said franchises to pay the ninth sheaf, fleece and lamb where no such ninth or tenth nor any other sort of tax was ever paid in those places. He craves a discharge from such taxes, never previously paid, lest his church be disinherited (AP 2151).

A nostre seignur le Roi et son conseil moustre leuesqe de Duresme qe come lui et ses predecessours de tout temps si bien en temps nostre seignur le Roi qore est come en temps de touz ses progenitours ont tenuz touz lour terres et tenementz deinz lours fraunchises de Norham'shire, Bedlyngton'shire et Halieland en

Contee de Northumbr' et de Crayke en le Contee de Euerwyk'
quites de tout manere de taxe et de talliage, de nefnismes et
quindezismes, come parcelle de lour Roial fraunchise de Duresme
entre Tyne et Tese ou ... Count de Pal[at] ... nul bref ne court
illoeqes forsqe brief le dit Euesqe, la le viscont de Northumbr' par
commandement et garaunt hors de Lescheker [entrent] ... come
Ministre nostre seignur le Roi destrent les tenantz le dit Euesqe
deinz les franchises susdites de paier la nefnisme des garbes, des
tysons et des aigneux la ou tiele nefnisme ne disme ne nul autre
manere de taxe ne feust vnqes paie en les lieux susdits: Dount il prie
en oeure de Charite en saluacion del droit de sa eglise de seint
Cutbert de Dinelme [sic] qe lui et ses tenauntz puissent estre
deschargez de tieles taxes et talliages qeconqes, qe ne furont vnqes
paiez auant ces heures, issint qe sa dite eglise ne soit desherite.

Endorsed: Quant a les terres de Northumbr' qe sont de la Roial
franchise de Duresme, soient serchez les remembrances de la
Tresorie touchant ceste bosoigne, et enquis sur busoigne la verite
ou faus et sur ce le Roi et son cunsoil enfourme, soit autre fait
ce qe droit voet.

Quant a les terres de Crayke qe sont deinz les teres du Countee
de Eurewyk', paient sicome les autres du Counte si Leuesqe ne
puisse moustrere qe les soient enfranches et donent de droit.

c. 1345. A grant of the ninth sheaf, fleece and lamb was made in
parliament in March 1340. On 14 February 1346 the Treasurer and
Barons of the Exchequer were ordered to examine the rolls and
memoranda of the Exchequer in respect of the claim that the men
of Crayke in Yorkshire were within the liberty of Durham and
quit of aids granted by the commons of the realm. If so found, they
were to supersede the demand for a ninth, for which they were
being distrained by the sheriff of York (CCR 1346–49, p. 3). The
freedom of the franchise of Durham from national taxation
was notional rather than real, as the King expected the Bishop to
act as his collecting agent (Lapsley, pp. 118–20; Willaid, p. 29;
cf. Reg. Pal Dun iv, 225–28).

204

Information to the King and Council that whereas William son of William de Prendregest inherited through Isabel his mother in the township of Cornhill in Norhamshire within the franchise of Durham and [lived] in the counties of Berwick and Roxburgh in the faith of [the Scots] until he was 30 and more, all his lands should belong to the King as forfeiture of war and be so seized. May a writ be issued under the great seal to certain liegemen to enquire and return their findings for preservation of the King's right (AP 8627).

Pleise a nostre seignur le Roi et son conseil entendre qe come William fiz William de Prendregest [enherite] depar Isabelle sa mere en la ville de Cornhale on Norhamshire deinz la franchise de Duresme ... [on] les Countees de Berewyk et Rokesburgh' a lour foi feust demorant tanqe il estoit del age de trente [ans et plus et] totes les terres auandites deussent apartenir a nostre dit seignur le Roi come sa forfeiture de guerre, queles terres ... dit seignur le Roi et de sa Corone, par quoi pleise au nostre dit seignur le Roi et son conseil pur le droit nostre dit seignur le Roi [sauuer, qe] le grant seal soit fait as certeins gentz et loiaux denquere des choses susdites et lenqueste retourne qe entre ... a faire en sauuacioun du droit nostre seignur le Roi auandit.   Responcio patet in dorso

Endorsed: Soient certeins gens dignes de foy et nient suspecciounous assignes denquere sur les pointz contenuz en cestes peticions et lenqueste retourne en Chancellarie outre soit fait droit sibien au Roi come la partie.

1348–51. In 1328 Bishop Beaumont granted two-thirds of Cornhill to William son of William de Denum, Isabel his wife, and Edmund their son, from whom it passed to the Herons of Ford (J Raine, *North Durham* (1852), pp. 320–1 and note n). On 18 November 1348 the lands in Cornhill of Roger de Aulton and Isabel de Cornhale, and of William de Prendergast, his wife and son, following their seizure as forfeitures, were granted to William Heroun for his good service and by fine of 200 marks. William Prendergast senior seems to have married the eldest of co-heiresses to an estate in Cornhill. The Prendergasts had property in Glendale (*CPR 1348–50*, pp. 208, 245; *NCH* xi, 230-33). See no. 205 below.

205

His liege William de Prendregast petitions the King that whereas William de Prendregast his father married an Isabel de Cornhall, heiress of certain lands in Cornhill within the franchises of Durham in Norhamshire, which Isabel died faithful to the King, and thereafter William, holding by courtesy of England, adhered to the King's Scottish enemies, by reason of which forfeiture Bishop Louis granted the same lands to a William de Denum on the supposition that William the son had forfeited with his father, although he was but seven and never suffered forfeiture. After the death of his father, William brought an assize of *mort dancestor* in the court of the present Bishop of Durham at Norham against Edmund son of the said William à Denome and recovered his mother's tenements by verdict of the assize, but through a false suggestion made to the King a writ was issued to seize the tenements into the King's hand through the son's forfeiture. He craves a commission to try the issue of forfeiture, so that he be not evicted by false suggestion (AP 8626).

A nostre seignur le Roy pri soun leige hom William de Prendregest qe come William de Prendregast pier mesme ceste William prist a femme vne Isabele de Cornhall', enherite de certeynes terres e tenementz en Cornhall' e deins les franchises de Doresme en Norhamschire, la quel Isabele morust a la foy nostre seignur le Roy, apres le mort le dit William tenant par la curtosy dengleterre senherdy a les enemys descoce, par cause de quel forfaiture Leuesque Lowys graunte par sa chartre meismes les terres avn William de Denum, Supposeunt par sa chartre qe meisme cesti William de Prendregast le fitz au[oit] forfait ensemblement od soun pier ou il fust del agee de septe aunz e vnqes ne forfist, e ou apres la mort William de Prendregast le pier le dit William le fitz porta vn assise de mort de auncestre de la mort la dite Isabele sa mere en la courte leuesqe de Doresme qe ore est a Norham deuer Eadmund' fitz le dit William a Denome e recouery meismes le tenementz del heritage sa mere par veredit dassise e vnqor est tenaunt, sur qoy par feynt sugestioun fait a nostre seignur le Roy bref est issu de seiser meismes lez tenementz en la mayne le Roy par la forfaiture le dit William le fitz: Par qoy pleise a nostre seignur le Roy comaunder Comissioun a qi qe ly plerra pur trier si le dit

William le fitz forfist ou noun, issint qe le dit William le fitz ne soit pas oste de sa terre par faus sugestion.

Endorsed: Veignent certeins gentz.

1350–51. See no. 204 above. If Prendergast were seven years of age in 1328 he would have been 'thirty years and more' in 1351. William de Denome died in 1350 (Surtees i, 192).

206

Margaret de Cornale petitions the King that whereas she lived as an infant among her friends in Scotland during the war, he may order the Bishop of Durham and his bailiffs of Norham to give her seisin of tenements in Cornhill of which her father John de Cornhale died seised, as she is next heir (AP 4963).

W[illiam] de Cotes sues this petition

A nostre seignour le Roi prie Margarete de Cornale qe ad demore entre ses amis Descoce durant la guer[e comme en]faunt deinz age, qil la voille si li plest graunter bref al Eueske de Dureme et a ses Baillifs de Norham qe eux la facent seisine des tenementz en Cornale od les aprestenaunces dount ⟨Johan de Cornhale⟩ son piere morut seisi et ele est son prochein heir.

W. de Cotes sequitur istam petitionem

Endorsed: Coram Cancellario   Fiat

?post 1348. See no. 204 note above.

APPENDIX

Subsequent to the editing of Ancient Petition 10882 in *Northumberland Petitions* (no 21) new information came to hand. This confirmed the logic of the dating that 'the contract for [the erection of Staward pele] would suggest [royal] ownership at the date of the agreement', but proved that Edward II did not acquire the site until 22 April 1326, when the pele and half the village of Staward was granted him by Sir Hugh de Louthre. Seisin was given on 24 April, and the same day the contract for repairs was made with Thomas de Fetherstanhalgh after tender by Thomas on 19 April. The terms of the contract were as follows:

Ceste endenture faite a kenilworth le .xxiij. iour Dauerill Lan del Regne nostre seignur le Roi .xixme parentre mesme nostre seignur et Thomas de Fetherstanhalgh tesmoigne qe mesme celui Thomas ad empris afaire et reparailler le Peel de Staworth en la forme qe sensuyt: Cest a sauer qil fra faire oyt Rodes de Mur de Pere et de Chauce en certein lieu, et qe mesme le Mur serra de oyt peedz de lee et de vint et qatre peedz de haut od le batailler, et fra auxint de nouel vne porte de fust, bone et couenable en dit peel, od treis estages dont le souerein estage serra bataillez, et il fra le remenant de mesme le Peel de fust de vint et qatre peedz de haut od le batailler. Et qe tote ceste oueraigne serra faite entre cy et la goule Daugst, par vieue et tesmoignance sire Antoigne de Lucy ou de celui qil assignera pur mesmes les oueraignes surueer, et qe nostre seignur le Roi lui trouera merrym. Et pur mesme les coustages faire il prendra de nostre seignur le Roi Cent liures es lieux ou le Tresorier et les Barons del Escheqier lui assigneront a prendre, et ce de temps en temps, solonc ce qe les oueraignes auantdites serront faites par vieue et tesmoignance auantdites: et qil fra garder le dit Peel tantque mesmes les oueraiges soient faites. Et a cestes choses bien et lealment faire le dit Thomas se oblige par ceste endenture. En tesmoignance de queu chose le dit nostre seignur le Roi a Lune parte de mesme ceste Endenture ad mis son priue seal, et le dit

APPENDIX   277

Thomas son seal a lautre partie. Don' as lieu, iour et an auantditz.
The documentation was enrolled on the Memoranda Roll of
the Exchequer on 29 April 1326 (PRO, E159/102 mm 56, 117).
From the petition, now datable to June/July 1326, it appears that
like many another speculative builder Fetherstanhalgh had under-
estimated his costs and was facing ruin 'par sa fole empris' (North'd
Pet, p. 25; cf. pp. 14–15). Antony de Lucy had earlier commanded
the garrison at Staward in 1316 (ibid. 25).

INDEX OF PERSONS AND PLACES

INDEX OF PERSONS AND PLACES
Bold type indicates that the entry refers to a petitioner

Brom, Adam de, 175–6
Brough under Stainmore, (West'd),
  121–2
Bruges, Flanders, 58; burgomaster and
  échevins, 168–9
Brun, Ada la, 94–5; William le, 94–5
Bruntoft, Andrew de, 163; Nicholas
  de, 163, 178, 228
Brus, David de, king of Scotland
  (1329–71), 2, 35–7, 147–8, 186;
  Peter de, 165; Robert de, king of
  Scotland (1306–29), 12, 15–17,
  21–3, 34–5, 38–9, 41, 81, 138, 160,
  173–5, 177–8, 245, 249, 255–6,
  264
Buchan, earl of, 124
Bulmer, Sir John, 240
Burdon, John de, chamberlain of Ber-
  wick, 70, 71
Burgh, Thomas de, chamberlain of
  Berwick, 26;—clerk, 117–18
Burghman, John, gaoler of Cocker-
  mouth castle, 124–5
Burne, William del, burgess of Ber-
  wick, 69–70
Burnton, William de, merchant
  of Newcastle upon Tyne, 88–
  90
Burton Agnes, John of, 236
Burton, Robert de, collector of cus-
  toms at Hull, 161–2;—keeper of
  St Mary Magdalen hospital, Ber-
  wick, 88
Bury, Richard de, bishop of Durham
  (1333–45), 36–7, 41, 160–1, 184,
  192–3, 196, 231, 264–5, 267, 268,
  270–2
Byntele, William de, 10
Bywell [on Tyne], 229

Caldew, river (Cumb), 120
Callet, Tweed salmon fishery, 74
Camberton, Alan de 131, Mary
  widow of, 131
Cambridge, parliament at, 154–5
Campbell, Neil, 93
Canterbury, 71; archbishop, 86–7,
  222–3

Carbonel, John, 60
Cardoill, Robert de, King's yeoman,
  95
Carlisle 104, 108–19; castle, 113, 115–
  117, 149; hospital of St Nicholas,
  108, 110–11, brethren of, 110–11;
  men of, 109, 111–12, 113, 114–15,
  118–19; parliament at, 47, 244–5;
  parts of, 62
Carlisle, bishop, 107–8, 110–11, 133,
  135, 153–5—see also Appleby,
  Thomas, Halton, John; bishopric,
  3, 134–5; clergy of, 134,
  135
Carnarvon, 121
Castre, John de, 97
Catwick, (Yorks), vicarage, 205
Champion, Richard, 102, 106
Charing, (Mx), manor, 220, 221
Chaumbre, John del, 199, Joan widow
  of, 174–5; Thomas del, 159, 197–
  199
Chesham, Henry de, merchant of
  London, 27
Chester le Street, (Dur), collegiate
  church, 204–5
Chilton, John de, 12–14, burgess of
  Berwick, 45–6, 68–70
Cinque Ports, 164
Clare, Thomas de, 264
Clarence, duke of, 239–40
Clarendon, (Wilts), 231
Claxton, Thomas de, 199–201; Wil-
  liam de, 239–40
Cleator, (Cumb), 100
Clertene, Richard de, 100, Isabel
  widow of 92, 99–100
Cleveland, 181; archdeaconry, clergy
  of, 141–3
Cliderhou, Robert de, escheator north
  of Trent, 97–8, 212, 245
Clifford, Lady, 62; Lord, 155; Robert
  de, 120, 122, 126, 129, 245, 264,
  Maud widow of, 97, 246–7;
  Robert son of, 264–5; Roger de
  150, 255–6
Clifton (Cumb), 131–2
Clipston (Northants), 62

Londeham, John son and heir of John de, 49
London, 93, 96; bishop, 137; Tower of, 251, 261
Longnewton (Dur), 226–9, 248
Loundres, Edmund de, 80–81; Robert de, burgess of Berwick, **69–70**
Louther, Hugh de, 115–16, 276
Louthwait, (Cumb), 124
Louwedre, Sir Robert de, junior, 16, 18;—senior, 15, 16
Luceby, Henry de, intruded prior of Durham, 207, 241–3
Lucy, Antony de, 99, 100, 115–16, 123, 140, **143**, 276–7, keeper of Berwick, 26, 40, warden of the Marches, 144–5; John de, collector in Cumberland, **103–4**; Thomas de, 106–7, 123, **125–7, 128–9**
Lue, Roger de, **38–40**, Joan wife of, **38–40**
Lundres, John de, 15
Lyndeseye, Richard, 166–8
Lynn (Norf), 71, 227–8; men of, 151
Lynton, William de, clerk, 202
Lythum, John de, 236–7

Magna Carta, 225–6
Maidenestan, John son of John de, **222–4**
Maison Dieu, Berwick, 15, 79–80; brethren of **80–81**; master and brethren of, **82**
Malorre, Peter, 131
Manceux, Amand, 155—*see also* Mounceux, Amand
March, earl of Scottish, 3, 35, 146–147, 149, 151–2, 185–6; wardens of the 71, 147–8—*see also* Greystoke, Ralph de, Lucy, Antony de, Nevill, John de
Marchaunt, John, of Berwick, **72–3**
Mareys, Peter del, 163
Marmaduke, John, 182, Ida widow of 257; Richard, 179, 182, 246, 247, heirs of, 259
Marmyon, John, 150

Marshalsea prison (London), 228
Mauldesson, Robert, 13
Maunsel, Simon, 23–4, 26
Mayden, bro William, master of the Bridge House at Berwick, 15
Mayden, William, 17
Melmerby, (Cumb), tower, 137
Melrose, abbot, 15
Melton, William de, archbishop of York (1317–40), 72
Menevill, Henry de, 105
Merkingfeld, John de, keeper of dies, 251
Middelburg, Zeeland, 49, 58
Middilton, Robert de, 225–6, Robert son of, 225–6
Middleton on Tees (Dur), 225–6
Middleton One Row (Dur), 226
Middleton St George (Dur), church, 195
Middleton, Gilbert de, 249
Miridon, Thomas of, 236
Mitford (North'd), 255, 259, 266–7
Mitford, John de, 153–5
Mohaut, Hugh de, master of Kepier Hospital, **189–90**
Monboucher, Bertram, 43
Montague, John, steward of King's household, 201
Montfort, Peter de, 264
Monthermer, Ralph, 65
Moorsley (Dur), 168
Moray, bishop of, 44
Moray, Thomas de, keeper of Scotland, 35
Moresby, Christopher de, 153–4
Moriley, Thomas son of Thomas de la, **128**
Morpath, John de, 108–9, **113–14**
Mortemer, Roger de, keeper of Barnard Castle, 261–2
Mortone, Henry, 60
Moubray, John de, 41; Roger de, 49, 50
Mounceux, Amand 155, sheriff of Cumberland, 119
Moyses, Nicholas, 12
Mulecastre, William de, 97